D0500800

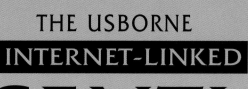

# THE USBORNE
## INTERNET-LINKED
# ESSENTIAL
# ATLAS
## OF THE WORLD

### Stephanie Turnbull

Designers: Stephen Moncrieff and Helen Wood
Consultant cartographic editor: Craig Asquith

Cartography by European Map Graphics Ltd
Map design by Laura Fearn and Keith Newell

# CONTENTS

*This page: African elephants graze on plains south of the Sahara Desert.*

*Title page: Evening sunlight shines on Mount Rainier, in Washington, northwestern U.S.A.*

*Endpapers: This picture of the world at night has been made by combining many satellite images.*

# INTERNET LINKS

This book contains descriptions of many interesting websites where you can find out more about maps and places around the world. For links to these sites, go to the Usborne Quicklinks Website at **www.usborne-quicklinks.com** and enter the keywords "essential atlas". There you will find links to take you to all the sites.

## Site availability

The links on the Usborne Quicklinks Website will be reviewed and updated regularly. If any sites become unavailable, we will, if possible, replace them with suitable alternatives.

Occasionally, you may get a message saying that a website is unavailable. This may be temporary, so try again a few hours later, or even the next day.

> ### Internet links
> For links to all the websites described in this book, go to **www.usborne-quicklinks.com** and enter the keywords "essential atlas".

## Help

For general help and advice on using the Internet, go to the Usborne Quicklinks Website and click on "Net Help".

To find out more about using your web browser, click on your browser's Help menu and choose "Contents and Index". You'll find a searchable dictionary containing tips on how to find your way around the Internet easily.

## What you need

The websites described in this book can be accessed using a standard home computer and a web browser (the software that enables you to display information from the Internet). Here's a list of the basic requirements:

- A PC with Microsoft® Windows® 98 or a later version, or a Macintosh computer with System 9.0 or later

- 64Mb RAM

- A web browser such as Microsoft® Internet Explorer 5, or Netscape® 6, or later versions

- Connection to the Internet via a modem (preferably 56kbps) or a faster digital or cable line

- An account with an Internet Service Provider (ISP)

- A sound card to hear sound files

> ### Computer not essential
> If you don't have use of the Internet, don't worry. This atlas is a complete, self-contained reference book on its own.

# Extras

Some websites need additional free programs, called plug-ins, to play sounds, or to show videos, animations or 3-D images. If you go to a site and you do not have the necessary plug-in, a message should come up on the screen.

There is usually a button on the site that you can click on to download the plug-in. Alternatively, go to Usborne Quicklinks and click on "Net Help". There you can find links to download plug-ins. Here is a list of plug-ins that you might need:

- **QuickTime** – lets you play video clips.

- **RealOne™ Player** – lets you play video clips and sound files.

- **Flash™** – lets you play animations.

- **Shockwave®** – lets you play animations and enjoy interactive sites.

# Computer viruses

A computer virus is a program that can damage your computer. A virus can get into your computer when you download programs from the Internet, or in an attachment (an extra file) that arrives with an email. We strongly recommend that you buy anti-virus software to protect your computer and that you update the software regularly. You can buy anti-virus software at computer stores or download it from the Internet. To find out more about viruses, go to Usborne Quicklinks and click on "Net Help".

*Macintosh and QuickTime are trademarks of Apple computer, Inc., registered in the U.S.A. and other countries.*

*RealOne Player is a trademark of RealNetworks, Inc., registered in the U.S.A. and other countries.*

*Flash and Shockwave are trademarks of Macromedia, Inc., registered in the U.S.A. and other countries.*

# Internet safety

When using the Internet, make sure you follow these simple safety rules.

- Ask your parent's or guardian's permission before you connect to the Internet. They can then stay nearby if they think they should do so.

- If you write a message in a website guest book or on a website message board, do not include your email address, real name, address or telephone number.

- If a website asks you to log in or register by typing your name or email address, ask the permission of an adult first.

- If you receive email from someone you don't know, tell an adult and do not reply to the email.

- Never arrange to meet anyone you have talked to on the Internet.

# Note for parents

The websites described in this book are regularly checked and reviewed by Usborne editors and the links in Usborne Quicklinks are updated. However, the content of a website may change at any time and Usborne Publishing is not responsible for the content of any website other than its own.

We recommend that children are supervised while on the Internet, that they do not use Internet chat rooms and that you use Internet filtering software to block unsuitable material. Please ensure that your children follow the safety guidelines above. For more information, go to the Net Help area on the Usborne Quicklinks Website at **www.usborne-quicklinks.com**

# MAPS AND ATLASES

An atlas is a collection of maps, along with useful information about the areas shown. The maps in this atlas cover the whole world and are grouped by continent.

## What maps show

A map is an image that represents an area of the Earth's surface, usually from above. Unlike a photograph, which shows exactly what an area looks like, a map can show features of the area in a clear, simplified way. It can also give different information, such as place names. Symbols are often used to mark features such as volcanoes and waterfalls.

## Which way is up?

Although the Earth doesn't have a top and a bottom, north is usually at the top of maps. But it is sometimes more convenient to reposition a map, so north might not necessarily be at the top. Some maps have a compass symbol that indicates where north lies.

Wolf volcano

Darwin volcano

San Salvador

Fernandina

Alcedo volcano

La Cumbre volcano

Santa Cruz

Isabela

Sierra Negra volcano

Cerro Azul volcano

*This simple map of the central Galapagos Islands names the main islands and their volcanoes.*

Floreana

*This is a satellite image of part of the Galapagos Islands. Using the map on this page, can you identify the islands shown in the satellite photo?*

## Physical and political

Physical maps indicate natural features such as mountains, deserts, rivers and lakes. Political maps focus on the division of the Earth's surface into different countries. Look on pages 16–17 for a political map of the world, and on pages 18–19 for a physical map. Most of the maps in this atlas show physical features as well as country borders, cities and towns.

# Using satellites

Today, scientists can make more accurate maps of the world than ever before, using information from artificial satellites in space. These devices travel around, or orbit, the Earth, and send back pictures of its surface. Satellite images provide detailed views of the Earth, and are often artificially shaded to highlight certain features, for example forests or deserts, so they are easier to see. They are used for a variety of purposes, such as monitoring weather conditions and natural hazards.

# Map scales

The size of a map in relation to the area it shows is called its scale. Some maps have a scale bar, which is a rule with measurements. It tells you how many miles or km are represented by a certain distance on the map. Other maps show these relative distances just as numbers. For example, the figure 1:100 means that 1cm on the map represents 100cm on the Earth's surface.

The scale of a map depends on its purpose. A map showing the whole world is on a very small scale, but a town plan is on a much larger scale so that features such as roads can be shown clearly.

## Internet links

For links to the following websites, go to **www.usborne-quicklinks.com**

**Website 1** Find physical and political maps of different countries.

**Website 2** Look at detailed satellite pictures of any part of the world.

*This illustration shows a satellite that monitors weather conditions on Earth. It collects data using powerful radar.*

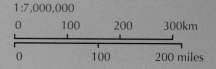

*This map of Europe is on a small scale so that it all fits onto one small map.*

*This map of Denmark is on a larger scale to show more detail.*

# DIVIDING LINES

The Earth is divided up with imaginary lines that help us measure distances and find where places are. There are two sets of lines, called latitude and longitude.

*This arctic fox lives in northern Canada, very near the Arctic Circle line of latitude.*

## Latitude lines

Lines of latitude run around the globe. They are parallel to each other and get shorter the closer they are to the two poles. The latitude line that runs around the middle of the Earth is called the Equator. It is the most important line of latitude as all other lines are measured north or south of it.

## Longitude lines

Lines of longitude run from the North Pole to the South Pole. All the lines are the same length, and they all meet at the North and South Poles.

The most important line of longitude is the Prime Meridian Line, which runs through Greenwich, in England. All other lines of longitude are measured east or west of this line.

## Other lines

The Equator is not the only named line of latitude. The Tropic of Cancer is a line north of the Equator. The Tropic of Capricorn is at the same distance south of the Equator. Between these lines are the hottest, wettest parts of the world. This region is called the tropics.

The Arctic Circle is a latitude line far north of the Equator. The area north of this includes the North Pole and is called the Arctic. On the other side of the globe is the Antarctic Circle. The area south of this includes the South Pole and is known as the Antarctic.

*Latitude lines*

*Longitude lines*

*This drawing of the Earth shows some of the main latitude and longitude lines.*

North Pole

Arctic Circle (66°30'N)

Prime Meridian Line (0°)

Tropic of Cancer (23°27'N)

Equator (0°)

Lines of longitude

Lines of latitude

Tropic of Capricorn (23°27'S)

### Internet link

For a link to a website where you can find out more about the Earth's lines of latitude and longitude, and test your knowledge with a great latitude and longitude quiz, go to **www.usborne-quicklinks.com**

# Using the lines

Lines of latitude and longitude are measured in degrees (°). The positions of places are described according to which lines of latitude and longitude are nearest to them. For example, a place with a location of 50°S and 100°E has a latitude 50 degrees south of the Equator, and a longitude 100 degrees east of the Prime Meridian Line.

# Exact locations

The distance between degrees is divided up to give even more precise measurements. Each degree is divided into 60 minutes ('), and each minute is divided into 60 seconds ("). The subdivisions allow us to locate any place on Earth. For example, the city of New York, U.S.A., is at 40°42'51"N and 74°00'23"W.

*The steamy rainforests of Malaysia lie near the Equator. Many apes, like the one shown here, live in these rainforests.*

*This is a map of New Zealand, with a grid formed by lines of latitude and longitude.*

# Using a grid

Lines of latitude and longitude form grids on maps. The maps in this book look similar to the one on the left. The columns that run from top to bottom are formed by lines of longitude and marked with letters. The rows running across the page are formed by lines of latitude and are numbered.

All the places listed in the map index on page 98 have a letter and a number reference that tell you where to find them on a particular page. For example, on the map on the left, the city of Christchurch would have a grid reference of C3.

# HOW MAPS ARE MADE

The process of making maps is called cartography. Map-makers, or cartographers, compile each map by gathering information about the area and representing it as an image as accurately as possible.

**Internet link**

For a link to a website where you can see examples of all kinds of different map projections, including cylindrical, conical and azimuthal projections, go to
**www.usborne-quicklinks.com**

## Creating maps

Many sources are used to create maps. These include satellite images and aerial photographs. Cartographers often visit the area to be mapped, where they take many extra measurements.

In addition, cartographers use statistics, such as population figures, from censuses and other documents. As the maps are being made, many people check them to make sure they are accurate and up to date.

## Map projections

Cartographers can't draw maps that show the world exactly as it is, because it is impossible to show a curved surface on a flat map without distorting (stretching or squashing) some areas. A representation of the Earth on a map is called a projection. Projections are worked out using complex mathematics.

There are three basic types of projections – cylindrical, conical and azimuthal, but there are also variations on these. They all distort the Earth's surface in some way, either by altering the shapes or sizes of areas of land or the distance between places.

*A cartographer uses an electronic distance measurer to check the measurements of an area of land.*

# Cylindrical projections

A cylindrical projection is similar to the image created by wrapping a piece of paper around a globe to form a cylinder and then shining a light inside the globe. The shapes of countries would be projected onto the paper. Near the middle they would be accurate, but farther away they would be distorted.

Cartographers often alter the basic cylindrical projection to make the distortion less obvious in certain areas, but they can never make a map that is completely accurate.

*This picture of a piece of paper wrapped around a globe illustrates how a cylindrical projection is made.*

*Below is a type of cylindrical projection called the Mercator projection, which was invented in 1596 by a cartographer named Gerardus Mercator. It makes countries the right shape, but makes those near the poles too big.*

*This cylindrical projection makes countries the right size in relation to each other, but some parts are too long. The projection was created in 1973 by Arno Peters. It is called the Peters Projection.*

# Conical projections

A conical projection is similar to the image you would get if you wrapped a cone of paper around part of a globe, then shone a light inside the globe. Where the cone touches the globe, the projection will be most accurate.

*This picture of a cone of paper over a globe illustrates how a conical projection is made.*

*This is a conical projection. The land nearest the top is the most distorted in shape.*

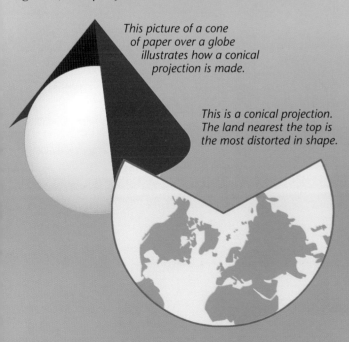

# Azimuthal projections

An azimuthal projection is like an image made by holding paper in front of a globe, and shining a light through it. Land projected onto the middle of the paper would be accurate, but areas farther away would be distorted.

*This picture of a piece of paper placed in front of a globe illustrates how an azimuthal projection is made.*

*This is an azimuthal projection. The farther away land is from the middle, the more distorted it is.*

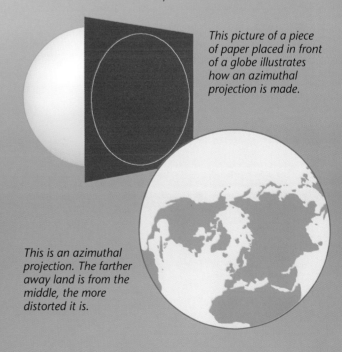

# THEMATIC MAPS

Maps that represent information on particular themes, like the ones on these pages, are known as thematic maps. They help you to identify patterns and make comparisons between the features of different areas.

## Earth's resources

The Earth contains all kinds of useful resources. Rocks and minerals can be used as building materials, and fuels such as coal, oil and gas contain energy that can be turned into heat and electricity.

Countries with large amounts of natural resources can become very rich. For example, Saudi Arabia, in western Asia, has large oil and gas reserves, which it exports all over the world.

*This is an oil field, where oil is extracted from the ground using pumps. It is then piped to refineries and turned into products such as motor fuel.*

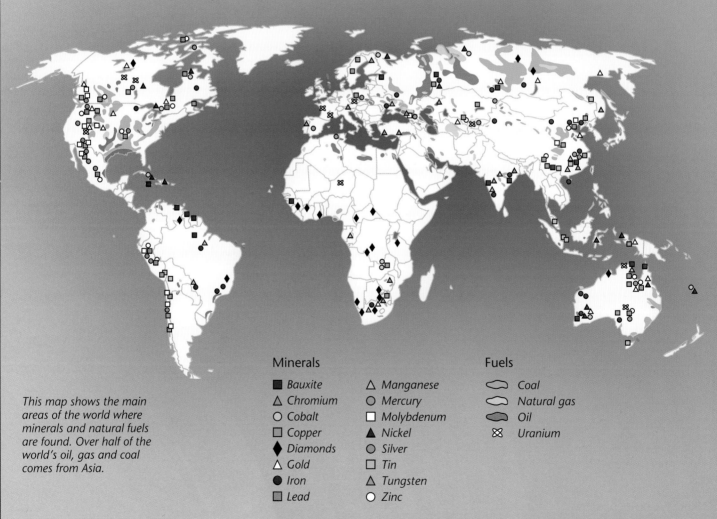

*This map shows the main areas of the world where minerals and natural fuels are found. Over half of the world's oil, gas and coal comes from Asia.*

**Minerals**

■ Bauxite
△ Chromium
○ Cobalt
□ Copper
◆ Diamonds
△ Gold
● Iron
▣ Lead
△ Manganese
○ Mercury
□ Molybdenum
▲ Nickel
◉ Silver
□ Tin
△ Tungsten
○ Zinc

**Fuels**

◠ Coal
◠ Natural gas
◗ Oil
⊠ Uranium

# Different climates

The long-term or typical pattern of weather in a particular area is known as its climate. Climates vary across the world and depend largely on each area's latitude. The hottest parts of the world are those closest to the Equator.

Climate is also affected by other factors, such as wind and the height of the land. Oceans influence climate too – places near the sea normally have a milder, wetter climate than areas farther inland.

*On this map, land is divided into five climate types. Dry areas are generally hot, but temperatures there can fall very low too. Some dry places, such as the Gobi Desert in eastern Asia, are extremely cold in winter.*

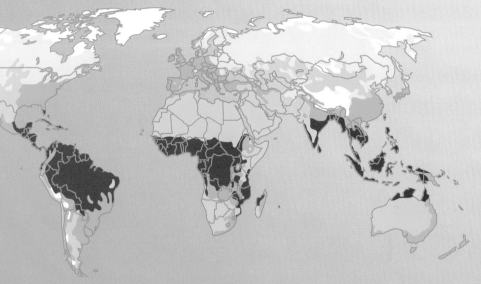

- ☐ Polar
- ☐ Cold
- ☐ Temperate
- ☐ Dry
- ■ Tropical

# World population

There are more than six billion people in the world, and the population is still growing. Experts think it may reach more than nine billion by 2050. The number of people living in a given area is known as its population density. Europe and Asia are the most densely populated continents in the world. About a third of the world's population lives in China and India alone.

## Internet link

For a link to a website where you can discover how many people there were on Earth when you were born, and find out about the effects of population growth, go to
**www.usborne-quicklinks.com**

*This map shows the average population density by country. The shading indicates the number of people per sq km (0.386 sq miles).*

- ■ Over 500 people
- ■ 200–500 people
- ☐ 100–200 people
- ☐ 50–100 people
- ☐ 10–50 people
- ☐ Fewer than 10 people

# HOW TO USE THE MAPS

Each continent section in this atlas begins with a political map showing the whole continent. The rest of the maps are larger scale maps showing the various parts of the continent in more detail.

## Political maps

The shading on the political maps in this atlas is there to help you see clearly the different countries that make up each continent. The main purpose of these maps is to show country borders and capital cities. Alongside them there are facts and figures about the continents and their features.

*This is a section of the political map of South America. You can see the whole map on pages 28–29.*

## Environmental maps

The majority of the maps in this atlas are environmental maps, like the one on the right. The shading on these maps shows different types of land, or environments, such as desert, mountain or wetland.

The main key on the opposite page shows what the different shading means. It also shows the symbols used to represent towns, cities and other features. There is a smaller key on each environmental map repeating the most important information from this key.

## Finding places

To find a particular place or feature on the environmental maps, look up its name in the index on pages 98–111. Its page number and grid reference is given next to the name. You can find out how to use the grid on page 9.

*The map on the right is part of the environmental map of the U.S.A. The numbered labels at the top explain some important features of these maps.*

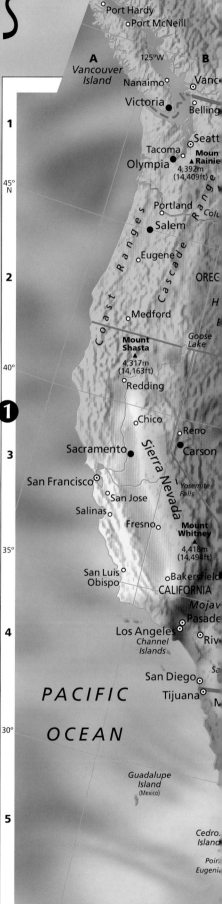

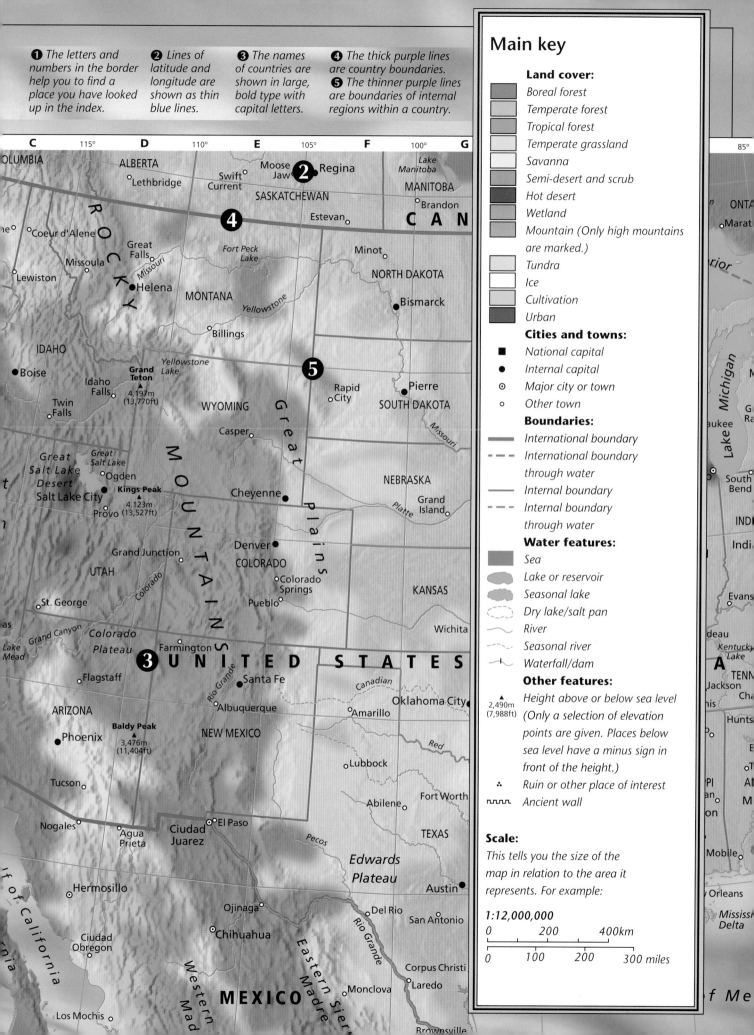

❶ The letters and numbers in the border help you to find a place you have looked up in the index.

❷ Lines of latitude and longitude are shown as thin blue lines.

❸ The names of countries are shown in large, bold type with capital letters.

❹ The thick purple lines are country boundaries.

❺ The thinner purple lines are boundaries of internal regions within a country.

# Main key

### Land cover:
*Boreal forest*
*Temperate forest*
*Tropical forest*
*Temperate grassland*
*Savanna*
*Semi-desert and scrub*
*Hot desert*
*Wetland*
*Mountain (Only high mountains are marked.)*
*Tundra*
*Ice*
*Cultivation*
*Urban*

### Cities and towns:
■ *National capital*
● *Internal capital*
⊙ *Major city or town*
○ *Other town*

### Boundaries:
── *International boundary*
--- *International boundary through water*
── *Internal boundary*
--- *Internal boundary through water*

### Water features:
*Sea*
*Lake or reservoir*
*Seasonal lake*
*Dry lake/salt pan*
*River*
*Seasonal river*
*Waterfall/dam*

### Other features:
▲ 2,490m (7,988ft) *Height above or below sea level (Only a selection of elevation points are given. Places below sea level have a minus sign in front of the height.)*
⁂ *Ruin or other place of interest*
ⲛⲛⲛⲛ *Ancient wall*

### Scale:
*This tells you the size of the map in relation to the area it represents. For example:*

**1:12,000,000**

| 0 | 200 | 400km |

| 0 | 100 | 200 | 300 miles |

GREENLAND
(Denmark)

Arctic Circle

ALASKA
(U.S.A.)

ICELAND

60°

C A N A D A

IRELAND
UNITED
KINGDO

40°

UNITED STATES
OF AMERICA

Azores
(Portugal)

SPAIN

PORTUGAL

MOROCCO

Canary Islands
(Spain)

ALG

Tropic of Cancer

THE BAHAMAS

WESTERN SAHARA
(Morocco)

20°
N

Hawaiian
Islands
(U.S.A.)

MEXICO

CUBA

DOMINICAN
REPUBLIC

HAITI

MAURITANIA

MALI

CAPE VERDE

SENEGAL

BURKINA
FASO

JAMAICA

BELIZE
GUATEMALA HONDURAS
EL SALVADOR NICARAGUA

Caribbean Sea

DOMINICA

THE GAMBIA
GUINEA-BISSAU

GUINEA

P A C I F I C

COSTA RICA
PANAMA

TRINIDAD AND TOBAGO

SIERRA LEONE

LIBERIA

IVORY
COAST

TOG

GHAN
EC

VENEZUELA

GUYANA
SURINAM

SAO TOME A
PRINCIPE

COLOMBIA

FRENCH GUIANA
(France)

Equator

Galapagos Islands
(Ecuador)

ECUADOR

A T L A N T I C

O C E A N

KIRIBATI

PERU

B R A Z I L

O C E A N

Cook
Islands
(New Zealand)

French
Polynesia
(France)

BOLIVIA

20°
S

Tropic of Capricorn

Pitcairn
Islands
(U.K.)

PARAGUAY

CHILE

URUGUAY

ARGENTINA

40°

1:80,000,000

0    1,000   2,000   3,000   4,000  5,000km

0         1,000        2,000       3,000 miles

Falkland Islands
(U.K.)

South Georgia
(U.K.)

60°

Antarctic Circle

Weddell
Sea

80°

160°    140°    120°    100°    80°    60°    40°    20° W

40° 60° 80° 100° 120° 140° 160° 180°

**Abbreviations used on map:**

| ARM. | ARMENIA |
|---|---|
| AUST. | AUSTRIA |
| AZER. | AZERBAIJAN |
| BELG. | BELGIUM |
| B.H. | BOSNIA AND HERZEGOVINA |
| CRO. | CROATIA |
| CZECH REP. | CZECH REPUBLIC |
| LEB. | LEBANON |
| LUX. | LUXEMBOURG |
| MAC. | MACEDONIA |
| NETH. | NETHERLANDS |
| S.M. | SERBIA AND MONTENEGRO |
| SLOV. | SLOVENIA |
| SWITZ. | SWITZERLAND |
| U.A.E. | UNITED ARAB EMIRATES |

Arctic Circle

80°

FINLAND

RUSSIA

60°

ESTONIA
LATVIA
LITHUANIA
BELARUS
ND
KIA
UKRAINE
GARY MOLDOVA
ROMANIA
S.M. BULGARIA
MAC.
GREECE TURKEY

Black Sea

GEORGIA
ARM. AZER.
Caspian Sea

KAZAKHSTAN

UZBEKISTAN KYRGYZSTAN

MONGOLIA

NORTH KOREA

40°

TURKMENISTAN

CYPRUS LEB. SYRIA
ISRAEL
JORDAN
IRAQ
IRAN
ranean Sea

TAJIKISTAN

AFGHANISTAN

PAKISTAN

CHINA

SOUTH KOREA

JAPAN

PACIFIC

OCEAN

EGYPT

KUWAIT
BAHRAIN
QATAR
U.A.E.
SAUDI ARABIA

OMAN

NEPAL
BHUTAN
BANGLA-
DESH

INDIA

BURMA
(MYANMAR)

TAIWAN

Tropic of Cancer

20° N

AD

SUDAN

ERITREA
YEMEN

DJIBOUTI

LAOS

THAILAND

VIETNAM

CAMBODIA

PHILIPPINES

Northern Mariana Islands (U.S.A.)

MARSHALL ISLANDS

entral
FRICAN
EPUBLIC
N

ETHIOPIA

SOMALIA

SRI LANKA

BRUNEI

MALAYSIA

PALAU

FEDERATED STATES OF MICRONESIA

CONGO
EMOCRATIC
REPUBLIC)

UGANDA
KENYA
RWANDA
BURUNDI
TANZANIA

MALDIVES

SEYCHELLES

INDIAN

SINGAPORE

INDONESIA

Equator 0°

NAURU

KIRIBATI

PAPUA
NEW GUINEA

SOLOMON ISLANDS

TUVALU

LA

ZAMBIA

MALAWI

ZIMBABWE

COMOROS

OCEAN

EAST TIMOR

Coral Sea Islands Territory (Australia)

SAMOA

VANUATU

FIJI TONGA 20° S

BOTSWANA MOZAMBIQUE
MADAGASCAR MAURITIUS

Reunion (France)

New Caledonia (France)

Tropic of Capricorn

SWAZILAND

AUSTRALIA

A LESOTHO
OUTH AFRICA

40°

Kerguelen Islands (France)

NEW ZEALAND

60°

OUTHERN OCEAN

Antarctic Circle

80°

ANTARCTICA

The shading on this map is there to help you see the different countries clearly.

40° 60° 80° 100° 120° 140° 160° 180°

Copyright © Usborne Publishing Ltd.

17

160° 140° 120° 100° 80° 60° 40° 20° W

Ellesmere Island

80°

*Beaufort Sea*

Victoria Island

Queen Elizabeth Islands

Baffin Island

Baffin Bay

*Greenland*

Greenland Sea

Arctic Circle

*Alaska*

60°

**Mount McKinley**
▲
6,194m
(20,321ft)

Yukon

Gulf of Alaska

Aleutian Islands

Hudson Bay

Labrador Sea

Iceland

British Isles

40°

**NORTH AMERICA**

Rocky Mountains

Great Plains

Great Lakes

Newfoundland

Appalachian Mountains

Azores

Mississippi

Tropic of Cancer

Gulf of Mexico

Canary Islands

Atlas Mo

20° N

Hawaiian Islands

Cuba

West Indies

Greater Antilles

Cape Verde Islands

Caribbean Sea

Lesser Antilles

0° Equator

*Polynesia*

PACIFIC OCEAN

Galapagos Islands

Guiana Highlands

Amazon Basin

Amazon

ATLANTIC OCEAN

Selvas

**SOUTH AMERICA**

20° S

Tahiti

Andes

Tropic of Capricorn

Easter Island

Atacama Desert

**Aconcagua**
▲
6,959m
(22,831ft)

Pampas

40°

1:80,000,000

0   1,000   2,000   3,000   4,000   5,000km

0        1,000        2,000        3,000 miles

Patagonia

Falkland Islands

South Georgia

Cape Horn

60°

Antarctic Circle

Antarctic Peninsula

*Weddell Sea*

80°

160° 140° 120° 100° 80° 60° 40° 20° W

ARCTIC OCEAN

Svalbard
Novaya Zemlya
Kara Sea
Severnaya Zemlya
Laptev Sea
New Siberia Islands
East Siberian Sea
Cape
Barents Sea

Scandinavia
North European Plain
Ural Mountains
Ob
Yenisey
Siberia
Verkhoyansk Range
Arctic Circle

60°

EUROPE
Volga
ASIA
Lake Baikal
Altai Mountains
Sea of Okhotsk
Kamchatka Peninsula

Danube
Black Sea
Mount Elbrus
5,642m (18,510ft)
Caspian Sea
Aral Sea
Gobi Desert
Huang He (Yellow)
Sea of Japan
Hokkaido

Mediterranean Sea
Zagros Mountains
Himalayas
Chang Jiang (Yangtze)
Yellow Sea
Honshu

40°

Arabian Peninsula
Red Sea
Ganges
Mount Everest
8,850m (29,035ft)
East China Sea
Tropic of Cancer

AFRICA
Ethiopian Highlands
Arabian Sea
Deccan Plateau
Bay of Bengal
Mekong
Taiwan
20° N

Lake Victoria
Seychelles
Sri Lanka
South China Sea
Philippine Islands
Micronesia
PACIFIC OCEAN

Congo Basin
Kilimanjaro
5,895m (19,340ft)
Celebes Sea
Borneo

Rift Valley
Comoro Islands
INDIAN OCEAN
Sumatra
Greater Sunda Islands
Java
New Guinea
Mount Wilhelm
4,509m (14,793ft)
Solomon Islands
Melanesia
Equator

Madagascar
Mauritius
Reunion
Lesser Sunda Islands
Arafura Sea
Coral Sea
New Caledonia
Fiji Islands
20° S

Kalahari Desert
Great Sandy Desert
AUSTRALASIA AND OCEANIA
Great Barrier Reef
Tropic of Capricorn

Drakensberg
of Good Hope
Great Victoria Desert
Great Dividing Range
Tasman Sea
North Island
40°

Kerguelen Islands
Tasmania
South Island

SOUTHERN OCEAN

60°

Antarctic Circle

See page 15 for key.

ANTARCTICA
80°

40° 60° 80° 100° 120° 140° 160° 180°

Copyright © Usborne Publishing Ltd.

# NORTH AMERICA

The name "North America" can be used to mean several different things. In this atlas, North America includes Greenland, Canada, the U.S.A., the Caribbean, and the countries of Central America, which run along the narrow strip of land between the U.S.A. and South America. The continent has over 20 countries, including Canada, the second-largest country in the world.

These are columns of rock called hoodoos in Bryce Canyon National Park, U.S.A.

Arctic Circle

**ARCTIC OCEAN**

Bering
Sea

Beaufort
Sea

Yukon

**ALASKA**
(U.S.A.)

⊙ Anchorage

Victoria
Island

**CANAD**

Vancouver ⊙

Columbia

**PACIFIC**

**OCEAN**

Hawaiian
Islands
(U.S.A.)

**UNITED STAT**

Colorado

Los Angeles ⊙

Rio Grande

Tropic of Cancer

**MEXICO**

Mexico ●

Copyright © Usborne Publishing Ltd.

The shading on this map is
there to help you see clearly
the different countries that
make up the continent.

**Internet link**

For a link to a website where you
can find out about the history and
geography of each U.S. state, go to
www.usborne-quicklinks.com

GREENLAND
(Denmark)

*mere*
*d*

*Baffin
Island*

**Godthab** ■

*beth
ds*

*Hudson
Bay*

*Newfoundland*

*Arctic Circle*

*St. Lawrence*

Montreal ⊙
**Ottawa** ■

*Great
Lakes*

⊙ New York

Chicago ⊙

■ **Washington D.C.**

**AMERICA**

*ATLANTIC
OCEAN*

*Mississippi*

*Tropic of Cancer*

*Houston*

**THE
BAHAMAS**

*Gulf of
Mexico*

**Havana** ■
**CUBA**

*Puerto Rico*
(U.S.A.)

*Guadeloupe*
(France)

**HAITI**   **DOMINICAN
REPUBLIC**

**DOMINICA**
*Martinique* (France)

**JAMAICA**

**BARBADOS**

**BELIZE**

*Caribbean Sea*

**TRINIDAD
AND TOBAGO**

**HONDURAS**

**UATEMALA**

**NICARAGUA**

**EL SALVADOR**

**COSTA RICA**   **PANAMA**

# Facts

**Total land area**  22,656,190 sq km
(8,745,289 sq miles)
**Total population**  487 million
**Biggest city**  Mexico City, Mexico
**Biggest country**  Canada  *9,970,610
sq km (3,849,653 sq miles)*
**Smallest country**  Saint Kitts and
Nevis  *269 sq km (104 sq miles)*

**Highest mountain**  Mount
McKinley, Alaska, U.S.A.  *6,194m
(20,321ft)*
**Longest river**  Mississippi/Missouri,
U.S.A.  *6,019km (3,741 miles)*
**Biggest lake**  Lake Superior,
between the U.S.A. and
Canada  *82,414 sq km (31,820
sq miles)*
**Highest waterfall**  Yosemite Falls,
on the Yosemite Creek, California,
U.S.A.  *739m (2,425ft)*
**Biggest desert**  Great Basin Desert,
U.S.A.  *492,000 sq km (190,000
sq miles)*
**Biggest island**  Greenland
*2,175,600 sq km (840,000 sq miles)*

**Main mineral deposits**  Silver, gold,
copper, lead, zinc, graphite,
molybdenum, nickel
**Main fuel deposits**  Oil, coal,
natural gas, uranium

*The bald eagle is the national bird
of the U.S.A. It is not really bald,
but has white feathers
on its head.*

21

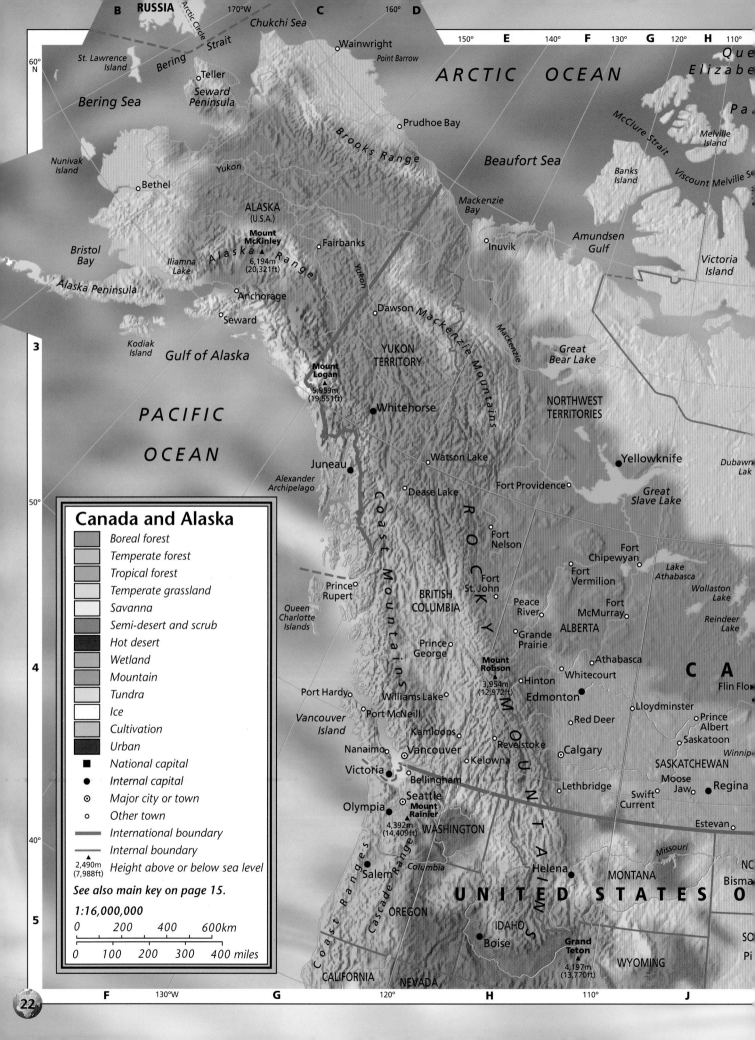

## Canada and Alaska

| | |
|---|---|
| | Boreal forest |
| | Temperate forest |
| | Tropical forest |
| | Temperate grassland |
| | Savanna |
| | Semi-desert and scrub |
| | Hot desert |
| | Wetland |
| | Mountain |
| | Tundra |
| | Ice |
| | Cultivation |
| | Urban |
| ■ | National capital |
| ● | Internal capital |
| ⊙ | Major city or town |
| ○ | Other town |
| | International boundary |
| | Internal boundary |
| ▲ 2,490m (7,988ft) | Height above or below sea level |

See also main key on page 15.

1:16,000,000

0   200   400   600km

0   100   200   300   400 miles

### Map labels

RUSSIA
Arctic Circle
Chukchi Sea
Bering Strait
St. Lawrence Island
Teller
Seward Peninsula
Bering Sea
Wainwright
Point Barrow
ARCTIC OCEAN
Quee Elizabe Pa
Nunivak Island
Bethel
Yukon
ALASKA (U.S.A.)
Prudhoe Bay
Brooks Range
Beaufort Sea
McClure Strait
Melville Island
Banks Island
Viscount Melville S
Bristol Bay
Iliamna Lake
Mount McKinley 6,194m (20,321ft)
Alaska Range
Fairbanks
Mackenzie Bay
Inuvik
Amundsen Gulf
Victoria Island
Alaska Peninsula
Anchorage
Yukon
Seward
Kodiak Island
Gulf of Alaska
Dawson
YUKON TERRITORY
Mackenzie Mountains
Mackenzie
Great Bear Lake
NORTHWEST TERRITORIES
PACIFIC OCEAN
Mount Logan 5,959m (19,551ft)
Whitehorse
Yellowknife
Dubawn Lak
Juneau
Watson Lake
Fort Providence
Great Slave Lake
Alexander Archipelago
Dease Lake
ROCKY
Fort Nelson
Fort Chipewyan
Lake Athabasca
Wollaston Lake
Prince Rupert
Queen Charlotte Islands
BRITISH COLUMBIA
Fort St. John
Fort Vermilion
Reindeer Lake
Peace River
Fort McMurray
ALBERTA
Grande Prairie
Prince George
Mount Robson 3,954m (12,972ft)
Athabasca
C A
Port Hardy
Williams Lake
Hinton
Whitecourt
Flin Flo
Vancouver Island
Port McNeill
Edmonton
Lloydminster
Prince Albert
Kamloops
Red Deer
Saskatoon
Winnip
Nanaimo
Vancouver
Revelstoke
Calgary
SASKATCHEWAN
Victoria
Kelowna
Moose Jaw
Regina
Bellingham
Lethbridge
Swift Current
Seattle
Olympia
Mount Rainier 4,392m (14,409ft)
WASHINGTON
Estevan
Salem
Coast Ranges
Columbia
Helena
MONTANA
NO Bisma
Cascade Range
OREGON
UNITED STATES O
Boise
IDAHO
Grand Teton 4,197m (13,770ft)
CALIFORNIA
NEVADA
WYOMING
Pi
SO
Missouri
Coast Mountains

60°N
50°
40°
170°W
160°
150°   E   140°   F   130°   G   120°   H   110°
130°W   120°   110°
B   C   D   E   F   G   H
F   G   H   J
3
4
5

90° **L** 80° **M** 70° **N** 60° **P** 50° **Q** 40° **R** 30° **S** 60°

*Ellesmere Island*

*Devon Island*

*Lancaster Sound*

*...erset Island*

*...othia ...insula*

*Gulf of Boothia*

*Baffin Bay*

**A** 180° **B** 170°W **C** 160°

*Bering Sea*

55°N

**Shishaldin Volcano** 55°N

2,857m (9,372ft) ▲ *Unimak Island*

**3** *Attu Island*

*Near Islands*

*A l e u t i a n   I s l a n d s*

*Fox Islands*

**3**

*Unalaska Island*

*Rat Islands*

*Andreanof Islands*

*Atka Island*

*Umnak Island*

**Same scale as main map**

**A** 180° **B** 170°W **C**

**1** *Baffin Bay*

*Baffin Island*

*Cumberland Peninsula*

*Nettling Lake*

**2**

*Davis Strait*

**GREENLAND** *Cape Farewell*
(Denmark)

**3**

*Melville Peninsula*

*Foxe Basin*

*Foxe Peninsula*

*Amadjuak Lake*

●*Iqaluit*

*Labrador Sea*

*ATLANTIC*

*OCEAN*

**NUNAVUT**

*Southampton Island*

*Hudson Strait*

○*Ivujivik*

*Ungava Peninsula*

*Ungava Bay*

*Cape Chidley*

*Nain* ○

50°

*Makkovik* ○

○*Kuujjuaq*

**NEWFOUNDLAND**

*Cartwright* ○

All islands within Hudson Bay, James Bay and Ungava Bay lie within Nunavut.

○*Inukjuak*

*Smallwood Reservoir*

*Happy Valley-Goose Bay* ○

**Hudson Bay**

*Churchill Falls* ○

*Gander* ○

*St. John's* ●

●*Churchill*

*Belcher Islands*

*Labrador City* ○

*Newfoundland*

*Corner Brook* ○

**...TOBA**

*...ompson*

*Fort Severn* ○

*La Grande Reservoir*

**D A**

*James Bay*

○*Radisson*

**QUEBEC**

*Manicouagan Reservoir*

*Anticosti Island*

*St. Pierre and Miquelon* (France)

**4**

*Lake Winnipeg*

*...s*

*Fort Albany* ○

○*Waskaganish*

*Baie-Comeau* ○

*Gulf of St. Lawrence*

*Gaspe* ○

*Sydney* ○

*...peg*

*Lake of the Woods*

*Dryden* ○

○*Kenora*

**ONTARIO**

*Lake Nipigon*

*Kirkland Lake* ○

*Lake Mistassini*

*Chicoutimi* ○

*Val-d'Or* ○

*Quebec* ●

*Bathurst* ○

**PRINCE EDWARD ISLAND**

*Charlottetown* ●

*...ba*

○*Marathon*

*Edmundston* ○

**NEW BRUNSWICK**

*Moncton* ○

*Halifax* ●

*Thunder Bay* ○

*Trois-Rivieres* ○

*Fredericton* ○

**NOVA SCOTIA**

**MINNESOTA**

**A**

*Lake Superior*

*Sudbury* ○

*Montreal* ○

*St. Lawrence*

**MAINE**

*Saint John* ○

*Yarmouth* ○

**MERICA**

*Sault Ste. Marie* ○

*North Bay* ○

**Ottawa** ■

*Montpelier* ○

*Augusta* ○

40°

*Huntsville* ○

*Concord* ○

*St. Paul* ○

**WISCONSIN**

**MICHIGAN**

*Owen Sound* ○

*Kingston* ○

*Lake Ontario*

*Albany* ○

**VERMONT**

**NEW HAMPSHIRE**

*Boston* ●

**MASSACHUSETTS**

*Providence* ●

**5**

*Minneapolis* ●

*Lake Huron*

*Toronto* ●

*Niagara Falls*

**NEW YORK**

*Hartford* ●

**RHODE ISLAND**

*Madison* ●

*Lansing* ○

*Hamilton* ○

*Buffalo* ○

**CONNECTICUT**

*New York* ●

*London* ○

*Detroit* ●

*Lake Erie*

*Trenton* ●

**NEW JERSEY**

**K**

*Chicago* ●

*Windsor* ○

*Erie* ○

**PENNSYLVANIA**

*Harrisburg* ○

*Philadelphia* ●

*Dover* ●

70° **N**

**ILLINOIS**

**INDIANA**

*Cleveland* ○

*Pittsburgh* ○

*Annapolis* ○

**DELAWARE**

*Columbus* ●

**OHIO**

**Washington D.C.** ■

*Mississippi*

*Lake Michigan*

90° 80°

Copyright © Usborne Publishing Ltd.

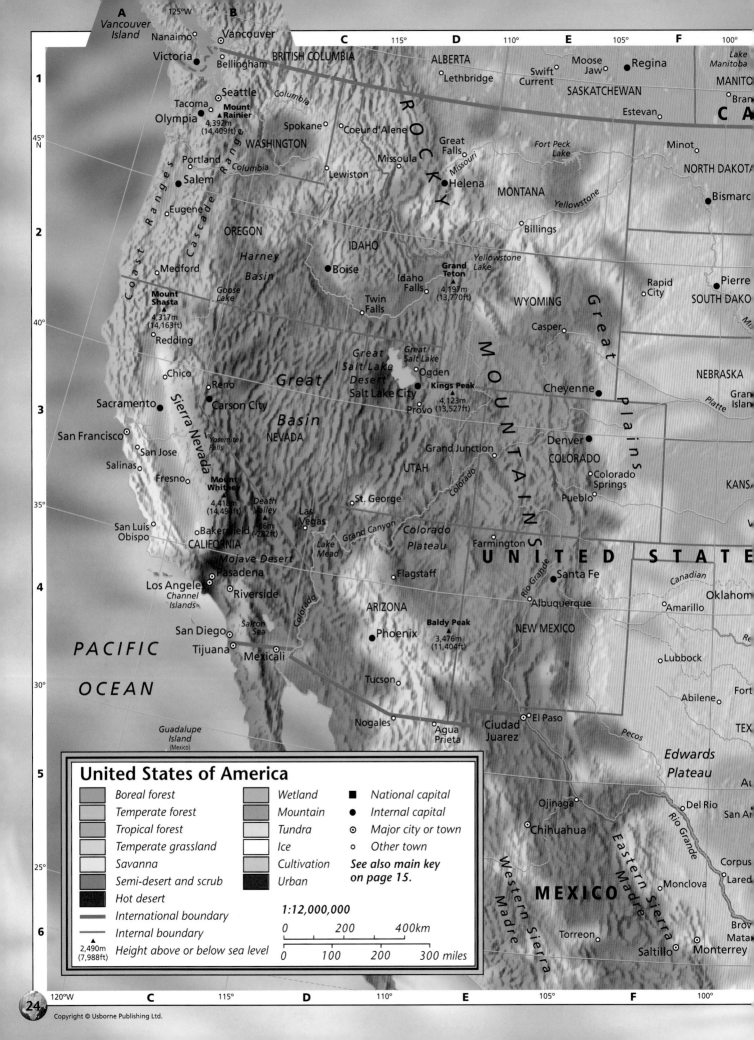

A B 125°W C 115° D 110° E 105° F 100°

**Vancouver Island** Nanaimo ●Vancouver
Victoria ○Bellingham BRITISH COLUMBIA ALBERTA Swift Moose ●Regina Lake Manitoba MANITO
1 Lethbridge Current Jaw Estevan Bran C A
SASKATCHEWAN

Tacoma● ○Seattle Columbia Coeur d'Alene Great ○Minot NORTH DAKOTA
Olympia● ▲Mount Spokane Falls Missouri
Rainier ○Missoula R Fort Peck ●Bismarc
4,392m WASHINGTON Lewiston Helena● O Lake
(14,409ft) Portland● Columbia Helena● C Yellowstone Billings
45°N Salem● MONTANA
Eugene○ OREGON K ●Rapid Pierre●
2 City
Harney Boise Yellowstone Y SOUTH DAKO
Medford○ Basin ●Boise Lake ●Casper
Mount Goose Idaho Grand WYOMING Great NEBRASKA
Shasta Lake Falls○ Teton Cheyenne●
4,317m Twin 4,197m M Platte Gran
(14,163ft) Falls○ (13,770ft) Islan
40° Redding○ O
Chico○ Great U Great Denver●
Reno○ Salt Lake Salt Lake N Grand Junction COLORADO KANS
3 Sacramento● Carson City● Desert ○Ogden T Colorado
Salt Lake City○ Kings Peak A Springs
San Francisco○ Basin Provo○ 4,123m I Pueblo○
San Jose○ NEVADA (13,527ft) N
Salinas○ St. George○ UTAH S
Fresno○ Mount Colorado Farmington○ Santa Fe●
Whitney Death ○ Plateau U N I T E D S T A T E
4,418m Valley Las Flagstaff○
(14,494ft) -86m Vegas○ Grand Canyon Albuquerque○ Canadian Oklahom
San Luis (-282ft) Lake Colorado ●Santa Fe
4 Obispo○ Bakersfield○ Mead Plateau Amarillo○
CALIFORNIA Mojave Desert ARIZONA NEW MEXICO Re
Pasadena● Lubbock○
Los Angeles● Riverside● Baldy Peak
Channel Salton ●Phoenix 3,476m Abilene○ Fort
Islands Sea (11,404ft) TEX
San Diego○ Tucson○ Pecos
Tijuana○ Mexicali○ El Paso○ Edwards
PACIFIC Nogales○ Ciudad Plateau
Juárez A
Agua Ojinaga○ Del Rio○ San A
OCEAN Prieta○ Rio Grande
Guadalupe Chihuahua○ Corpus
Island W
(Mexico) e Lared
s
t Monclova○
e
5 r Western Sierra Saltillo○ Monterrey●
n
S MEXICO Torreon○
i
e Eastern Sierra Madre
r
r
a
6

**United States of America**

Boreal forest ☐ Wetland ■ National capital
Temperate forest ☐ Mountain ● Internal capital
Tropical forest ☐ Tundra ⊙ Major city or town
Temperate grassland ☐ Ice ○ Other town
Savanna ☐ Cultivation *See also main key*
Semi-desert and scrub ■ Urban *on page 15.*
Hot desert

━━━ International boundary 1:12,000,000
─── Internal boundary 0 200 400km
▲ 2,490m Height above or below sea level 0 100 200 300 miles
(7,988ft)

Copyright © Usborne Publishing Ltd.

120°W C 115° D 110° E 105° F 100°

95° H 90° J 85° K 80° L 75° M 70° N 65°

1

Chicoutimi  Bathurst
Edmundston
Gouin Reservoir
QUEBEC  NEW BRUNSWICK
Winnipeg  Kenora  Dryden  Lake Nipigon  ONTARIO  Val-d'Or  Quebec  Fredericton
Lake of the Woods  Marathon  Kirkland Lake  St. Lawrence  MAINE  Saint John
Thunder Bay  Cabonga Reservoir  Trois-Rivieres  St. Stephen  45°N
Lake Superior  Sudbury  North Bay  Montreal  Bangor

2
Duluth  Sault Ste. Marie  Huntsville  Ottawa  VERMONT  Augusta
MINNESOTA  Lake Huron  Kingston  Montpelier  NEW HAMPSHIRE  Portland  Gulf of Maine
Owen Sound  NEW YORK  Concord
Minneapolis  St. Paul  MICHIGAN  Toronto  Lake Ontario  Albany  Boston
Green Bay  Hamilton  Niagara Falls  Rochester  Syracuse  MASSACHUSETTS  Cape Cod
Madison  Milwaukee  WISCONSIN  London  Buffalo  Springfield  Providence
Grand Rapids  Lansing  Lake Erie  Jamestown  Hartford  RHODE ISLAND  40°
Sioux City  Rockford  Detroit  Erie  CONNECTICUT
Cedar Rapids  Chicago  Windsor  Cleveland  Newark  New York
IOWA  South Bend  Toledo  PENNSYLVANIA  Trenton  Philadelphia
Omaha  Des Moines  Fort Wayne  OHIO  Pittsburgh  Harrisburg  NEW JERSEY  Atlantic City  3
Lincoln  Peoria  Columbus  Baltimore  Dover  DELAWARE
ILLINOIS  INDIANA  WEST VIRGINIA  MARYLAND  Annapolis
Quincy  Springfield  Indianapolis  Cincinnati  Charleston  Washington D.C.
Kansas City  Frankfort  Ohio  Charlottesville
eka  Jefferson City  St. Louis  Lexington  VIRGINIA  Richmond  35°
MISSOURI  Evansville  Roanoke  Virginia Beach
Cape Girardeau  KENTUCKY
Springfield  Kentucky Lake  Knoxville  Greensboro  Raleigh  Cape Hatteras
Ozark Plateau  Nashville  Tennessee  NORTH CAROLINA  ATLANTIC
Tulsa  AMERICA  Jonesboro  Jackson  Chattanooga  Charlotte  OCEAN  4
as  Memphis  TENNESSEE  Appalachian Mountains  Columbia
OHOMA  Little Rock  Tupelo  Huntsville  Clark Hill Lake  SOUTH CAROLINA
ARKANSAS  Mississippi  Atlanta  Charleston  160°W  Same scale as main map
Texarkana  Greenville  Birmingham  Macon  GEORGIA  Hawaiian Islands
llas  Shreveport  Tuscaloosa  ALABAMA  Columbus  Savannah  Kauai  Oahu  Molokai
MISSISSIPPI  Meridian  Montgomery  Albany  7  Honolulu  Kahului  Maui  7
Vicksburg  Jackson  Valdosta  HAWAII (U.S.A.)  4,205m (13,796ft)▲  20°N
ston  Beaumont  LOUISIANA  Hattiesburg  Mobile  Jacksonville  20°N  PACIFIC OCEAN  Hilo
Sam Rayburn Reservoir  Toledo Bend Reservoir  Pensacola  Daytona Beach  8  P  Hawaii  8
Galveston  Baton Rouge  New Orleans  Apalachee Bay  160°W  155°
Mississippi Delta  Orlando  Cape Canaveral
Gulf of Mexico  FLORIDA  Grand Bahama  Abaco  THE BAHAMAS
Tampa  Freeport City  25°
St. Petersburg  Lake Okeechobee  Eleuthera
The Everglades  Fort Lauderdale  Nassau  Cat Island
Miami  Andros  6
Key West  Florida Keys  Tropic of Cancer
Straits of Florida  Long Island
Acklins Island
95° H 90° J  Matanzas  Santa Clara  75°
Havana  CUBA  Ciego de Avila
Cienfuegos  Camaguey
85°  Pinar del Rio  80°

25

120°W **A** 115° **B** 110° **C** 105° **D** 100° **E** 95° **F** 90°

CALIFORNIA

San Diego
Tijuana
Mexicali
ARIZONA
Phoenix
Tucson
NEW MEXICO
**UNITED STATES OF AMERICA**
OKLAHOMA
Lubbock
Little Rock
ARKANSAS
Tupel
MISSISSIPPI

Nogales
Agua Prieta
Ciudad Juarez
El Paso
Texarkana
Fort Worth
Dallas
Abilene
Shreveport
Jackso

TEXAS
Pecos
Waco
LOUISIANA
Hattiesburg

Guadalupe Island (Mexico)
Cedros Island
Hermosillo
Edwards Plateau
Austin
Houston
San Antonio
Baton Rouge
New Orlea

Point Eugenia
Ciudad Obregon
Ojinaga
Galveston
Missis Del

30°N

25°

Chihuahua
Rio Grande
Corpus Christi
Laredo

Tropic of Cancer

Los Mochis
Plateau of Mexico
Monclova
Brownsville
Matamoros

La Paz
Culiacan
Durango
Torreon
Saltillo
Monterrey
4,054m (13,300ft)
Ciudad Victoria
**Gulf of Mexico**

Cape San Lucas
Mazatlan
**MEXICO**
Matehuala
San Luis Potosi
Tampico

20°

Revillagigedo Islands (Mexico)
Aguascalientes
Merida
Yuca Penin

Puerto Vallarta
Leon
Bay of Campeche
Campec

Guadalajara
Celaya
Ciudad del Carm

Colima
Morelia
Teotihuacan
**Mexico City**
Coatzacoalcos
Villahermosa
Belmopa

15°

Uruapan
Puebla
Orizaba 5,610m (18,405ft)
Veracruz
Tehuacan
Oaxaca
Isthmus of Tehuantepec
Tuxtla Gutierrez
Tikal
B

Acapulco
Southern Sierra Madre
Juchitan
Gulf of Tehuantepec
Tajumulco 4,220m (13,845ft)
**GUATEMAL**

Tapachula
Quezaltena
**Guatemala City**
**San Salvador**
EL SALVA

**PACIFIC OCEAN**

Galapagos Islands (Ecuador)

Equator

Puerto Ayora

90°

---

## Inset map

**L** 65°W **M** 60° **N**

Virgin Islands (U.K.)
Anguilla (U.K.)
**ATLANTIC OCEAN**

San Juan
Virgin Islands (U.S.A.)
St. Martin (France and Netherlands)
**ANTIGUA AND BARBUDA**
Leeward Islands

Puerto Rico (U.S.A.)
**Basseterre**
**ST. KITTS AND NEVIS**
**St. John's**

Montserrat (U.K.)
Guadeloupe (France)
Windward Islands

**1:8,000,000**

Basse-Terre

0   100   200km
0   50   100 miles

**Roseau**
**DOMINICA**

15°N

Martinique (France)
Fort-de-France

Caribbean Sea

5°N
**Castries**
**ST. LUCIA**

**Kingstown**
**BARBADOS**
**ST. VINCENT AND THE GRENADINES**
**Bridgetown**

Lesser Antilles

15°N

**St. George's**  **GRENADA**

0°

Margarita Island
Porlamar
Tobago

**Port-of-Spain**
**TRINIDAD AND TOBAGO**

Cumana
**VENEZUELA**
Trinidad

**L** 65°W **M** 60° **N**

115°W **B** 110° **C** 105° **D** 100° **E** 95°

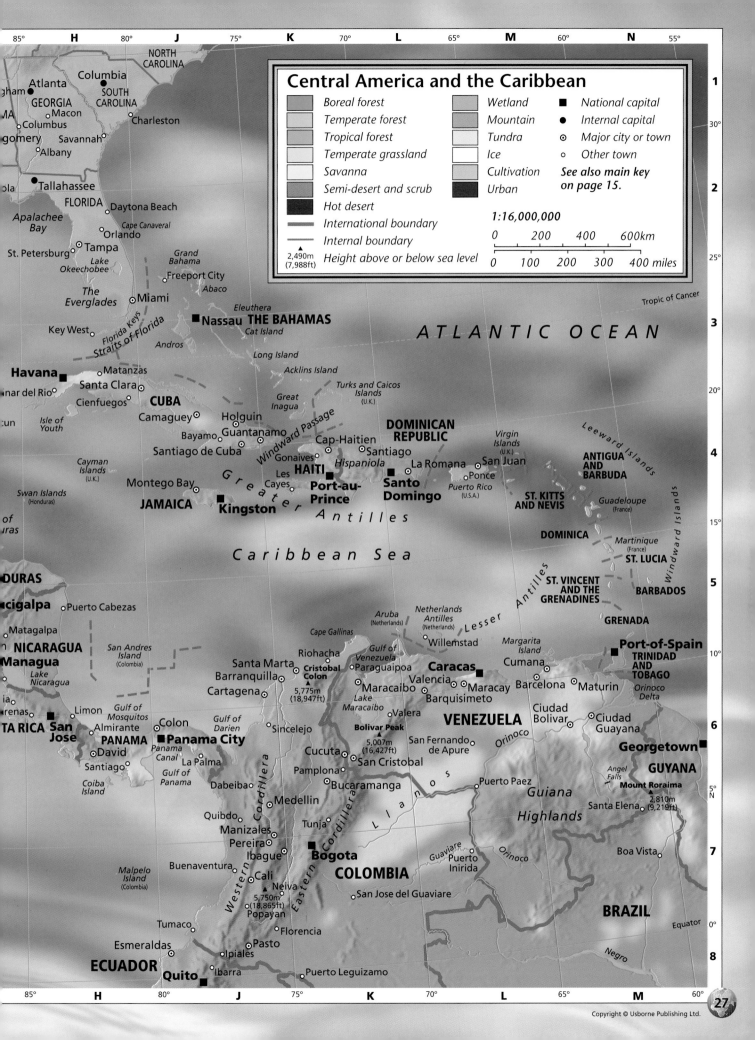

# SOUTH AMERICA

South America is made up of 12 independent countries, along with French Guiana, which belongs to France. The continent's biggest and most industrialized country is Brazil, which covers about half of the total land. Brazil is also home to half of South America's population.

*This is a guanaco. Guanacos are members of the camel family that live in South America. Guanaco hair is used to make textiles.*

Caribbean Sea

Caraca

**VENEZUEL**

Medellin° **Bogota**

Orinoco

**COLOMBIA**

Equator

Galapagos
Islands
(Ecuador)

**Quito**

**ECUADOR**

Guayaquil°

**PERU**

**Lima**

**BOLIV**

**La Paz**

S

Tropic of Capricorn

**CHILE**

PACIFIC

OCEAN

**Santiago** °Mendoza

**ARGEN**

Cape H

Drake Pa

The shading on this map is there to help you see clearly the different countries that make up the continent.

orgetown
**Paramaribo**
**Cayenne**
**IA**
**RINAM** **FRENCH**
**GUIANA**
(France)

on

Equator

○Recife

**B R A Z I L**

■ **Brasilia**

○Belo Horizonte

Parana

**AGUAY**
Sao Paulo ○Rio de Janeiro

**suncion**
Tropic of Capricorn

○Porto Alegre

**A T L A N T I C**

**JGUAY**
**Montevideo**      **O C E A N**
**nos Aires**

land Islands
(U.K.)

This is a red-eyed tree frog. These frogs live in rainforests in South and Central America.

# Facts

**Total land area** 17,866,130 sq km (6,898,113 sq miles)

**Total population** 346 million

**Biggest city** Sao Paulo, Brazil

**Biggest country** Brazil *8,547,400 sq km (3,300,151 sq miles)*

**Smallest country** Surinam *163,270 sq km (63,039 sq miles)*

**Highest mountain** Aconcagua, Argentina *6,959m (22,831ft)*

**Longest river** Amazon, mainly in Brazil *6,440km (4,000 miles)*

**Biggest lake** Lake Maracaibo, Venezuela *13,312 sq km (5,140 sq miles)*

**Highest waterfall** Angel Falls, on the Churun River, Venezuela *979m (3,212ft)*

**Biggest desert** Patagonian Desert, Argentina *673,000 sq km (260,000 sq miles)*

**Biggest island** Tierra del Fuego *46,360 sq km (17,900 sq miles)*

**Main mineral deposits** Copper, tin, molybdenum, bauxite, emeralds

**Main fuel deposits** Oil, coal

## Internet link

For a link to a website where you can discover the sights and sounds of the Amazon rainforest, go to **www.usborne-quicklinks.com**

Copyright © Usborne Publishing Ltd.

**A** 85°W **B** 80° **C**

1

Liberia
Puntarenas
Limon
**San Jose**
**COSTA
RICA**
David
Almirante
Puerto
Armuelles
Santiago
**Panama City**
*Panama
Canal*
Penonome
**PANAMA**
*Gulf of Panama*
*Coiba
Island*

Cape Gallinas
Riohacha
Santa Marta
Barranquilla
**Cristobal
Colon**
5,775m
(18,947ft)
Paraguaipoa
Aruba 70°
(Netherlands)
*Netherlands Antilles*
(Netherlands)
Willemstad
*Lesser Antilles*
**GRENADA**
65°
**TRINIDAD
AND TOBAGO**
Cartagena
Sincelejo
*Gulf of
Darien*
Maracaibo
Coro
*Gulf of
Venezuela*
Paraguaipoa
Lagunillas
*Lake
Maracaibo*
Maracay
**Caracas**
Barcelona
Cumana
Guiria
Valencia
Barquisimeto
Maturin
Tucupita
**Port
Spa**
Magangue
Turbo
*Mosquitos*
*Gulf of*
Caceres
Cucuta
**Bolivar Peak**
5,007m
(16,427ft)
Valera
Araure
Zaraza
Barinas
**VENEZUELA**
San Fernando
de Apure
Ciudad
Bolivar
Ciudad
Guayan
Dabeiba
Pamplona
San Cristobal
*Cordillera*
*Western*
Nuqui
**Medellin**
Bucaramanga
Cravo
Norte
Caicara
Orinoco
Quibdo
Duitama
Tunja
*L  l  a  n  o  s*
Puerto
Paez
Angel
Falls
Pereira
**Manizales**
*Cordillera*
*Eastern*
**Mount Ro**
2,810r
(9,219)
Buga
Ibague
**Bogota**
Buenaventura
Cali
**COLOMBIA**
Guaviare
Puerto
Inirida
Santa Elena
Neiva
5,750m
(18,865ft)
Popayan
San Jose del Guaviare
Orinoco
Boa Vi
*Guiana*
*Highlands*
Tumaco
Florencia
Ipiales
Pasto
Esmeraldas
*Cape
San Francisco*
Ibarra
**Quito**
Nueva Loja
Puerto Leguizamo
Santo Domingo de los Colorados
La Chorrera
*Negro*
Manta
Quevedo
Ambato
**ECUADOR**
6,310m
(20,702ft)
*Japura*
Babahoyo
Montalvo
La Libertad
Guayaquil
Cuenca
*Gulf of
Guayaquil*
Machala
*Amazon*
Iquitos
Leticia
Amazon
Tumbes
Loja
Atalaia do Norte
Talara
Zumba
*Maranon*
Sullana
Piura
Chulucanas
Yurimaguas
*Ucayali*
*S  e  l  v  a  s*
Cape Negro
Moyobamba
*Jurua*
Chiclayo
**PERU**
Purus
*Madeira*
Pacasmayo
Cajamarca
Cruzeiro do Sul
Trujillo
Huacrachuco
Pucallpa
Porto Velho
Chimbote
**Mount Huascaran**
6,746m
(22,132ft)
Huanuco
Rio Branco
**PACIFIC**
Cerro de Pasco
Riberalta
**OCEAN**
La Oroya
Cobija
Huancayo
Puerto
Maldonado
**Lima**
*Cordillera*
*Western*
Mala
*A  N  D  E  S*
Quillabamba
*Eastern
Cordillera*
Chincha Alta
Ayacucho
Machu Picchu
Magdalena
Ica
Cusco
Nazca
Sicuani
Rurrenabaque
**Mount
Coropuna**
6,425m
(1,079ft)
Juliaca
Trinidad
Chala
Puno
Concepcion
Mollendo
*Lake
Titicaca*
**La Paz**
**BOLIVIA**
Arequipa
**Mount Illimani**
6,402m
(21,004ft)
Cochabamba
**San Jo
Chio**
Tacna
Oruro
**Santa
Cruz**
*Lake
Poopo*
Challapata
Challagua
*Gulf of
Arica*
Arica
**Sucre**
Potosi
Camiri
**CHILE**

N 90°W P
*Same scale as main map*
9 9
*Galapagos Islands*
(Ecuador)
0° Equator 0°
*Fernandina*
San Salvador
Santa Cruz
*Isabela*
Puerto
Ayora
San Cristobal
10 10
*PACIFIC OCEAN*
N 90°W P

**A** 85°W **B** 80° **C** 75° **D** 70° **E** 65° **F**

10°
5°
N
Equator
0°
5°
S
5°
10°
15°
20°

1
2
3
4
5
6
7

G  55°  H  50°  J  45°  K  40°  L  35°  M

1

2

3

4

5°N

5°S

6

7

0°

10°

15°

20°

## Northern South America

| | | | | |
|---|---|---|---|---|
| Boreal forest | | Wetland | ■ | National capital |
| Temperate forest | | Mountain | ● | Internal capital |
| Tropical forest | | Tundra | ⊙ | Major city or town |
| Temperate grassland | | Ice | ○ | Other town |
| Savanna | | Cultivation | | **See also main key** |
| Semi-desert and scrub | | Urban | | **on page 15.** |
| Hot desert | | | | |
| International boundary | | | | |
| Internal boundary | | | | 1:14,000,000 |

2,490m
(7,988ft) ▲ Height above or below sea level

0        200        400km

0    100    200    300 miles

Georgetown
New
Amsterdam
Nieuw Nickerie
**Paramaribo**
ANA
Brokopondo
**SURINAM**
Sinnamary
**Cayenne**
Regina
Cape Orange
**FRENCH
GUIANA**
(France)

**ATLANTIC  OCEAN**

Equator

Amazon
Delta
Macapa

Braganca

bina
ervoir

Amazon

Belem
Cameta

Sao Luis
Parnaiba
aus
Santarem
Altamira
Sobral
Fortaleza
Bacabal

Itaituba
Tucurui
Reservoir
Teresina
Cape
Sao Roque

Tapajos
Maraba
Imperatriz
Mossoro
Natal

Xingu
Floriano
Campina
Grande
Joao
Pessoa

**B R A Z I L**

Araguaina
Urucui
Juazeiro
do Norte
Recife
Caruaru

Tocantins
Petrolina
Sao Francisco
Maceio

Araguaia
Tocantins
Juazeiro
Arapiraca

**P l a t e a u   o f**

Sobradinho
Reservoir
Aracaju

Gurupi
Barreiras
Morpara
Feira de
Santana

**M a t o   G r o s s o**

Salvador
(Bahia)

Espinosa
Vitoria da
Conquista
Ilheus

Cuiaba

Caceres
**Brasilia**
**B r a z i l i a n**

Rondonopolis
Montes Claros

Goiania
**H i g h l a n d s**

Jatai

Teofilo Otoni

erto
uarez
Patos de Minas
Governador Valadares

Corumba
Uberlandia
Linhares

Uberaba
Tres Marias
Reservoir
Belo Horizonte

Parana
Sao Jose do
Rio Preto
Ribeirao
Preto
Furnas
Reservoir
Cachoeiro de
Itapemirim
Vitoria

Barbacena

Copyright © Usborne Publishing Ltd.

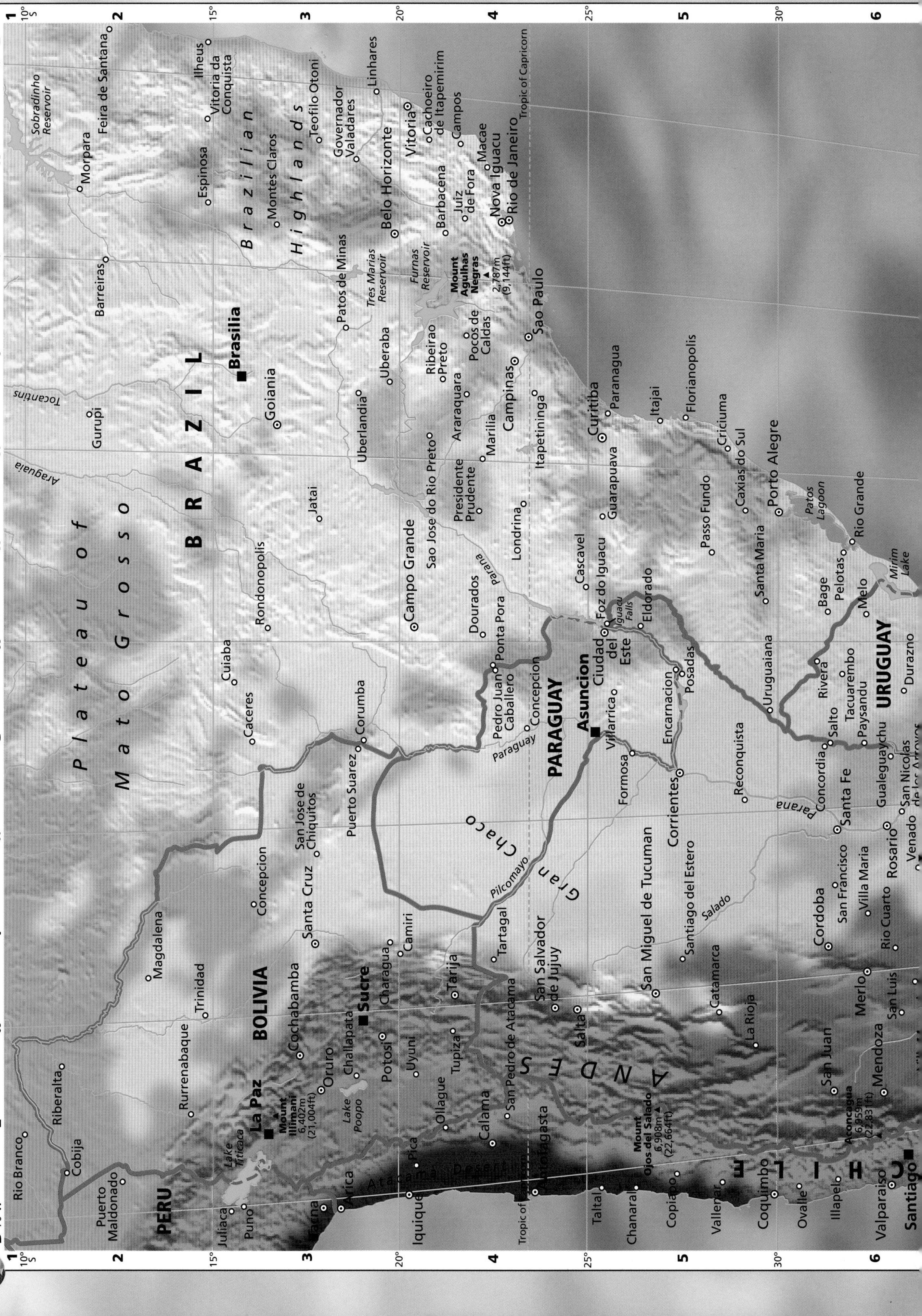

L

K

J

H

G

F

E

D

**Coordinate labels (top):**
10° S · 15° · 20° · 25° · 30° · Tropic of Capricorn

1 · 2 · 3 · 4 · 5 · 6

40°

45°

50°

55°

60°

65°

70°W

10° S

**Place names:**

Sobradinho Reservoir

Morpara

Feira de Santana

Ilheus

Vitoria da Conquista

Linhares

Teofilo Otoni

Espinosa

Montes Claros

*Brazilian Highlands*

Governador Valadares

Vitoria

Cachoeiro de Itapemirim

Campos

Macae

Belo Horizonte

Barbacena

Juiz de Fora

Nova Iguacu

Rio de Janeiro

Tropic of Capricorn

Barreiras

Patos de Minas

Tres Marias Reservoir

Furnas Reservoir

Mount Agulhas Negras 2,787m (9,144ft)

Sao Paulo

**Brasilia**

Goiania

Uberaba

Ribeirao Preto

Pocos de Caldas

Campinas

*Tocantins*

*B  R  A  Z  I  L*

Uberlandia

Sao Jose do Rio Preto

Araraquara

Marilia

Itapetininga

Curitiba

Paranagua

*Araguaia*

Jatai

Presidente Prudente

Londrina

Guarapuava

Itajai

Florianopolis

*Plateau of Mato Grosso*

Rondonopolis

Campo Grande

*Parana*

Cascavel

Foz do Iguacu

Iguacu Falls

Eldorado

Passo Fundo

Caxias do Sul

Criciuma

Porto Alegre

Cuiaba

Dourados

Ponta Pora

Ciudad del Este

Posadas

Santa Maria

*Patos Lagoon*

Rio Grande

Caceres

Corumba

Concepcion

Pedro Juan Caballero

**Asuncion**

Villarrica

Encarnacion

Uruguaiana

Bage

Pelotas

Melo

*Mirim Lake*

Magdalena

San Jose de Chiquitos

Puerto Suarez

*paraguay*

**PARAGUAY**

Formosa

Reconquista

Concordia

Rivera

Tacuarembo

Paysandu

**URUGUAY**

Trinidad

Concepcion

Santa Cruz

Charagua

Camiri

*Gran Chaco*

*Pilcomayo*

Tartagal

Corrientes

*Parana*

Salto

Gualeguaychu

San Nicolas

Venado de los Arroyos

Rurrenabaque

**BOLIVIA**

Cochabamba

**Sucre**

Tarija

San Salvador de Jujuy

San Miguel de Tucuman

Santiago del Estero

*Salado*

Santa Fe

Rosario

Riberalta

Cobija

Challapata

Potosi

San Pedro de Atacama

Salta

*A  N  D  E  S*

Cordoba

San Francisco

Villa Maria

Rio Cuarto

Rio Branco

Puerto Maldonado

**La Paz**

Mount Illimani 6,402m (21,004ft)

Oruro

Challapata

Uyuni

Tupiza

Calama

Mount Ojos del Salado 6,908m (22,664ft)

Catamarca

La Rioja

Merlo

San Luis

Mendoza

Aconcagua 6,959m (22,831ft)

San Juan

**PERU**

*Lake Titicaca*

*Lake Poopo*

Ollague

Pica

*Desierto de Atacama*

Antofagasta

Taltal

Chanaral

Copiapo

Vallenar

*C  H  I  L  E*

Coquimbo

Ovalle

Illapel

Valparaiso

**Santiago**

Juliaca

Puno

Tacna

Arica

Iquique

*Atacama*

Tropic of Capricorn

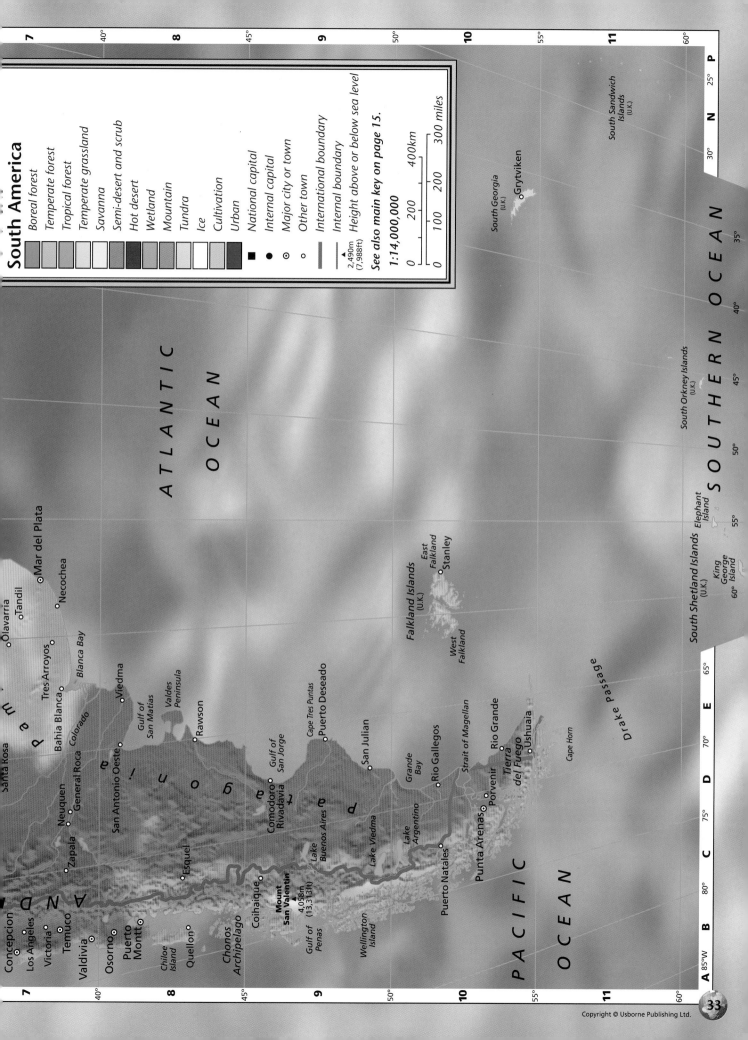

Copyright © Usborne Publishing Ltd.

# AUSTRALASIA AND OCEANIA

Australasia is made up of Australia, New Zealand and Papua New Guinea. Oceania is a collection of over 20,000 islands stretching out into the Pacific Ocean.

International Date Line

Northern Mariana Islands (U.S.A.)

Guam (U.S.A.)

MARSHALL ISLANDS

Koror ■

Palikir ■

■ Majuro

PALAU

FEDERATED STATES OF MICRONESIA

■ Bairiki

Equator

■ Yaren

NAURU

KIRI

PAPUA NEW GUINEA

INDIAN

New Guinea

OCEAN

Arafura Sea

Port Moresby ●

SOLOMON ISLANDS

TUVALU
Funafuti ■

SA

Honiara ■

Coral Sea Islands Territory (Australia)

VANUATU

Wallis and Futuna (France)

Coral Sea

New Caledonia (France)

Port-Vila ■

FIJI

○ Noumea

■ Suva

TO

Nukualofa ■

Tropic of Capricorn

AUSTRALIA

Brisbane ◉

Darling

Perth ◉

Adelaide ◉

Murray

◉ Sydney
■ Canberra

Melbourne ◉

Tasmania

Tasman

Sea

Auckland ◉

NEW ZEALAND

North Island

■ Wellington

○ Christchurch
South Island

International Date Line

*This small island belongs to Papua New Guinea.*

PACIFIC OCEAN

*The shading on this map is there to help you see clearly the different countries that make up the continent.*

Line Islands

Equator

au
land)

an

e
aland)

Cook Islands
(New Zealand)

Society
Islands

Marquesas
Islands

French
Polynesia
(France)

Pitcairn Islands
(U.K.)

Tropic of Capricorn

## Facts

**Total land area** 8,564,400 sq km (3,306,715 sq miles)

**Total population** 31 million

**Biggest city** Sydney, Australia

**Biggest country** Australia 7,686,850 sq km (2,967,124 sq miles)

**Smallest country** Nauru 21 sq km (8 sq miles)

**Highest mountain** Mount Wilhelm, Papua New Guinea *4,509m (14,793ft)*

**Longest river** Murray/Darling River, Australia *3,718km (2,310 miles)*

**Biggest lake** Lake Eyre, Australia *9,000 sq km (3,470 sq miles)*

**Highest waterfall** Sutherland Falls, on the Arthur River, New Zealand *580m (1,904ft)*

**Biggest desert** Great Victoria Desert, Australia *388,500 sq km (150,000 sq miles)*

**Biggest island** New Guinea *800,000 sq km (309,000 sq miles)* (Australia is counted as a continental land mass and not as an island.)

**Main mineral deposits** Iron, nickel, precious stones, lead, bauxite

**Main fuel deposits** Oil, coal, uranium

*The Moorish idol fish is found in shallow waters throughout the Pacific. It has very bold stripes and a long, distinctive snout.*

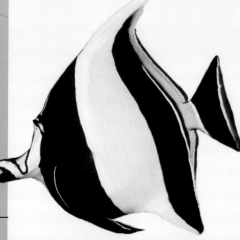

### Internet link

For a link to a website where you can take a virtual tour of New Zealand and find out all about its sights, cities and landscape, go to **www.usborne-quicklinks.com**

Copyright © Usborne Publishing Ltd.

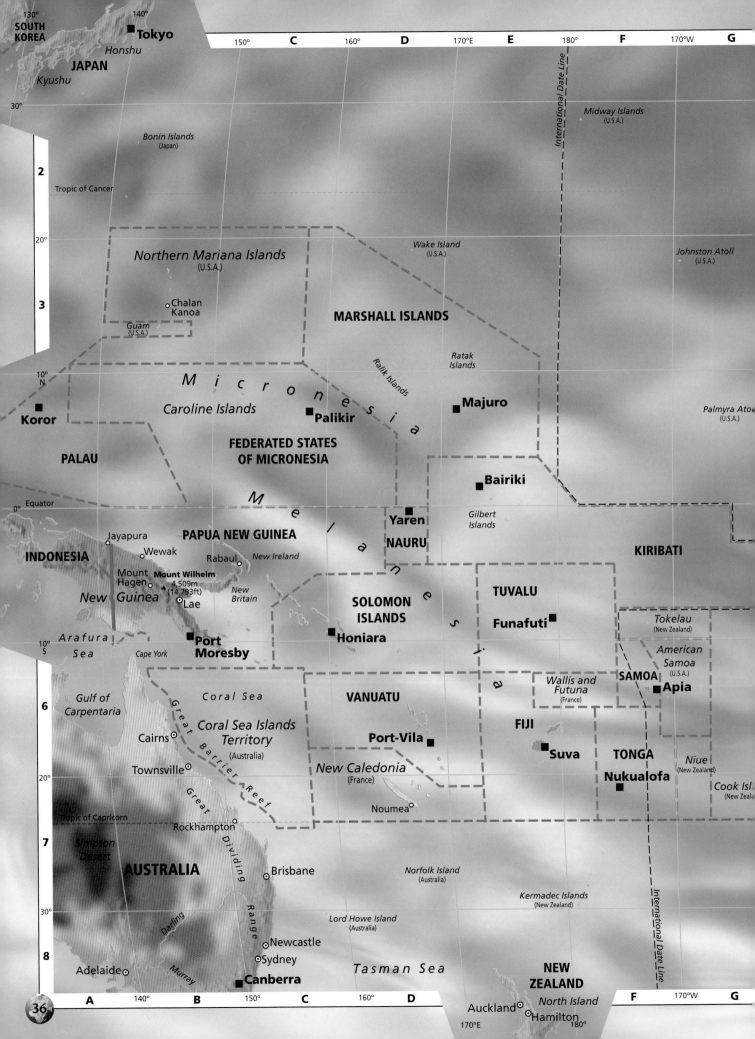

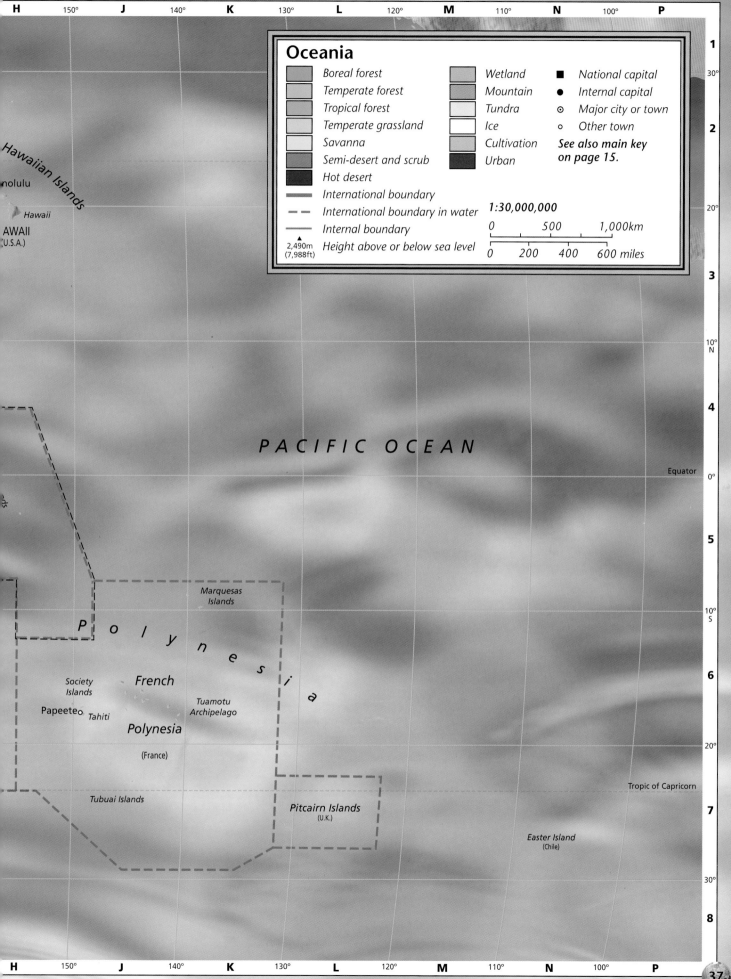

## Oceania

| | | | |
|---|---|---|---|
| Boreal forest | | Wetland | ■ National capital |
| Temperate forest | | Mountain | ● Internal capital |
| Tropical forest | | Tundra | ⊙ Major city or town |
| Temperate grassland | | Ice | ○ Other town |
| Savanna | | Cultivation | **See also main key** |
| Semi-desert and scrub | | Urban | **on page 15.** |
| Hot desert | | | |

International boundary

– – – International boundary in water

——— Internal boundary

▲ 2,490m (7,988ft) Height above or below sea level

**1:30,000,000**

0 — 500 — 1,000km

0 — 200 — 400 — 600 miles

Hawaiian Islands

nolulu

*Hawaii*

AWAII
(U.S.A.)

PACIFIC OCEAN

Equator — 0°

Marquesas
Islands

P o l y n e s i a

Society
Islands

French

Papeete○ ○ *Tahiti*

Tuamotu
Archipelago

Polynesia

(France)

Tubuai Islands

Pitcairn Islands
(U.K.)

Tropic of Capricorn

Easter Island
(Chile)

30°N
20°
10°N
Equator 0°
10°S
20°
30°

Copyright © Usborne Publishing Ltd.

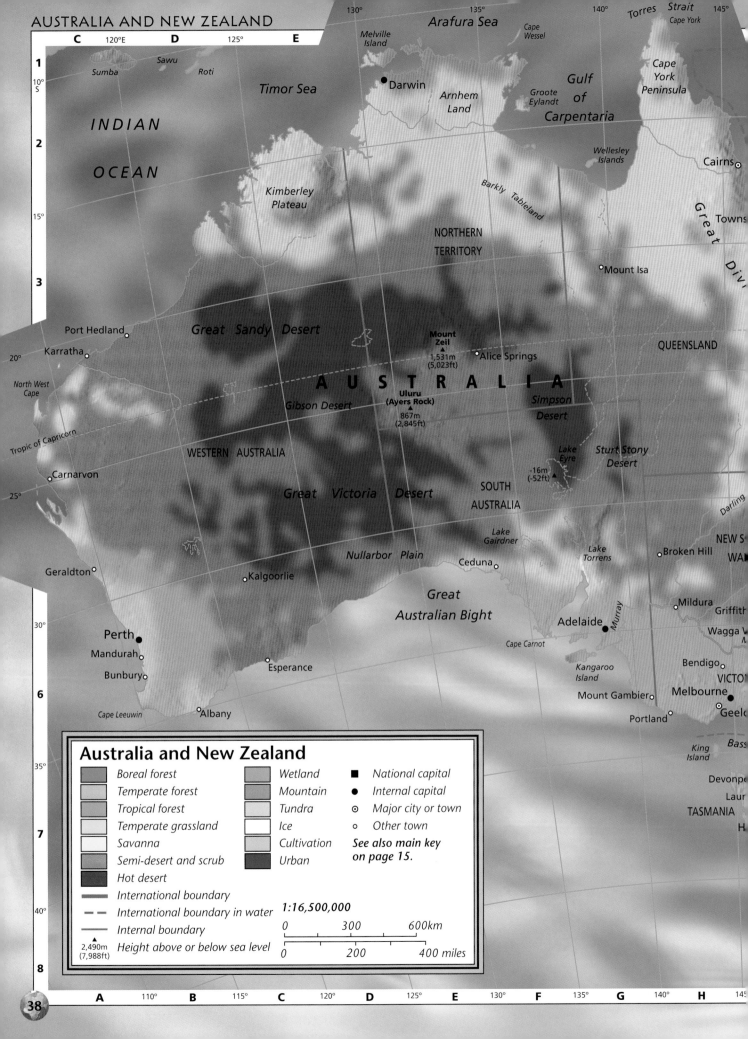

130°   135°   140°   145°

Torres Strait

Arafura Sea

Cape York

C  120°E  D  125°  E

Cape Wessel

**1**
10°S

Sumba

Sawu

Roti

Melville Island

INDIAN

Timor Sea

Darwin

Arnhem Land

Gulf of Carpentaria

Cape York Peninsula

**2**

OCEAN

Kimberley Plateau

Groote Eylandt

Wellesley Islands

Cairns

15°

NORTHERN

Barkly Tableland

Great Divi

Towns

**3**

TERRITORY

Mount Isa

QUEENSLAND

Port Hedland

Great  Sandy  Desert

Mount Zeil 1,531m (5,023ft) ▲

Alice Springs

20°

Karratha

AUSTRALIA

North West Cape

Gibson Desert

Uluru (Ayers Rock) ▲ 867m (2,845ft)

Simpson Desert

Tropic of Capricorn

WESTERN  AUSTRALIA

Lake Eyre

Sturt Stony Desert

Carnarvon

-16m (-52ft) ▲

25°

Great  Victoria  Desert

SOUTH AUSTRALIA

Darling

Lake Gairdner

Lake Torrens

NEW S

WA

Geraldton

Nullarbor  Plain

Ceduna

Broken Hill

Mildura

Kalgoorlie

Griffith

Great Australian Bight

Adelaide

Murray

Wagga W

30°

Perth

Cape Carnot

Bendigo

Mandurah

Kangaroo Island

VICTO

Bunbury

Esperance

Mount Gambier

Melbourne

**6**

Portland

Geelo

Cape Leeuwin

Albany

Bass

35°

King Island

Devonpe

Laur

TASMANIA

### Australia and New Zealand

| | | |
|---|---|---|
| ▦ Boreal forest | ▦ Wetland | ■ National capital |
| ▦ Temperate forest | ▦ Mountain | ● Internal capital |
| ▦ Tropical forest | ▦ Tundra | ⊙ Major city or town |
| ▦ Temperate grassland | ▦ Ice | ○ Other town |
| ▦ Savanna | ▦ Cultivation | *See also main key on page 15.* |
| ▦ Semi-desert and scrub | ▦ Urban | |
| ▦ Hot desert | | |

**7**

───── International boundary

────── International boundary in water

1:16,500,000

0        300        600km

───── Internal boundary

▲ 2,490m (7,988ft) Height above or below sea level

0        200        400 miles

**8**

A  110°  B  115°  C  120°  D  125°  E  130°  F  135°  G  140°  H  145

Copyright © Usborne Publishing Ltd.

# ASIA

Asia is the largest continent and has over 40 countries, including Russia, the biggest country in the world. As well as large land masses, it has thousands of islands and inlets, giving it over 160,000km (100,000 miles) of coastline. Turkey and Russia are partly in Europe and partly in Asia, but both are shown in full on the map on the right.

## Internet link

For a link to a website where you can read about the Great Wall of China and see a photo of it taken from space, go to www.usborne-quicklinks.com

*This is a type of Chinese boat called a junk, sailing in the sea off Singapore.*

*The shading on this map is there to help you see clearly the different countries that make up the continent.*

ARCTIC OCEA

Franz Josef Land

Novaya Zemlya

Barents Sea

Kar

Ob

Moscow

R U S

Volga

Black Sea

Ankara

Astana

TURKEY

GEORGIA

Caspian Sea

KAZAKHSTAN

CYPRUS

ARMENIA

Aral Sea

AZERBAIJAN

UZBEKISTAN

LEBANON

SYRIA

TURKMENISTAN

Bishkek

Beirut

Damascus

Tashkent

KYRGYZSTAN

Jerusalem

Amman

Ashgabat

ISRAEL

JORDAN

Baghdad

Tehran

Dushanbe

TAJIKISTAN

IRAQ

IRAN

Kabul

Islamabad

Tropic of Cancer

KUWAIT

AFGHANISTAN

SAUDI

ARABIA

BAHRAIN

PAKISTAN

Riyadh

QATAR

Doha

Indus

New Delhi

NEPAL

Abu Dhabi

Kathmand

UNITED ARAB

Muscat

Ganges

EMIRATES

Thi

BANGL

Sana

OMAN

Arabian

INDIA

YEMEN

Sea

Socotra

(Yemen)

Bay

Ben

INDIAN OCEAN

SRI LAN

Sri Jayewardenepura Kotte

Equator

Colombo

MALDIVES

Male

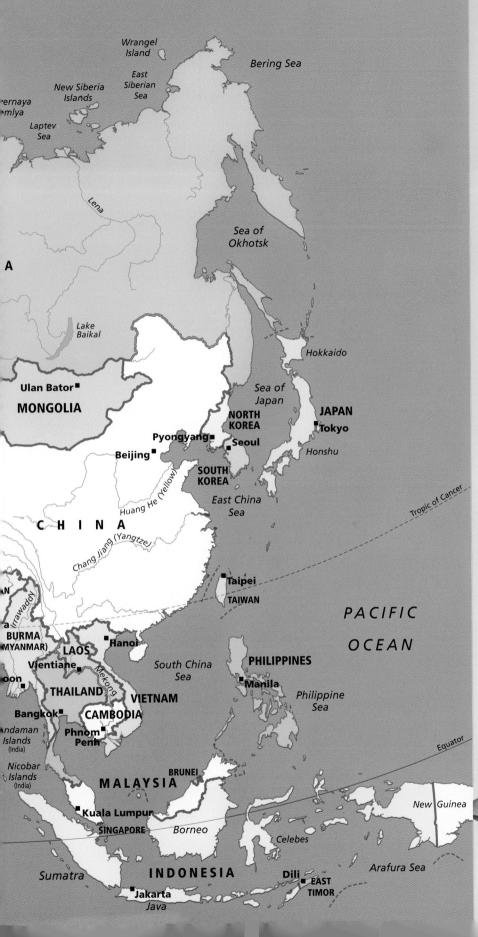

Wrangel
Island

*Bering Sea*

*New Siberia
Islands*

East
Siberian
Sea

*vernaya
mlya*

*Laptev
Sea*

*Lena*

*Sea of
Okhotsk*

A

*Lake
Baikal*

*Hokkaido*

Ulan Bator■

**MONGOLIA**

*Sea of
Japan*

**JAPAN**
■Tokyo

**NORTH
KOREA**

Pyongyang●

Beijing●                    ●Seoul

*Honshu*

**SOUTH
KOREA**

**C H I N A**

*Huang He (Yellow)*

*East China
Sea*

*Tropic of Cancer*

*Chang Jiang (Yangtze)*

■Taipei

**TAIWAN**

N

*Irrawaddy*

**BURMA
(MYANMAR)**

■Hanoi

**LAOS**

*South China
Sea*

**PHILIPPINES**

*P A C I F I C*

*O C E A N*

Vientiane●

*Mekong*

●Manila

**THAILAND**

**VIETNAM**

*Philippine
Sea*

Bangkok■

**CAMBODIA**

■Phnom
Penh

*ndaman
Islands*
(India)

*Nicobar
Islands*
(India)

**BRUNEI**

*Equator*

**M A L A Y S I A**

■Kuala Lumpur

**SINGAPORE**

*Borneo*

*New Guinea*

*Celebes*

*Sumatra*

**I N D O N E S I A**

Dili■

**EAST
TIMOR**

*Arafura Sea*

■Jakarta

*Java*

# Facts

**Total land area** 44,537,920 sq km
(17,196,090 sq miles)
**Total population** 3.8 billion
(including all of Russia)
**Biggest city** Tokyo, Japan
**Biggest country** Russia *Total area:
17,075,200 sq km (6,592,735 sq
miles) Area of Asiatic Russia:
12,780,800 sq km (4,934,667 sq miles)*
**Smallest country** Maldives *300 sq km
(116 sq miles)*

**Highest mountain** Mount Everest,
Nepal/China border *8,850m (29,035ft)*
**Longest river** Chang Jiang (Yangtze),
China *6,380km (3,964 miles)*
**Biggest lake** Caspian Sea, western
Asia *370,999 sq km (143,243 sq miles)*
**Highest waterfall** Jog Falls, on the
Sharavati River, India *253m (830ft)*
**Biggest desert** Arabian Desert, in and
around Saudi Arabia *2,230,000 sq km
(900,000 sq miles)*
**Biggest island** Borneo *751,100 sq km
(290,000 sq miles)*

**Main mineral deposits** Zinc, mica, tin,
chromium, iron, nickel
**Main fuel deposits** Oil, coal,
uranium, natural gas

*These are lotus flowers, a type of
water lily. In China they are
associated with purity and for
Buddhists they are sacred.*

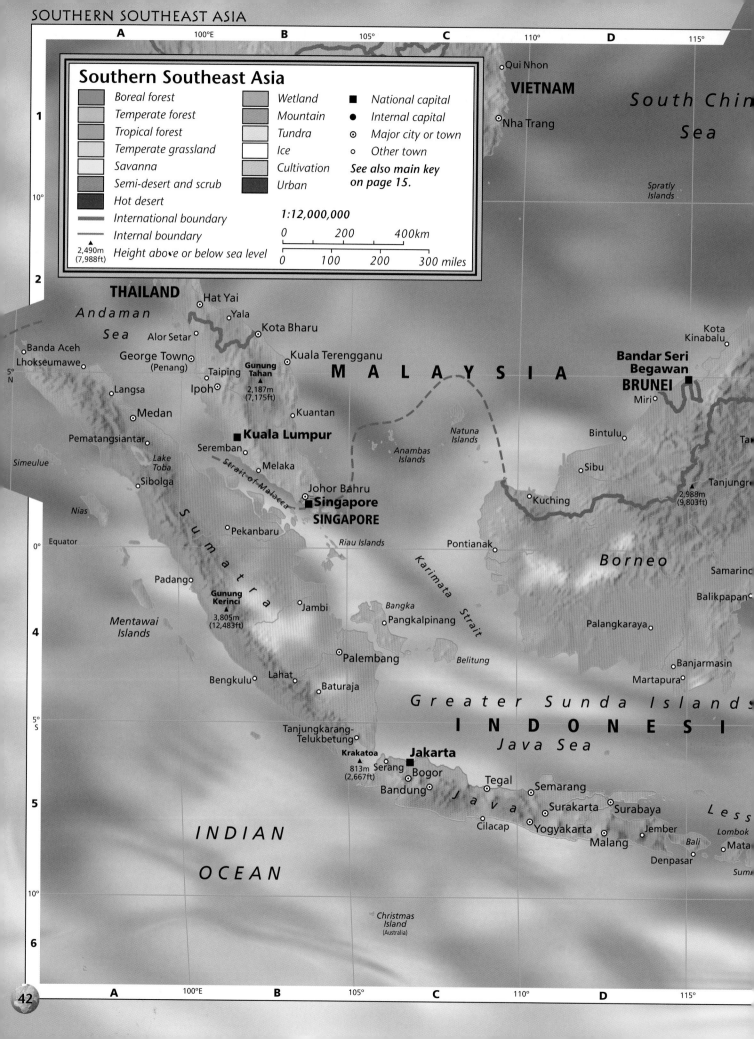

## Southern Southeast Asia

| | | |
|---|---|---|
| *Boreal forest* | *Wetland* | ■ National capital |
| *Temperate forest* | *Mountain* | ● Internal capital |
| *Tropical forest* | *Tundra* | ◉ Major city or town |
| *Temperate grassland* | *Ice* | ○ Other town |
| *Savanna* | *Cultivation* | |
| *Semi-desert and scrub* | *Urban* | See also main key on page 15. |
| *Hot desert* | | |

International boundary

Internal boundary

▲ 2,490m (7,988ft) Height above or below sea level

1:12,000,000

0    200    400km

0  100  200  300 miles

**VIETNAM**

Qui Nhon

Nha Trang

*South China Sea*

*Spratly Islands*

**THAILAND**

*Andaman Sea*

Hat Yai

Yala

Alor Setar

Kota Bharu

George Town (Penang)

Taiping

**Gunung Tahan** ▲ 2,187m (7,175ft)

Kuala Terengganu

**M A L A Y S I A**

Banda Aceh

Lhokseumawe

Langsa

Ipoh

Kuantan

Kota Kinabalu

**Bandar Seri Begawan**

**BRUNEI**

Miri

Medan

**Kuala Lumpur**

*Natuna Islands*

Bintulu

Pematangsiantar

*Lake Toba*

Seremban

Melaka

*Anambas Islands*

Sibu

*Simeulue*

Sibolga

*Strait of Malacca*

Johor Bahru

◉ **Singapore**

**SINGAPORE**

Kuching

▲ 2,988m (9,803ft)

Tanjungre

*Nias*

*Sumatra*

Pekanbaru

*Riau Islands*

Pontianak

*Borneo*

Samarin

Equator 0°

Padang

Karimata Strait

Balikpapan

**Gunung Kerinci** ▲ 3,805m (12,483ft)

Jambi

*Bangka*

Palangkaraya

*Mentawai Islands*

Pangkalpinang

**4**

Palembang

*Belitung*

Banjarmasin

Bengkulu

Lahat

Baturaja

Martapura

*G r e a t e r   S u n d a   I s l a n d s*

5° S

Tanjungkarang-Telukbetung

**I N D O N E S I A**

*Java Sea*

**Krakatoa** ▲ 813m (2,667ft)

Serang

**Jakarta**

Tegal

Semarang

*Less*

Bogor

Surakarta

Surabaya

Bandung

*J a v a*

Cilacap

Yogyakarta

Jember

*Lombok*

Malang

*Bali*

Mata

**5**

Denpasar

*Sum*

**INDIAN**

**OCEAN**

*Christmas Island (Australia)*

120° Cabanatuan
*Olongapo* *Luzon*
○ Quezon City
**Manila** ■
○ Lucena ○ Naga
Calapan○ ○ Legaspi
*Mindoro*
**PHILIPPINES**
Masbate○ ○ Calbayog
*Masbate* *Samar*
○ Roxas ○ Tacloban
*Panay*
○Taytay ○ Iloilo ○ Bacolod
○ Cebu
*Negros* ○ Surigao
*Bohol*
Puerto Princesa○ Dumaguete○ ○Butuan
*wan* ○ Cagayan de Oro
*Sulu Sea* Pagadian○ ○Iligan
*Mindanao*
○ Davao
○Zamboanga
○ Jolo ○ General Santos
*akan*
*Sulu*
*Archipelago*

*Philippine*
*Sea*

*Celebes Sea*
*Talaud*
*Islands*
*Sangihe*
*Islands*
○ Morotai
Manado○
Ternate○ *Halmahera*
Gorontalo○
*Molucca*
*Sea*
○Palu *Peleng*
*Obi*
*Celebes* *Sula*
*Islands* *Ceram Sea*
○Palopo *Buru* *Ceram*
*Buton* ○Ambon
*pare* ○ Kendari
○Watampone
○Ujung Pandang *Buton*
*Banda Sea*

*Flores Sea*
*Wetar*
*nda Islands*
■Dili
*Flores* **EAST TIMOR**
○Ende *Timor*
*Sumba* *Sawu Sea*
○Kupang
*Sawu*
*Roti*
*Timor Sea*

**PACIFIC**

**OCEAN**

**PALAU**

*Sorong*○ *Biak*

*Misool*
*Yapen*
Fakfak○
*Maoke Range*
**New**
▲Puncak Jaya
5,030m **Guinea**
(16,502ft)

*Aru*
*Islands*
*Tanimbar* *Dolak*
*Islands*
*Arafura Sea* *Torres Strait*

**AUSTRALIA**

● Darwin **NORTHERN TERRITORY**

Copyright © Usborne Publishing Ltd.

Inset map (top right):

J 140°E K 145° L 150° M Equator 155° N
*Admiralty* **PACIFIC**
*Islands* **OCEAN**
○ Jayapura
○ Wewak *Bismarck Sea* *New Ireland*
Mount Wilhelm ○Rabaul
4,509m
(14,793ft)▲ ○Madang *New Britain*
Mount Hagen○ ○Lae
**New Guinea** **PAPUA NEW GUINEA**
○Kerema *Solomon Sea*
*Gulf of* *D'Entrecasteaux*
*Papua* *Islands*
■ **Port**
*Torres Strait* **Moresby** *1:18,000,000*
*Cape York*
0 400km
○ Cape York
*Peninsula* **AUSTRALIA**
0 200 miles
J 140°E K 145° L 150° M 155° N

Jayapura (right edge)

**45**

A | 90°E | B | 95° | C | 100° | D | 105° | E

*Brahmaputra*  Lhasa  Chengdu  Wanxian

H i m a l a y a s  Gongga Shan  7,556m (24,790ft)  Leshan

Mount Everest 8,850m (29,035ft)  Neijiang  Chongqing

**Thimphu**  INDIA  Luzhou

NEPAL  Darjeeling  BHUTAN  Xichang  Yibin  C H

Biratnagar  Zunyi  Hu

Darbhanga  *Brahmaputra*  Dibrugarh  Zhaotong

Bhagalpur  Rangpur  Guwahati  Jorhat  Panzhihua  Guiyang

25° N  Shillong  Anshun

Asansol  Rajshahi  Sylhet  Dali  Kunming

Jamshedpur  BANGLADESH  Imphal  Baoshan  Liuzh

**Dhaka**  Myitkyina  Red  Kaiyuan  Nar

Kolkata (Calcutta)  Khulna  Gejiu  Ha Giang  Qinzhou

Chittagong  Lashio  Simao  Lao Cai

*Mouths of the Ganges*  Monywa  Mandalay  Phongsali  Thai Nguyen

Mount Victoria 3,053m (10,016ft)  BURMA (MYANMAR)  Son La  **Hanoi**

20°  Sittwe  Meiktila  Taunggyi  Hai Phong

*Bay of Bengal*  Pyinmana  Salween  *Mekong*  Louangphrabang  Thanh Hoa  *Gulf of Tonkin*

Pye  LAOS  Vinh  Sa

Sandoway  *Irrawaddy*  Chiang Mai

Henzada  **Vientiane**

Pathein  Pegu  Udon Thani  Savannakhet  Hue

15°  **Rangoon**  Thaton  Phitsanulok  Khon Kaen  Da N

Moulmein  Nakhon Sawan  Ubon Ratchathani

*Mouths of the Irrawaddy*  THAILAND  Pakxe  VIETN

Nakhon Ratchasima  Attapu

I N D I A N  Tavoy  **Bangkok**  Angkor  Stoeng Treng  Qui Nho

O C E A N  *Andaman Sea*  Pattaya  Tonle Sap  CAMBODIA  Buon M

5°  Andaman Islands (India)  Mergui  Batdambang  Kampong Cham  Thuot

Port Blair  Kampong Chhnang  Da Lat

*Mergui Archipelago*  Prachuap Khiri Khan  Krong Kaoh Kong  **Phnom Penh**  Bien Hoa

*Little Andaman*  Ho Chi Minh C (Saigon)

10°  *Ten Degree Channel*  Chumphon  Kampong Saom  Long Xuyen  *Mekong*  Can Tho

*Gulf of Thailand*  Bac Lieu

Nicobar Islands (India)  Nakhon Si Thammarat  *Con Son*

6°

Hat Yai

Yala

5°  Banda Aceh  Alor Setar  Kota Bharu  Kuala Terengganu

Lhokseumawe  George Town (Penang)  Gunung Tahan

*Sumatra*  Langsa  Taiping  Ipoh  MALAYSIA  *Natuna Islands (Indonesia)*

7°  INDONESIA  2,187m (7,175ft)

A | 90°E | B | 95° | C | 100° | D | 105° | E

## Northern Southeast Asia

**Boreal forest**
**Temperate forest**
**Tropical forest**
**Temperate grassland**
**Savanna**
**Semi-desert and scrub**
**Hot desert**
**Wetland**
**Mountain**
**Tundra**
**Ice**
**Cultivation**
**Urban**

■ National capital
● Internal capital
⊙ Major city or town
○ Other town
▬▬▬ International boundary
─── Internal boundary
▲ 2,490m
(7,988ft) Height above or below sea level

*See also main key on page 15.*

**1:12,000,000**

| 0 | 200 | 400km |
|---|-----|-------|

| 0 | 100 | 200 | 300 miles |
|---|-----|-----|-----------|

East China Sea

Yichang
Wuhan
Huangshi
Yueyang
*Dongting Lake*
Changsha
Zhuzhou
Shaoyang
Hengyang
Chenzhou
Shaoguan
Wuzhou
Canton (Guangzhou)
*Xi Jiang*
Macau
Hong Kong (Xianggang)

Luan
Hefei
Nanjing
Wuxi
Nantong
Wuhu
Shanghai
Anqing
Hangzhou
*Tai Lake*
Ningbo
*Chang Jiang (Yangtze)*
*Poyang Lake*
Nanchang
Quzhou
Jinhua
Linchuan
Wenzhou
Nanping
Yongan
Fuzhou
Ganzhou
Quanzhou
Zhangzhou
Xiamen
Meizhou
Shantou

*Taiwan Strait*
Chilung
**Taipei** ■
Taichung
Changhua
**TAIWAN**
▲ *Yu Shan* 3,997m (13,113ft)
Tainan
Kaohsiung

*Ryukyu Islands (Japan)*
*Sakishima Islands*
Tropic of Cancer

*Batan Islands*

Luzon Strait
*Babuyan Islands*

Laoag
Aparri
Tuguegarao
Ilagan
Mount Pulog ▲ 2,930m (9,613ft)

Dagupan
Cabanatuan
*Luzon*
Olongapo
Quezon City ⊙
**Manila** ■
Lucena

**South China Sea**

*Paracel Islands*

*Spratly Islands*

*Philippine Sea*

**PACIFIC OCEAN**

Calapan
*Mindoro*
Naga
Legaspi
Masbate
*Masbate*
Calbayog
*Samar*
Roxas
Tacloban
*Panay*
Iloilo
Bacolod
Cebu
Taytay
*Negros*
Surigao
*Bohol*
Dumaguete
Butuan
Cagayan de Oro
*Palawan*
Puerto Princesa
Iligan
Pagadian
*Mindanao*
Davao
**Sulu Sea**
Zamboanga
General Santos
Jolo
**MALAYSIA**
Kota Kinabalu
Sandakan
*Sulu Archipelago*
*Talaud Islands*
Bandar Seri Begawan
**BRUNEI** ■
Miri
Tawau
**Celebes Sea**
**INDONESIA**
Bintulu
*Borneo*
Tarakan

**PHILIPPINES**

Copyright © Usborne Publishing Ltd.

A · 80°E · B · 85° · C · 90° · D · 95° · E · 100° · F · 105° · G · 110°

**KAZAKHSTAN**
○ Almaty
Karamay ○
*Lake Issyk* ○ Yining
**2**
○ Kuytun
*Dzungarian Basin*
Altay ○
Bulgan ○
■ **Ulan Bator**

**KYRGYZSTAN**
Shihezi ○
○ Urumqi
**MONGOLIA**

▲ **Pik Pobedy**
7,439m
(24,406ft)
○ Aksu
*T i e n   S h a n*
Turpan ○
**40°N**
Korla ○
*Bosten Lake*
-154m
(-505ft)
*Turpan Depression*
Hami ○

**3**
*Tarim Basin*
*Lop Lake*
G o b i   D e s e r t
Baotou ○
Hoh

○ Hotan
*Taklimakan Desert*
⸪ Mogao Caves
Yumen ○
*The Great Wall of China*
○ Wuhai

*Altun Mountains*
▲ 5,547m
(18,199ft)
Yinchuan ○
Ta

**35°**
*Kunlun Mountains*
*Qaidam Basin*
*Qinghai Lake*
Xining ○
Lanzhou ○

Golmud ○
**C H I N A**
*Huang He (Yellow)*

**4**
*Plateau of Tibet*

*Siling Lake*
Mount Li
(Terracotta
Baoji ○

**30°**
**TIBET**
Yushu ○
Xian ⸪

*Nam Lake*
Shiyan ○

*Brahmaputra*
*Salween*
*Chang Jiang (Yangtze)*
Xian

*Himalayas*
Lhasa ○
Chengdu ○

**NEPAL**
■ **Kathmandu**
*Mekong*
**Gongga Shan**
Yichang

▲ **Mount Everest**
8,850m
(29,035ft)
Darjeeling ○
■ **Thimphu**
▲ 7,556m
(24,790ft)
Leshan ○
Chongqing ○
Changc

Darbhanga ○
○ Biratnagar
**BHUTAN**
Luzhou ○

○ Patna
*Ganges*
*Brahmaputra*
Dibrugarh ○
Xichang ○
*Chang Jiang (Yangtze)*
Zunyi ○
Huaihu

**25°**
○ Bhagalpur
Rangpur ○
Guwahati ○
Panzhihua ○
Guiyang ○
Hen

**INDIA**
Shillong ○
Dali ○

Ranchi ○
Asansol ○
Rajshahi ○
Sylhet ○
Kunming ○
Guilin

**6**
*Tropic of Cancer*
**BANGLADESH**
Imphal ○
Myitkyina ○
Liuzhou ○

■ **Dhaka**
Aizawl ○

Kolkata ○
(Calcutta)
○ Khulna
Wuzhou

Chittagong ○
*Red*
Gejiu ○
Nanning ○
Yulin

Cuttack ○
*Mouths of the Ganges*
Lashio ○
Simao ○
Wuzhou

**20°**
Monywa ○
Mandalay ○
Lao Cai ○
Zhanji

**Mount Victoria**
*Bay of Bengal*
3,053m
(10,016ft)
Phongsali ○
Son La ○
Thai
Nguyen
■ **Hanoi**

Sittwe ○
**BURMA
(MYANMAR)**
Taunggyi ○
Hai
Phong
*Gulf of Tonkin*
Haikou

**7**
*I N D I A N*
Pyinmana ○
*Mekong*

Sandoway ○
Pye ○
Louangphrabang ○
Thanh Hoa ○

*O C E A N*
*Irrawaddy*
*Salween*
Chiang
Mai
**LAOS**
**VIETNAM**

Henzada ○
Pegu ○
**THAILAND**
■ **Vientiane**
Vinh ○
*Haina*

Pathein ○
■ **Rangoon**
Udon Thani ○
Sanya ○

**46**
C · 90°E · D · *Mouths of the Irrawaddy* · F · 100° · G · 105° · 110°
Moulmein
95°

45°
N

115° **J** 120° **K** 125° **L** 130° **M** 135° **N** 140° **P** 145°

Hailar

*Hulun
Lake*

Yichun

Hegang

Jiamusi

*Amur*

**RUSSIA**

La Perouse Strait

*Kuril
Islands
(Russia)*

Qiqihar

Daqing

Asahikawa

*Hokkaido* Kushiro

2

Ulanhot

Harbin

Jixi

Sapporo

Tomakomai

Xilinhot

Mudanjiang

**MANCHURIA**

*Lake
Khanka*

Hakodate

**INNER
MONGOLIA**

Changchun

Jilin

Yanji

Vladivostok

Nakhodka

Aomori

40°

Tongliao

Liaoyuan

Chongjin

Akita

Chifeng

Fuxin

Fushun

Shenyang

Hyesan

*Sea of Japan*

Sendai

*Honshu*

3

China

Zhangjiakou

Jinzhou

Anshan

**NORTH
KOREA**

Kanggye

Kimchaek

Niigata

Fukushima

Dandong

Datong

**Beijing**

Tangshan

Qinhuangdao

Sinuiju

Hamhung

Toyama

Utsunomiya

35°

Tianjin

*Gulf of
Chihli*

Dalian

*Korea Bay*

Wonsan

**Pyongyang**

**JAPAN** **Tokyo**

Baoding

Nampo

Kanazawa

Fukui

**Mount Fuji**

Shijiazhuang

Yantai

**Seoul**

Inchon

Suwon

Shizuoka

3,776m
(12,388ft)

Handan

Zibo

Weifang

Qingdao

Chongju

Taejon

Nagoya

Kyoto

Hamamatsu

Dezhou

Taian

*Yellow*

**SOUTH
KOREA**

Taegu

Osaka

Wakayama

4

Jining

*Sea*

Kwangju

Pusan

Okayama

Hiroshima

Shijiazhuang

Zhengzhou

*Grand Canal*

Lianyungang

Kitakyushu

Matsuyama

*Shikoku*

Xuzhou

Cheju

Fukuoka

Pingdingshan

Yancheng

*Cheju*

Nagasaki

Kumamoto

Kagoshima

*Kyushu*

Nanjing

Wuxi

Hefei

Shanghai

*Huang He (Yellow)*

Wuhan

*Chang Jiang (Yangtze)*

Hangzhou

*Tai Lake*

5

Anqing

Ningbo

*Poyang
Lake*

Nanchang

Jinhua

*East*

Changsha

Linchuan

Wenzhou

*China*

*Amami*

Nanping

*Sea*

*R y u k y u  I s l a n d s
(Japan)*

25°

Ganzhou

Yongan

Fuzhou

*Okinawa*

Shaoguan

Quanzhou

**Taipei** Chilung

*Sakishima
Islands*

Tropic of Cancer

6

Canton
(Guangzhou)

Xiamen

Meizhou

*Taiwan Strait*

**TAIWAN**

Taichung

Changhua

Shantou

Tainan

**Yu Shan**

3,997m
(13,113ft)

*Batan
Islands*

**PACIFIC**

20°

Hong Kong
(Xianggang)

Kaohsiung

*South China Sea*

**OCEAN**

7

*Luzon Strait*

**PHILIPPINES**

*Babuyan
Islands*

Aparri

15°
N

Laoag

Tuguegarao

*Luzon*

115° **J** 120° **K** 125° **L** 130° **M** 135° **N**

## China, Korea
## and Japan

- Boreal forest
- Temperate forest
- Tropical forest
- Temperate grassland
- Savanna
- Semi-desert and scrub
- Hot desert
- Wetland
- Mountain
- Tundra
- Ice
- Cultivation
- Urban
- ■ National capital
- ● Internal capital
- ⊙ Major city or town
- ○ Other town
- ▬ International boundary
- ▬ Internal boundary
- ▲ 2,490m
(7,988ft) Height above or below sea level

*See also main key on page 15.*

1:14,000,000

0    200    400km

0    100    200    300 miles

Copyright © Usborne Publishing Ltd.

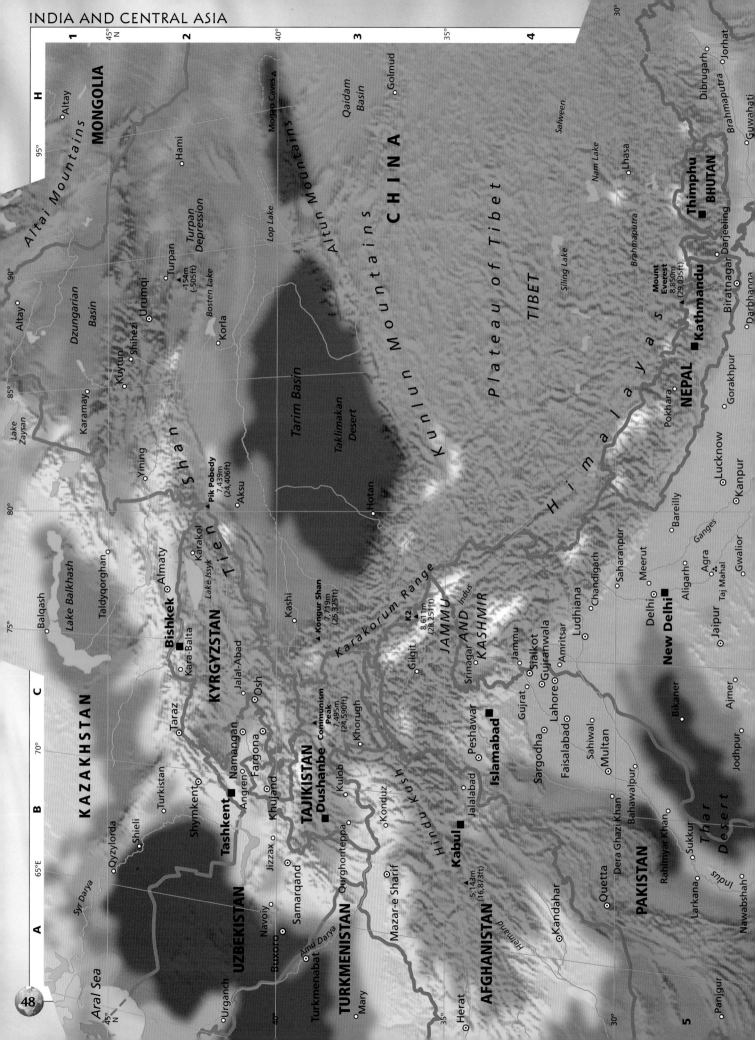

**MONGOLIA**

Altai Mountains

Altay

Altay

Hami

**CHINA**

Turpan

Urumqi

Shihezi

Mogao Caves

Altun Mountains

Turpan Depression

-154m (-505ft)

Bosten Lake

Korla

Qaidam Basin

Golmud

Lop Lake

Salween

Nam Lake

Lhasa

Dzungarian Basin

Kuytun

Lake Zaysan

Karamay

Yining

Tarim Basin

Taklimakan Desert

Siling Lake

**TIBET**

**Plateau of Tibet**

Brahmaputra

**Thimphu**

**BHUTAN**

Darjeeling

**Mount Everest 8,850m (29,035ft)**

Biratnagar

Darbhanga

**KAZAKHSTAN**

Balqash

Taldyqorghan

Lake Balkhash

*Shan*

Aksu

Hotan

Kunlun Mountains

Pokhara

**NEPAL**

**Kathmandu**

Gorakhpur

Dibrugarh

Jorhat

Brahmaputra

Guwahati

Lake Balkhash

Almaty

Karakol

Lake Issyk

Kashi

Kongur Shan 7,719m (25,325ft)

*Karakorum Range*

*Himalayas*

Lucknow

Kanpur

Bareilly

Qyzylorda

Shieli

Taraz

**Bishkek**

Kara-Balta

**KYRGYZSTAN**

Jalal-Abad

Osh

K2 8,611m (28,251ft)

Gilgit

**JAMMU**

**AND**

Srinagar

*Indus*

**KASHMIR**

Jammu

Saharanpur

Meerut

Ganges

Agra

Taj Mahal

Aligarh

Gwalior

Shymkent

Turkistan

Angren

Namangan

Fargona

**TAJIKISTAN**

Communism Peak 7,495m (24,590ft)

Khorugh

Sialkot

Gujranwala

Ludhiana

Chandigarh

**Delhi**

**New Delhi**

Jaipur

Ajmer

**UZBEKISTAN**

Jizzax

Khujand

**Dushanbe**

Kulob

Qurghonteppa

Konduz

Hindu Kush

Peshawar

**Islamabad**

Gujrat

Lahore

Faisalabad

Amritsar

Sahiwal

Multan

Bikaner

Jodhpur

**Tashkent**

Navoiy

Buxoro

Samarqand

Mazar-e Sharif

5,143m (16,873ft)

**Kabul**

Jalalabad

Sargodha

Dera Ghazi Khan

Bahawalpur

Rahimyar Khan

*Thar Desert*

Larkana

Nawabshah

Syr Darya

Urganch

Turkmenabat

**TURKMENISTAN**

Mary

Amu Darya

**AFGHANISTAN**

Herat

Kandahar

Quetta

*Helmand*

**PAKISTAN**

Sukkur

Rahimyar Khan

*Indus*

*Aral Sea*

45°N

45°N

**48**

Pik Pobedy 7,439m (24,406ft)

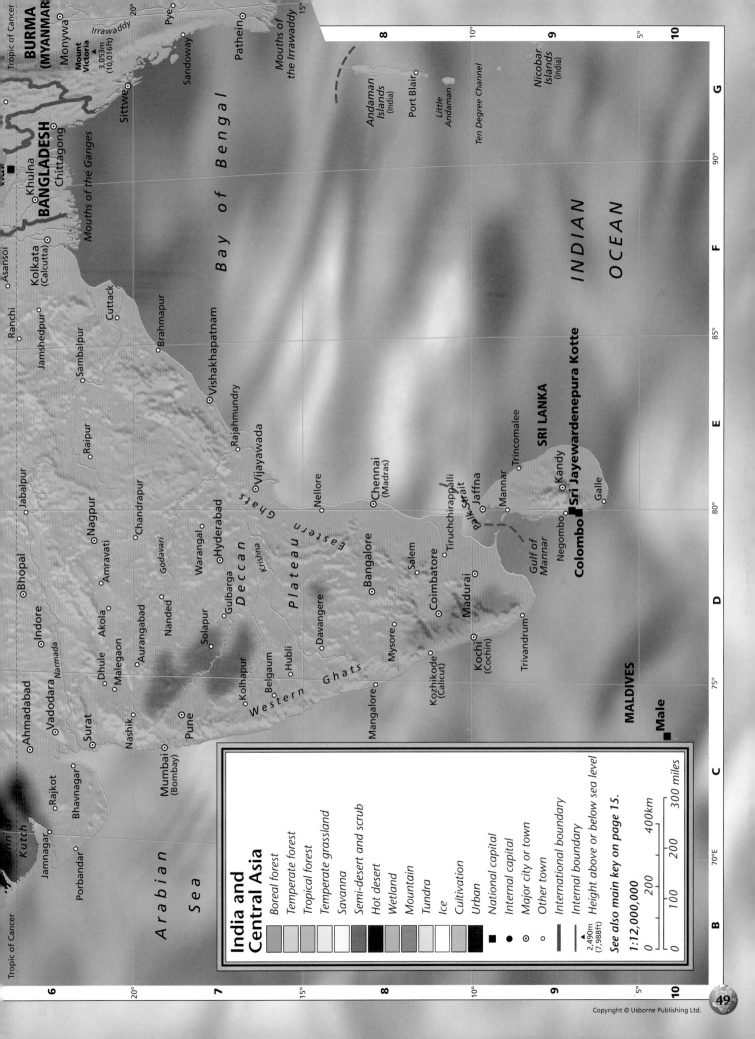

# India and Central Asia

Boreal forest
Temperate forest
Tropical forest
Temperate grassland
Savanna
Semi-desert and scrub
Hot desert
Wetland
Mountain
Tundra
Ice
Cultivation
Urban

■ National capital
● Internal capital
⊙ Major city or town
○ Other town

── International boundary
── Internal boundary
▲ 2,490m Height above or below sea level
(7,988ft)

**See also main key on page 15.**

**1:12,000,000**

0  100  200  300 miles
0  200  400km

## Map labels

BURMA (MYANMAR)
Monywa
Mount Victoria 3,053m (10,016ft)
Irrawaddy
Pye
Pathein
Mouths of the Irrawaddy
Sandoway
Sittwe
Chittagong
Khulna
BANGLADESH
Mouths of the Ganges
Asansol
Ranchi
Jamshedpur
Kolkata (Calcutta)
Cuttack
Sambalpur
Brahmapur
Raipur
Vishakhapatnam
Jabalpur
Bhopal
Nagpur
Rajahmundry
Chandrapur
Vijayawada
Eastern Ghats
Amravati
Warangal
Hyderabad
Godavari
Krishna
Nellore
Indore
Akola
Nanded
Gulbarga
Deccan Plateau
Chennai (Madras)
Dhule
Malegaon
Aurangabad
Solapur
Bangalore
Salem
Tiruchchirappalli
Ahmadabad
Vadodara
Narmada
Nashik
Pune
Belgaum
Hubli
Davangere
Mysore
Coimbatore
Madurai
Jaffna
Palk Strait
Mannar
Trincomalee
Surat
Kolhapur
Western Ghats
Mangalore
Kozhikode (Calicut)
Kochi (Cochin)
Trivandrum
Gulf of Mannar
Negombo
Kandy
SRI LANKA
Colombo ■ Sri Jayewardenepura Kotte
Galle
Rajkot
Bhavnagar
Jamnagar
Porbandar
Kutch
Mumbai (Bombay)
Arabian Sea
Bay of Bengal
Andaman Islands (India)
Port Blair
Little Andaman
Ten Degree Channel
Nicobar Islands (India)
INDIAN OCEAN
MALDIVES
■ Male
Tropic of Cancer

70°E  75°  80°  85°  90°
20°  15°  10°  5°  -5°

Copyright © Usborne Publishing Ltd.

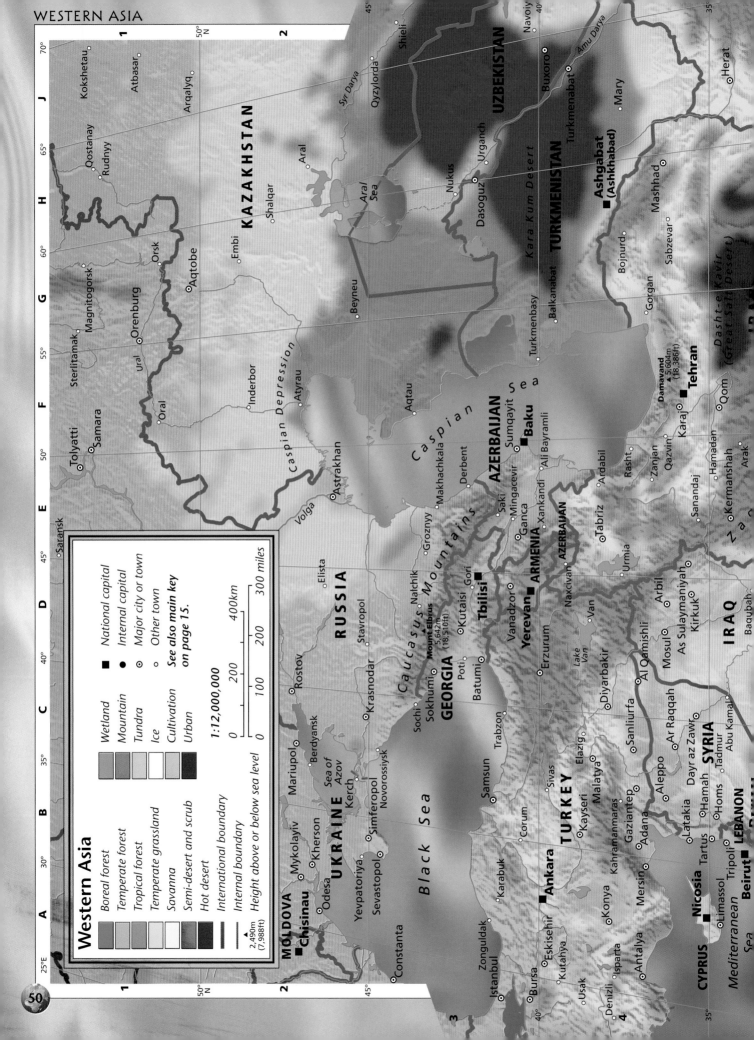

2    80°    1

UNITED
KINGDOM
London

**Paris**
BELGIUM
NETHERLANDS
FRANCE
LUXEMBOURG

*North
Sea*

*Norwegian
Sea*

Arctic Circle

NORWAY
**Oslo**

SWEDEN

*Svalbard*
(Norway)

A

20°

B

40°

ARCT

*Franz Josef
Land*

C

60°

D

80°

ARC

North Cape

*Barents
Sea*

*Novaya
Zemlya*

*Kara
Sea*

GERMANY
**Berlin**

*Baltic
Sea*

**Stockholm**

FINLAND

**Helsinki**

Murmansk

*Kola
Peninsula*

3

CZECH
REPUBLIC

AUSTRIA
SLOVAKIA
POLAND
**Warsaw**

LITHUANIA
LATVIA
**Vilnius**
ESTONIA

*Lake
Ladoga*

St. Petersburg

Arkhangelsk

**Budapest**
HUNGARY
**Minsk**
BELARUS

*Lake
Onega*

Cherepovets

Ukhta

Vorkuta

Lviv

**Moscow**

ROMANIA
**Kiev**
MOLDOVA
**Chisinau**
UKRAINE

Ryazan

Nizhniy Novgorod

*Volga*

Kazan

Perm

Novyy Urengoy

*Ural Mountains*

*Ob*

*West Siberian*

*Plain*

R   U

Odesa
Kharkiv

Voronezh

Samara

Yekaterinburg

Surgut

*Ob*

*Yenisey*

40°
N

Dnipropetrovsk

Simferopol

*Black
Sea*

Rostov

Volgograd

Oral

Orenburg

Chelyabinsk

*Irtysh*

Omsk

Tomsk

Krasn

**Ankara**

TURKEY

Krasnodar

Astrakhan

Mount Elbrus
5,642m
(18,510ft)

*Volga*

Aqtobe

Atyrau

Orenburg

KAZAKHSTAN

**Astana**

Pavlodar

Novosibirsk

Barnaul

Adana

GEORGIA
**Tbilisi**
ARMENIA
**Yerevan**
AZERBAIJAN
**Baku**

*Caspian Sea*

Aqtau

*Aral
Sea*

Qyzylorda

Qaraghandy

*Lake
Balkhash*

Uskemen

Altay

SYRIA

Mosul

Tabriz

Nukus

Dasoguz

Balqash

**Baghdad**

IRAQ

Damavand
5,604m
(18,386ft)

**Tehran**

TURKMENISTAN

UZBEKISTAN

Shymkent

**Ashgabat**
(Ashkhabad)

**Tashkent**

**Bishkek**
KYRGYZSTAN

Almaty

Urumqi

*Tien Shan*

4

Aleppo

Ahvaz

Esfahan

Mashhad

Turkmenabat

Samarqand

Osh

Aksu

*Tarim Basin*

**Kuwait City**
KUWAIT

**Dushanbe**
TAJIKISTAN

SAUDI
ARABIA

IRAN

Shiraz

*Persian
Gulf
(The Gulf)*

Herat

Mazar-e Sharif

*Taklimakan Desert*

Hotan

**Riyadh**

**Manama**

Bandar-e
Abbas

**Kabul**

AFGHANISTAN

K2
8,611m
(28,251ft)

QATAR
**Doha**

**Abu Dhabi**

Zahedan

Kandahar

**Islamabad**

Srinagar

PAKISTAN
*Indus*
Lahore
INDIA

*Plateau of Tibet*

C    60°E    D    80°    E

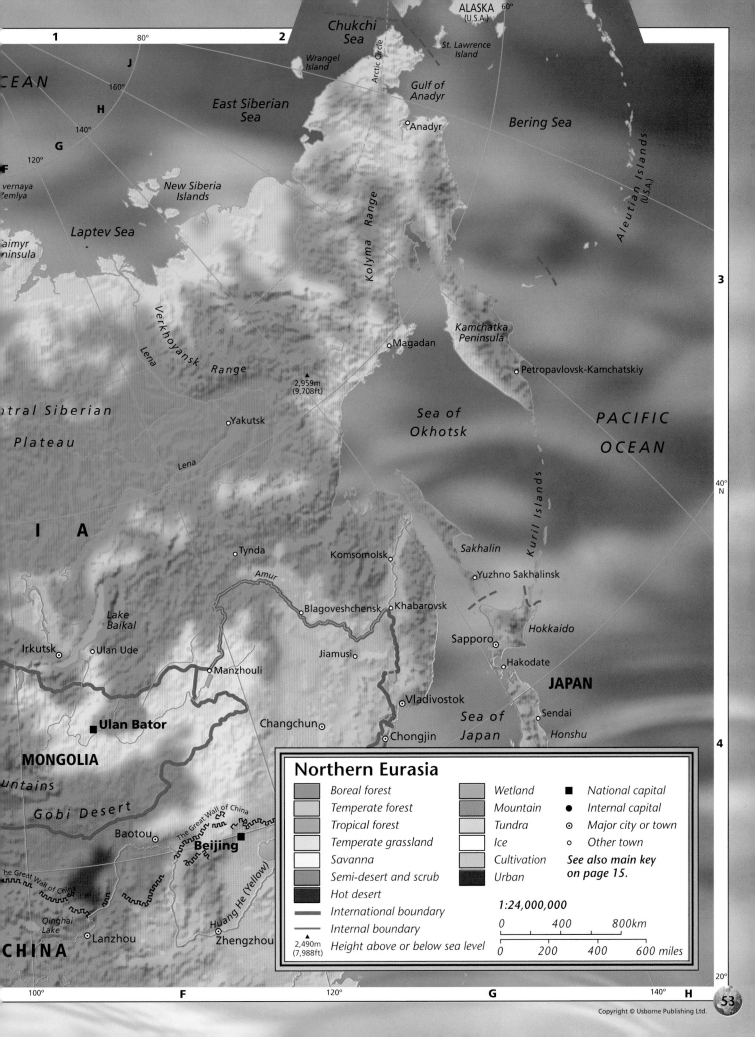

ALASKA 60°
(U.S.A.)

Chukchi
Sea

*Wrangel
Island*

Arctic Circle

*St. Lawrence
Island*

*Gulf of
Anadyr*

CEAN

J

160°

H

140°

G

120°

F

*East Siberian
Sea*

°Anadyr

*Bering Sea*

vernaya
Zemlya

*New Siberia
Islands*

*Laptev Sea*

aimyr
ninsula

*Verkhoyansk*

Lena

*Range*

Lena

*Central Siberian*

*Plateau*

I A

°Yakutsk

°Tynda

*Kolyma*

*Range*

2,959m
(9,708ft)

°Magadan

*Kamchatka
Peninsula*

°Petropavlovsk-Kamchatskiy

*Sea of
Okhotsk*

*Aleutian Islands*
(U.S.A.)

3

*PACIFIC

OCEAN*

40°
N

°Komsomolsk

*Amur*

°Blagoveshchensk °Khabarovsk

Jiamusi°

*Sakhalin*

°Yuzhno Sakhalinsk

*Kuril Islands*

Irkutsk°

*Lake
Baikal*

°Ulan Ude

°Manzhouli

Changchun°

°Vladivostok

°Chongjin

Sapporo°

*Hokkaido*

°Hakodate

**JAPAN**

*Sea of
Japan*

°Sendai

*Honshu*

4

■ **Ulan Bator**

**MONGOLIA**

ntains

*Gobi Desert*

The Great Wall of China

Baotou°

**Beijing** ■

The Great Wall of China

*The Great Wall of China*

*Qinghai
Lake*

°Lanzhou

*Huang He (Yellow)*

°Zhengzhou

**CHINA**

## Northern Eurasia

| | | | |
|---|---|---|---|
| Boreal forest | Wetland | ■ | National capital |
| Temperate forest | Mountain | ● | Internal capital |
| Tropical forest | Tundra | ⊙ | Major city or town |
| Temperate grassland | Ice | ○ | Other town |
| Savanna | Cultivation | | |
| Semi-desert and scrub | Urban | | |
| Hot desert | | | |

***See also main key
on page 15.***

International boundary

Internal boundary

▲ 2,490m
(7,988ft)  *Height above or below sea level*

**1:24,000,000**

0      400      800km

0    200    400    600 miles

20°

1        80°        2

100°        F        120°        G        140°        H

**53**

Copyright © Usborne Publishing Ltd.

# EUROPE

Europe is a small continent, packed with over 40 countries and more than 700 million people. Russia is an enormous country, spanning two continents. Its western part is in Europe, while its eastern part is in Asia. The European part of Russia is larger than any other country in Europe.

*The shading on this map is there to help you see clearly the different countries that make up the continent.*

## Internet link

For a link to a website where you can find out about the European Union and read key facts about each of its member states, go to www.usborne-quicklinks.com

*Arctic Circle*

ARCTIC OCEAN

Reykjavik
**ICELAND**

*Norwegian Sea*

*Faroe Islands (Denmark)*

**SWEDE**

*Shetland Islands*

**NORWAY**

Oslo ■

*Orkney Islands*

**Stockholm**

*North Sea*

**DENMARK**
Copenhagen ■

**IRELAND**
Dublin ■

**UNITED KINGDOM**

London ■

The Hague ■

Amsterdam ■
**NETHERLANDS**

Berlin ■

**POL**

Brussels ■
**BELGIUM**

**GERMANY**

LUXEMBOURG
Luxembourg ■

Prague ■
**CZECH REPUBLIC**

Paris ■

*Rhine*

Vienna ■
**LIECHTENSTEIN** **Bratislava**

Bern ■ Vaduz ■ **AUSTRIA** **Buda**

*Bay of Biscay*

**FRANCE** **SWITZERLAND**

**SLOVENIA** **HUN**
Ljubljana ■ Zagr
**CROA**

ATLANTIC

OCEAN

**MONACO**

**SAN MARINO**

**BOSNIA A HERZEGOV**
Sarajevo ■

**ANDORRA** ■
Andorra la Vella ■

**ITALY**

**PORTUGAL**

*Corsica*

**VATICAN CITY**

Lisbon ■

Madrid ■

Rome ■

**SPAIN**

**ALE**
Ti

*Sardinia*

*Balearic Islands*

*Mediterranean Sea*

*Sicily*

**MALTA**
Valletta ■

54

Barents Sea

Murmansk

Arctic Circle

Arkhangelsk

FINLAND

RUSSIA

aki

St. Petersburg

Tallinn
ESTONIA

Nizhniy Novgorod

Kazan

a

LATVIA

Moscow

UANIA
Vilnius

Minsk

Volga

BELARUS

saw

Kiev

Volgograd

UKRAINE

Dnieper

KIA

MOLDOVA

Chisinau

ROMANIA

de

Bucharest

Black Sea

Danube

A AND
NEGRO

BULGARIA

Sofia

opje

DONIA

TURKEY

CE

Athens

Crete

Copyright © Usborne Publishing Ltd

## Facts

**Total land area** 10,205,720 sq km (3,940,428 sq miles) (including European Russia)

**Total population** 727 million (including all of Russia)

**Biggest city** Moscow, Russia

**Biggest country** Russia *Total area: 17,075,200 sq km (6,592,735 sq miles) Area of European Russia: 4,294,400 sq km (1,658,068 sq miles)*

**Smallest country** Vatican City *0.44 sq km (0.17 sq miles)*

**Highest mountain** Elbrus, Russia *5,642m (18,510ft)*

**Longest river** Volga *3,700km (2,298 miles)*

**Biggest lake** Lake Ladoga, Russia *17,700 sq km (6,834 sq miles)*

**Highest waterfall** Utigard, on the Jostedal Glacier, Norway *800m (2,625ft)*

**Biggest desert** No deserts in Europe

**Biggest island** Great Britain *234,410 sq km (90,506 sq miles)*

**Main mineral deposits** Bauxite, zinc, iron, potash, fluorspar

**Main fuel deposits** Oil, coal, natural gas, peat, uranium

*A cow in Devon, in the south of England*

55

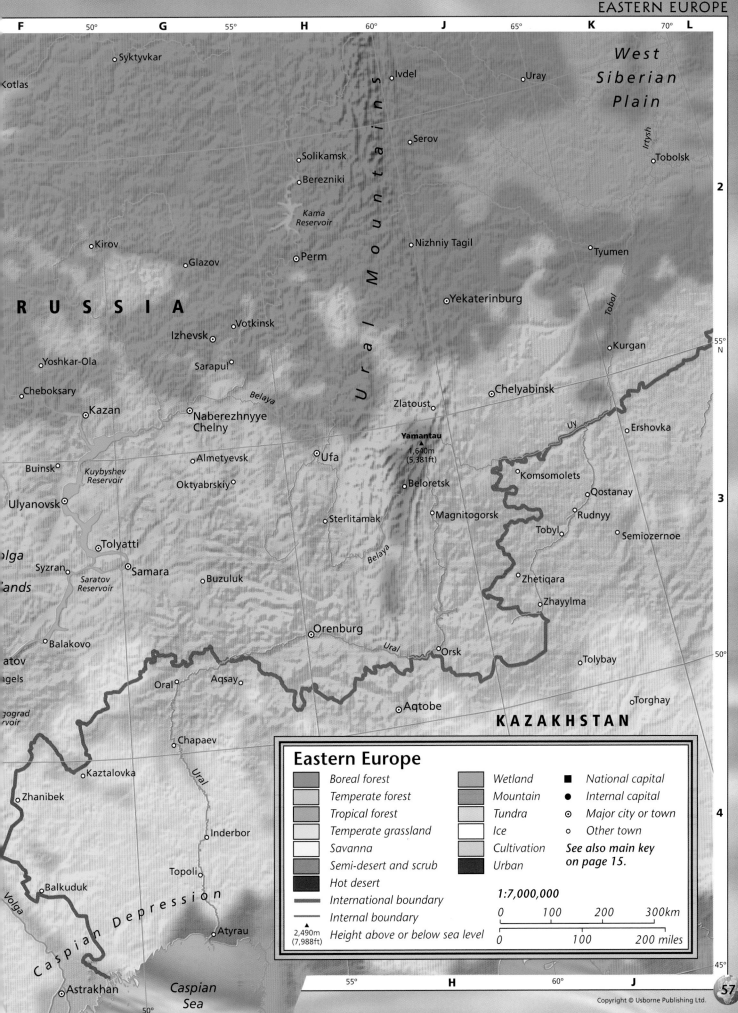

F  50°  G  55°  H  60°  J  65°  K  70°  L

*West Siberian Plain*

Kotlas

Syktyvkar

Ivdel

Uray

*Irtysh*

2

Solikamsk

Serov

Berezniki

Tobolsk

*Kama Reservoir*

Kirov

Nizhniy Tagil

Glazov

Perm

Tyumen

*U r a l   M o u n t a i n s*

**R U S S I A**

Yekaterinburg

Votkinsk

Izhevsk

*Tobol*

55° N

Yoshkar-Ola

Sarapul

Kurgan

Cheboksary

*Belaya*

Zlatoust

Chelyabinsk

Kazan

Naberezhnyye Chelny

*Uy*

Ershovka

Buinsk

Almetyevsk

Ufa

▲Yamantau
1,640m
(5,381ft)

Komsomolets

3

Ulyanovsk

*Kuybyshev Reservoir*

Oktyabrskiy

Beloretsk

Qostanay

Rudnyy

Magnitogorsk

Tobyl

Semiozernoe

Tolyatti

Sterlitamak

*olga*

Syzran

*Saratov Reservoir*

Samara

*Belaya*

Zhetiqara

*ands*

Buzuluk

Zhayylma

Balakovo

Orenburg

*Ural*

Orsk

Tolybay

50°

*atov*

Oral

Aqsay

Torghay

*gels*

Aqtobe

**K A Z A K H S T A N**

*jograd rvoir*

Chapaev

*Ural*

Kaztalovka

4

Zhanibek

Inderbor

Topoli

Balkuduk

*Volga*

*C a s p i a n   D e p r e s s i o n*

Atyrau

Astrakhan

*Caspian Sea*

50°

55°  H  60°  J

## Eastern Europe

| | | |
|---|---|---|
| Boreal forest | Wetland | ■ National capital |
| Temperate forest | Mountain | ● Internal capital |
| Tropical forest | Tundra | ⊙ Major city or town |
| Temperate grassland | Ice | ○ Other town |
| Savanna | Cultivation | ***See also main key*** |
| Semi-desert and scrub | Urban | ***on page 15.*** |
| Hot desert | | |

International boundary

Internal boundary

▲2,490m
(7,988ft) Height above or below sea level

1:7,000,000

0    100    200    300km

0         100       200 miles

Copyright © Usborne Publishing Ltd.

1    68°N    2    64°    3    60°

M   40°   L   36°   32°   K   28°   24°   G   20°   F   16°   E   12°   D   8°   C   16°   B   20°W   4°E   A   0°

*Barents Sea*

*Kola Peninsula*

▲1,191m 3,907ft

*White Sea*

Belomorsk

Severomorsk

Murmansk

Monchegorsk

Apatity

Kandalaksha

Lake Vyg

*Lake Onega*

R U S S I A

Tikhvin

Volkhov

Borovichi

Kirishi

Petrozavodsk

*Lake Seg*

Lieksa

Medvezhyegorsk

*Lake Ladoga*

St. Petersburg

Pushkin

Gatchina

Novgorod

Kingisepp

Narva

Vadso

Kirkenes

Utsjoki

Sevettijarvi

Kaamanen

*Lake Inari*

*Lokan Reservoir*

Sodankyla

Rovaniemi

Kuusamo

Kajaani

Kuhmo

*Lake Pya*

*Lake Top*

*Lake Kuyto*

Kostomuksha

*Pielis Lake*

*Hauki Lake*

Varkaus

Kuopio

Kiuruvesi

*Puula Lake*

Mikkeli

*Saimaa Lake*

Lappeenranta

Kouvola

Kotka

Vyborg

Zelenogorsk

Kohtla-Jarve

*Pihlaja Lake*

*Pajanne Lake*

*Arctic Circle*

Hammerfest

Alta

Tromso

*Soroya*

*North Cape*

*L a p l a n d*

Kiruna

*Stora Lule Lake*

*Horn Lake*

*Storavan Lake*

Boden

*Oulu Lake*

Raahe

Oulu

F I N L A N D

Kokkola

Vaasa

Kurikka

Saarijarvi

Alavus

Jyvaskyla

*Nasi Lake*

Tampere

Pori

Hameenlinna

Lahti

Helsinki

Espoo

Turku

Rauma

*Aland Islands*

*Gulf of Finland*

Tallinn

Haapsalu

*Hiiumaa*

ESTONIA

*Lake Peipus*

Narvik

▲ Kebnekaise 2,114m (6,935ft)

Svolvaer

Bodo

*Lofoten*

*Vesteralen*

*Vestfjorden*

Mo i Rana

*Ume*

*Umea*

Skelleftea

Umea

Sundsvall

Hudiksvall

Gavle

Borlange

Uppsala

Eskilstuna

*Lake Malar*

Stockholm

Sodertalje

*Gulf of Bothnia*

*Norwegian Sea*

Namsos

Steinkjer

*Vikna*

*Storlake*

Ostersund

*Stor Lake*

*Indals*

S W E D E N

Orebro

Karlstad

*Lake Vaner*

Vikna

Trondheim

*Froya*

*Hitra*

Oppdal

Lillehammer

*Klar*

*Glama*

Oslo

Drammen

Fredrikstad

Larvik

N O R W A Y

▲ Galdhopiggen 2,469m (8,100ft)

Honefoss

Alesund

Kristiansund

*Smola*

*Sula*

Bergen

Odda

*Sotra*

Stavanger

*Karmoy*

Varhaug

### Iceland inset

A   0°   N   20°W   B   P   16°   C   P   16°   Q   D   Q

1   68°N   2   64°N   3   64°N

*Langanes*

Siglufjordhur

Seydhisfjordhur

Isafjordhur

*Arctic Circle*

I C E L A N D

*Vatnajökull*

▲ Hvannadalshnukur 2,119m (6,952ft)

Reykjavik

Keflavik

*Faxafloi*

*ATLANTIC OCEAN*

*Same scale as main map*

*Arctic Circle*

24°W   20°   16°

1   68°N   2   64°   3   60°

4°W

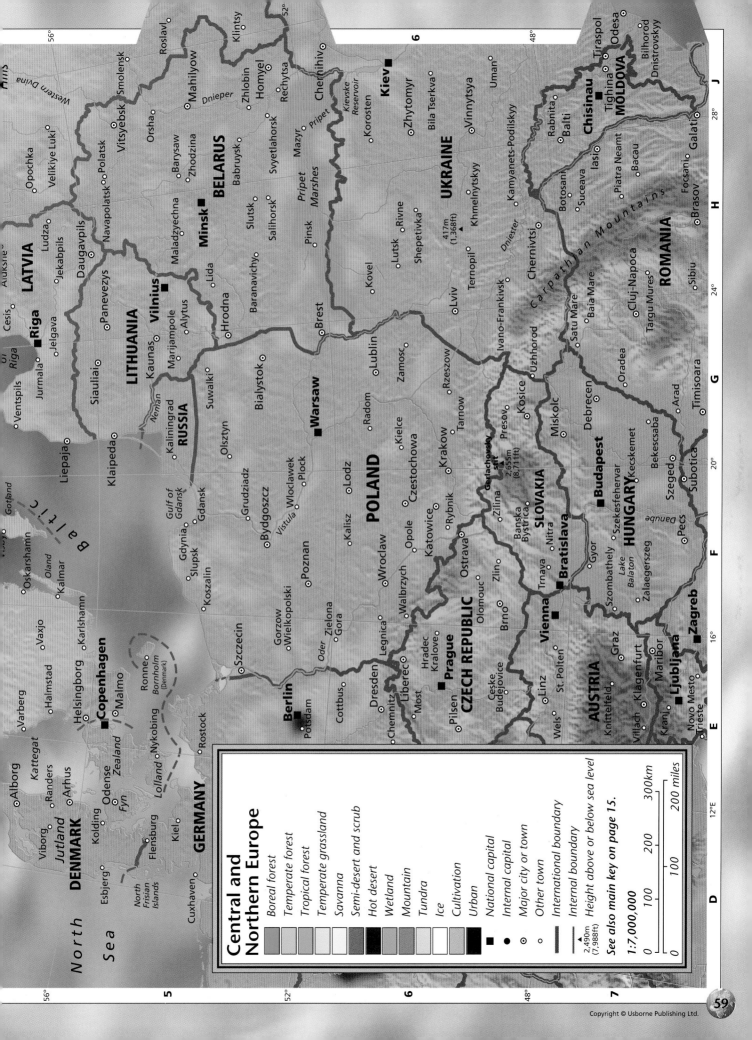

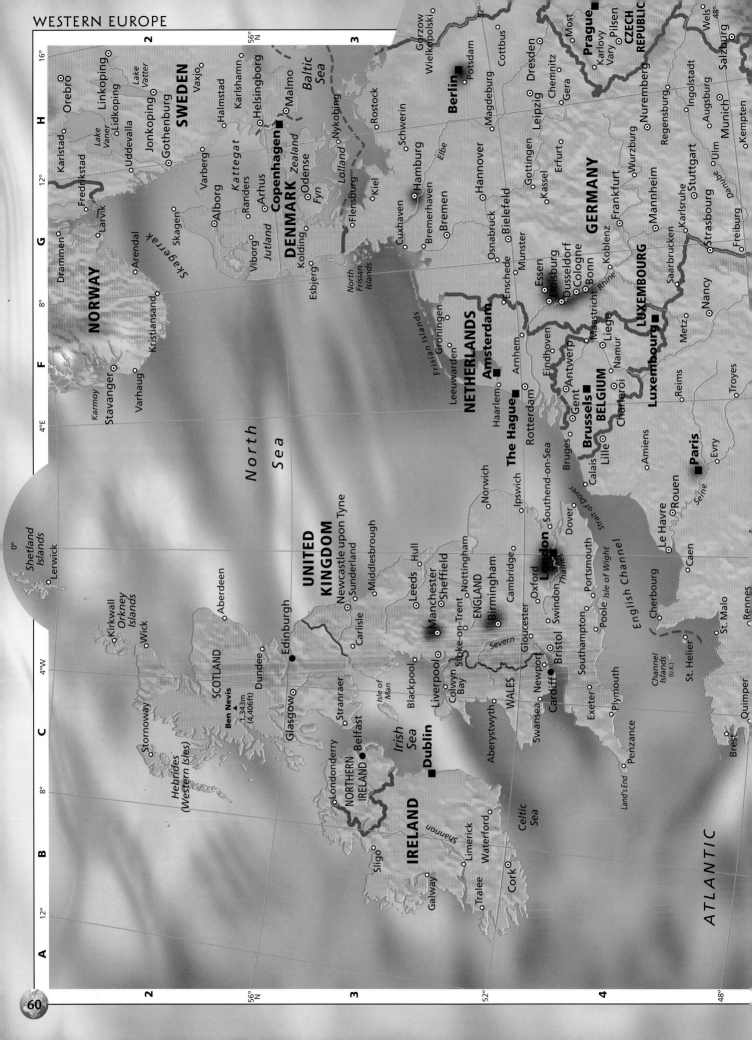

NORWAY
Orebró
Linköping
Lidköping
Jönköping
Karlshamn
Karlskrona
Helsingborg
SWEDEN
Vaxjö
Varberg
Halmstad
Karlstad
Fredrikstad
Larvik
Lake Vaner
Lake Vatter
Gothenburg
Uddevalla
Skagen
Arendal
Drammen
Kristiansand
Varhaug
Stavanger
Karmøy
Skagerrak

Malmö
Copenhagen Zealand
Odense
Fyn
Aborg
Randers
Arhus
Viborg
Jutland
Kolding
Flensburg
Esbjerg
DENMARK
Kattegat
Baltic Sea
Nykøbing
Lolland
Rostock
Schwerin
Kiel
Cuxhaven
Bremerhaven
Hamburg
Bremen
North Frisian Islands
Elbe

Berlin
Potsdam
Magdeburg
Cottbus
Dresden
Chemnitz
Gera
Leipzig
Erfurt
Göttingen
Kassel
Hannover
Bielefeld
Osnabrück
Münster
Enschede
GERMANY
Gorzow Wielkopolski
Prague
Karlovy Vary
Pilsen
CZECH REPUBLIC
Most
Nuremberg
Würzburg
Frankfurt
Koblenz
Cologne
Bonn
Düsseldorf
Duisburg
Essen
Rhine
Maastricht
Liège
Namur
LUXEMBOURG
Luxembourg
Saarbrücken
Karlsruhe
Mannheim
Stuttgart
Strasbourg
Freiburg
Nancy
Metz
Reims
Regensburg
Ingolstadt
Augsburg
Munich
Kempten
Ulm
Salzburg
Wels
Danube

NETHERLANDS
Groningen
Leeuwarden
Frisian Islands
Amsterdam
Haarlem
Arnhem
Eindhoven
Rotterdam
The Hague
Bruges
Gent
Antwerp
BELGIUM
Brussels
Charleroi
Lille
Calais
Strait of Dover
Amiens
Troyes
Paris
Evry
Rouen
Seine
Le Havre
Caen
Cherbourg
St. Malo
St. Helier
Channel Islands (U.K.)
Rennes
Brest
Quimper
ATLANTIC

North Sea

UNITED KINGDOM
Newcastle upon Tyne
Sunderland
Middlesbrough
Carlisle
Edinburgh
SCOTLAND
Aberdeen
Ben Nevis
1,343m (4,406ft)
Dundee
Glasgow
Stranraer
Kirkwall
Orkney Islands
Wick
Stornoway
Hebrides (Western Isles)
Shetland Islands
Lerwick

Leeds
Hull
Manchester
Sheffield
Nottingham
Stoke-on-Trent
ENGLAND
Birmingham
Cambridge
Norwich
Ipswich
London
Southend-on-Sea
Thames
Oxford
Swindon
Gloucester
Bristol
Cardiff
Newport
Swansea
WALES
Aberystwyth
Colwyn Bay
Liverpool
Blackpool
Isle of Man
Irish Sea
Belfast
NORTHERN IRELAND
Londonderry
Dublin
IRELAND
Sligo
Galway
Tralee
Limerick
Waterford
Cork
Shannon
Celtic Sea
Exeter
Plymouth
Penzance
Land's End
Poole
Portsmouth
Southampton
Isle of Wight
English Channel
Dover
Severn

0°
4°E
8°
12°
16°
52°N
56°N
0°
4°W
8°
12°
48°

H  G  F  C  B  A
2  3  4

60

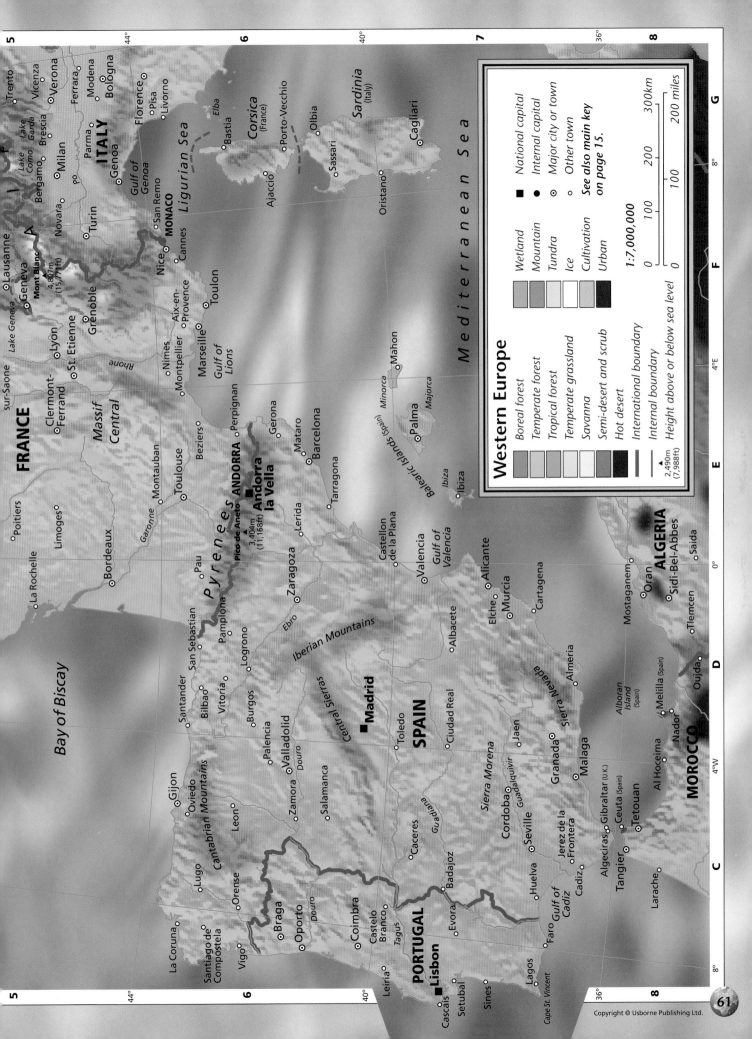

# Western Europe

|  |  |
|---|---|
| ■ | National capital |
| ● | Internal capital |
| ⊙ | Major city or town |
| ○ | Other town |
| ***See also main key on page 15.*** | |

**1:7,000,000**

| 0 | 100 | 200 | 300km |
|---|---|---|---|
| 0 | 100 | 200 miles | |

Wetland
Mountain
Tundra
Ice
Cultivation
Urban

Boreal forest
Temperate forest
Tropical forest
Temperate grassland
Savanna
Semi-desert and scrub
Hot desert

International boundary
Internal boundary

▲ 2,490m
(7,988ft)

Height above or below sea level

ITALY

Trento
Vicenza
Verona
Ferrara
Modena
Bologna
Parma
Brescia
Bergamo
Milan
Novara
Turin
Lake Como
Lake Garda
Po
Genoa
San Remo
**MONACO**
Nice
Cannes

Florence
Pisa
Livorno
Elba
Bastia

*Gulf of Genoa*

*Corsica*
(France)

Ajaccio

Porto-Vecchio
Olbia
Sassari

*Sardinia*
(Italy)

Oristano
Cagliari

*Ligurian Sea*

*Mediterranean Sea*

Lausanne
Geneva
Lake Geneva
▲ Mont Blanc
4,807m
(15,771ft)
Grenoble
sur-Saône
Clermont-Ferrand
Lyon
St. Etienne

**FRANCE**

*Massif Central*

*Rhône*

Nîmes
Aix-en-Provence
Montpellier
Marseille
Toulon

*Gulf of Lions*

Poitiers
Limoges
Montauban
Toulouse
Bordeaux
Pau

Béziers
Perpignan
Gerona

*Garonne*

*Pyrenees*

**ANDORRA**
■ **Andorra la Vella**
▲ Pic de Aneto
3,404m
(11,168ft)

Mataró
Barcelona
Tarragona

Minorca
Majorca
Palma
Mahon

*Balearic Islands (Spain)*

Ibiza
Ibiza

*Bay of Biscay*

La Rochelle

La Coruña
Santiago de Compostela
Lugo
Orense
Vigo

Gijón
Oviedo
Leon
*Cantabrian Mountains*

Santander
Bilbao
San Sebastian
Vitoria
Pamplona
Logroño
Burgos

*Iberian Mountains*

Zaragoza
Lérida
*Ebro*

Castellon
de la Plana

Valencia
*Gulf of Valencia*

Alicante
Elche
Murcia
Cartagena

Almería

*Sierra Nevada*

**SPAIN**

Palencia
Valladolid
*Douro*
Zamora
Salamanca

*Central Sierras*

■ **Madrid**
Toledo
Ciudad Real
Albacete

Jaén
Córdoba
*Guadalquivir*
*Sierra Morena*
*Guadiana*

Granada
Málaga

Braga
Oporto
*Douro*
Coimbra
Castelo Branco

**PORTUGAL**
■ **Lisbon**
Cascais
Setúbal
Sines

Cáceres
Badajoz
Évora

Mérida
Huelva
Seville
Jerez de la Frontera
Cádiz

*Gulf of Cádiz*
Faro
Lagos
*Cape St. Vincent*

Leiria

Algeciras
Gibraltar (U.K.)
Ceuta (Spain)
Tangier
Larache
Tetouan
Al Hoceima

Melilla (Spain)
Nador

*Alboran Island (Spain)*

**MOROCCO**

**ALGERIA**
Oran
Sidi-Bel-Abbes
Mostaganem
Saïda
Tlemcen
Oujda
Saida

Copyright © Usborne Publishing Ltd.

A  0°  B  4°E  C  8°  D  12°  E  16°

Cherbourg

Le Havre
Rouen
Caen
Amiens
Charleroi
Namur
BELGIUM
Koblenz
Erfurt
Gera
Dresden
Chemnitz
Most
Liberec
Wrocław
Walb

1

Paris
Reims
LUXEMBOURG
Luxembourg
Frankfurt
Wurzburg
Nuremberg
Karlovy
Vary
Pilsen
Hradec Kralove
Prague
CZECH REPUBLIC
Olomou

Evry
Metz
Saarbrucken
Mannheim
GERMANY
Ceske
Budejovice
Brno

48°
N
Le Mans
Nancy
Karlsruhe
Stuttgart
Regensburg
Ingolstadt
Linz
Vienna

Angers
Orleans
Troyes
Strasbourg
Rhine
Ulm
Danube
Augsburg
Wels
St. Polten
Brati

Tours

Freiburg
Munich
Salzburg

2
Poitiers
Nevers
Dijon
Besancon
Basel
Winterthur
Kempten
Innsbruck
AUSTRIA
Knittelfeld
Szomba

FRANCE
Chalon-
sur-Saone
Biel
Zurich
Lucerne
Vaduz
LIECHTENSTEIN
Grossglockner
3,798m
(12,461ft)
Villach
Graz
Klagenfurt
Zalae

Limoges
Bern
SWITZERLAND
Lausanne
Bolzano
S
p
Maribor

Clermont-Ferrand
Geneva
Lake Geneva
Mont Blanc
A
Trento
Kranj
SLOVENIA
Ljubljana

Lyon
4,807m
(15,771ft)
Lake
Como
Bergamo
Lake
Garda
Vicenza
Trieste
Novo
Mesto
Zagre

St. Etienne
Grenoble
Novara
Milan
Brescia
Verona
Venice
Rijeka
CROA

Massif
Central
Turin
Po
Karlovac
Sla

44°
Montauban
Genoa
Parma
Modena
Bologna
Ferrara
Ravenna
Pula
Zadar
Dinaric
BOSN
AND

Toulouse
Gulf of
Genoa
Rimini
ITALY
HERZEGO
Alps

Montpellier
Nimes
Aix-en-
Provence
MONACO
San Remo
Nice
Pisa
SAN MARINO
Ancona
Split

Beziers
Marseille
Cannes
Livorno
Florence
Perugia
Apennines
Pescara
Adriatic Sea

Andorra la Vella
Gulf of
Lions
Toulon
Ligurian Sea
Bastia
Elba
Terni
Foggia
Ba

3

Southern Europe

Boreal forest
Temperate forest
Tropical forest
Temperate grassland
Savanna
Semi-desert and scrub
Hot desert
Wetland
Mountain
Tundra
Ice
Cultivation
Urban

■  National capital
●  Internal capital
⊙  Major city or town
○  Other town
▬  International boundary
▬  Internal boundary
▲ 2,490m
(7,988ft)  Height above or below sea level

See also main key on page 15.
1:7,000,000

0      100     200     300km
0         100        200 miles

Corsica
(France)
Ajaccio
Porto-Vecchio
VATICAN CITY
Rome

Olbia
Sassari

Sardinia
(Italy)
Tyrrhenian

Oristano
Sea

Naples
Pompeii
Salerno
Taranto

Cosenza

40°

Cagliari

Lipari
Islands

4

Mediterranean  Sea
Catar

Annaba
Bizerte
Menzel
Bourguiba
Trapani
Palermo
Messina

Guelma
Carthage
Sicily
Mount Etna
3,323m
(10,902ft)
Catania

36°
Souk Ahras
Tunis
Agrigento
Syracuse

TUNISIA
Nabeul
Pantelleria
(Italy)
Ragusa

Tebessa
Kairouan
Sousse
MALTA

5
Kasserine
El Jem
Monastir
Pelagian Islands
(Italy)
Valletta

B  4°E  C  8°  D  12°  E  16°

62

# AFRICA

Africa is the second-biggest continent in the world, and has 53 countries. These range from the vast, dry Sudan, to small, tropical islands such as the Seychelles. More than a quarter of Africa's countries are landlocked, with no access to the sea except through other countries.

*Here is a group of Masai people from East Africa, silhouetted against a sunset over the flat grasslands of Africa.*

Algiers
Tunis
Rabat
Madeira
(Portugal)
MOROCCO
TUNISIA
Tripoli
Canary Islands
(Spain)
ALGERIA
LIBY
Laayoune
WESTERN
SAHARA
(Morocco)
Tropic of Cancer
MAURITANIA
Nouakchott
MALI
Niger
NIGER
CHAL
CAPE VERDE
Praia
Dakar
SENEGAL
THE GAMBIA
Banjul
Bamako
Niamey
Ndjam
Ouagadougou
GUINEA-BISSAU
Bissau
BURKINA FASO
Conakry
GUINEA
BENIN
NIGERIA
Freetown
IVORY
COAST
TOGO
Abuja
SIERRA LEONE
GHANA
Porto-Novo
CEM
AFF
REP
Monrovia
Yamoussoukro
Lome
CAMEROON
Bangui
LIBERIA
Accra
Malabo
Yaounde
EQUATORIAL
GUINEA
Equator
Libreville
CONGO
SAO TOME
AND PRINCIPE
GABON
Brazzaville
Kinsha
ATLANTIC
Luanda
OCEAN
ANGOLA
NAMIBI
Tropic of Capricorn
Windhoek
Or
Cape Town

Copyright © Usborne Publishing Ltd.

## Facts

**Total land area**  30,311,690 sq km (11,703,343 sq miles)
**Total population**  794 million
**Biggest city**  Lagos, Nigeria
**Biggest country**  Sudan  *2,505,810 sq km (967,493 sq miles)*
**Smallest country**  Seychelles  *455 sq km (176 sq miles)*

**Highest mountain**  Kilimanjaro, Tanzania  *5,895m (19,340ft)*
**Longest river**  Nile, running from to Burundi to Egypt  *6,671km (4,145 miles)*
**Biggest lake**  Lake Victoria, between Tanzania, Kenya and Uganda  *69,215 sq km (26,724 sq miles)*
**Highest waterfall**  Tugela Falls, on the Tugela River, South Africa  *610m (2,000ft)*
**Biggest desert**  Sahara, North Africa  *9,100,000 sq km (3,500,000 sq miles)*
**Biggest island**  Madagascar  *587,040 sq km (226,656 sq miles)*

**Main mineral deposits**  Gold, copper, diamonds, iron ore, manganese, bauxite
**Main fuel deposits**  Coal, uranium, natural gas

*The shading on this map is there to help you see clearly the different countries that make up the continent.*

*This greater flamingo is from the Transvaal National Park, South Africa.*

### Internet link

For a link to a website where you can find facts, photos and a quiz about Madagascar's amazing wildlife, go to **www.usborne-quicklinks.com**

A    0°    B    5°E

Saida

Djelfa

Atlas Mountains

Biskra

Batna    Tebessa    Kairouan

Annaba    Bizerte
Menzel    ♣Carthage
Bourguiba    ■ Tunis

Sicily    ○ Catania
(Italy)    ○ Syracuse

GREECE    At

20°

2

Ghardaia

Touggourt

El Oued

Gafsa
Tozeur

Ouargla

Chott
el Jerid

Gabes

Tataouine

TUNISIA

Sfax

Pantelleria
(Italy)

Kerkenah
Islands

Gulf of Gabes
Jerba

Sousse
○ Monastir
♣ El Jem

MALTA
■ Valletta

Pelagian
Islands
(Italy)

M e d i t e r r a n e

Tripoli

Al Khums

Gharyan    Leptis Magna ♣

○ Misratah

Cyrene
Al Bayda ♣    Darna

Benghazi

Tubru

30°
N

Tademait
Plateau

Ghadamis

Surt

Gulf of
Sidra

Ajdabiya

3

Great
Eastern Erg

ALGERIA

Illizi

Sabha

LIBYA

Liby

25°

Mount Tahat
2,918m
(9,573ft) ▲

Ahaggar
Mountains

Ghat

Murzuq

Tropic of Cancer

4

Tamanrasset

Al

20°

Djado
Plateau

Tibesti
Mountains

Emi Koussi
3,415m
(11,204ft) ▲

S    A    H    A    R    A

5

MALI

Agadez

NIGER

Faya-Largeau

Bodele
Depression

Ennedi
Plateau

15°

Tahoua

CHAD

6

Dosso

Sokoto

Birnin-Kebbi

Katsina

Maradi    ○ Zinder

Gusau

Kano

S    A    H    E    L

Mao

Lake Chad

Abeche

Mou

Kandi

Zaria

Kaduna

Kainji
Reservoir

NIGERIA

Maiduguri

Potiskum

Ndjamena

Mongo

Am Timan

10°

7

Saki

Niger    Bida

Minna

Jos

Kumo

■ Abuja

Maroua

CAMEROON ○ Bongor

Birao

B    5°E    C    10°    D    15°    E    20°    F

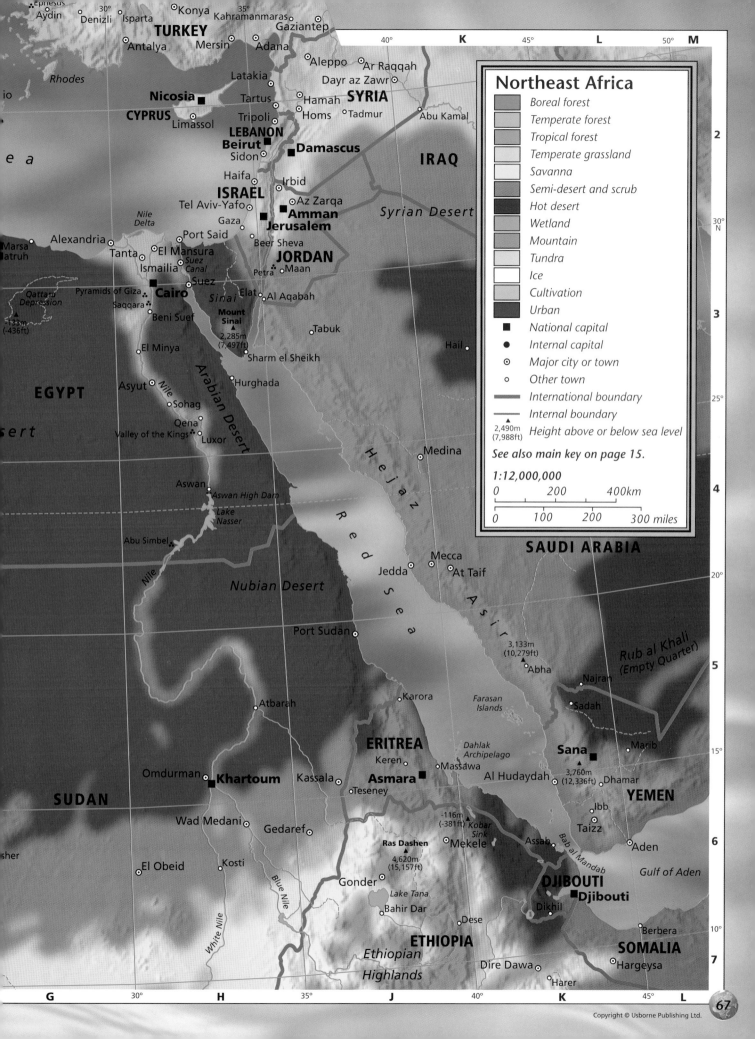

## Northeast Africa

**Boreal forest**
**Temperate forest**
**Tropical forest**
**Temperate grassland**
**Savanna**
**Semi-desert and scrub**
**Hot desert**
**Wetland**
**Mountain**
**Tundra**
**Ice**
**Cultivation**
**Urban**

■ National capital
● Internal capital
⊙ Major city or town
○ Other town
── International boundary
── Internal boundary
▲ 2,490m
(7,988ft) Height above or below sea level

*See also main key on page 15.*

**1:12,000,000**

0   200   400km
0   100   200   300 miles

---

TURKEY
Ephesus
Aydin
Denizli   Isparta   Konya   Kahramanmaras   Gaziantep
Antalya   Mersin   Adana
Aleppo   Ar Raqqah
Latakia   Dayr az Zawr
Rhodes   Tartus   Hamah   SYRIA   Tadmur   Abu Kamal
Nicosia   Homs
CYPRUS   Limassol   Tripoli
Sidon   Beirut   Damascus   IRAQ
LEBANON
Haifa   Irbid
Tel Aviv-Yafo   Az Zarqa   Syrian Desert
ISRAEL   Amman
Gaza   Jerusalem
Alexandria   Port Said   Beer Sheva   JORDAN
Marsa   Tanta   El Mansura   Petra   Maan
Matruh   Ismailia   Suez Canal
Qattara   Cairo   Sinai   Elat   Al Aqabah
Depression   Pyramids of Giza   Suez
-133m   Saqqara   Mount   Tabuk
(-436ft)   Beni Suef   Sinai
2,285m
(7,497ft)
El Minya   Sharm el Sheikh   Hail
EGYPT   Asyut   Hurghada
sert   Sohag   Arabian Desert
Qena   Valley of the Kings   Luxor
Medina
Aswan   Hejaz
Aswan High Dam
Lake   Red
Nasser
Abu Simbel   Mecca
Nubian Desert   Jedda   At Taif
SAUDI ARABIA
Nile   Sea
Port Sudan   3,133m
(10,279ft)
Rub al Khali
Abha   (Empty Quarter)
Atbarah   Karora   Najran
Farasan   Sadah
Islands
Keren   Dahlak   Sana   Marib
ERITREA   Archipelago
Omdurman   Khartoum   Kassala   Asmara   Massawa   3,760m
(12,336ft)   Dhamar
SUDAN   Teseney   Al Hudaydah   YEMEN
Ibb
Wad Medani   Gedaref   -116m   Taizz
(-381ft)   Kobar   Aden
Ras Dashen   Sink   Assab   Gulf of Aden
El Obeid   Kosti   4,620m   Mekele   Bab al Mandab   Berbera
(15,157ft)
Gonder   DJIBOUTI   Dikhil   Djibouti
White Nile   Lake Tana   Dese
Blue Nile   Bahir Dar   SOMALIA
ETHIOPIA   Hargeysa
sher   Ethiopian   Dire Dawa
Highlands   Harer

67

Copyright © Usborne Publishing Ltd.

A B C D E F G H

30°W 20° 15° 10° 5° 0° 5°E 10°

J K K 1

10 2

3 3

4 4

**ATLANTIC OCEAN**

Flores °
Terceira °
Angra do
Heroismo °
Pico ° Sao Miguel
Azores Ponta Delgada °
(Portugal)

*Same scale as main map*

40° N
40° N
25°

**PORTUGAL**
Lisbon ■

Sines °
Lagos °
Cadiz °
Seville °

**SPAIN**
Cordoba °
Granada °
Malaga °
Gibraltar (U.K.) °
Ceuta (Spain) °
Almeria °
Alicante °
Murcia °

Majorca
*Balearic Islands*
(Spain)

Ibiza

*Mediterranean Sea*

*Sardinia*
(Italy)
Cagliari °

10°

**Tunis** ■
Carthage
Bizerte
Menzel
Bourguiba
Annaba °
Sousse °
Monastir °
Kerkenah
Islands
Jerba
Sfax °
El Jem
Kairouan °
Gafsa °
Tozeur °
Chott
el Jerid
Tataouine

**TUNISIA**

Ghadamis °

**LIBYA**

35°

Madeira
(Portugal)
Funchal °

Canary Islands
(Spain)
La Palma Tenerife
La Gomera
El Hierro
Gran
Canaria
Fuerteventura
Lanzarote

**ATLANTIC OCEAN**

Tetouan °
Tangier °
Larache °
Al Hoceima °
Kenitra °
**Rabat** ■
Casablanca °
El Jadida °
Safi °
Essaouira °
Agadir °

Fes °
Meknes °
Beni Mellal °
Khouribga °
Marrakech °
**Toubkal**
4,165m
(13,665ft)
Ouarzazate °

**MOROCCO**

Taza °
Oujda °
Tlemcen °
Oran °
Melilla
(Spain)
Sidi-Bel-Abbes °
Mostaganem °
Saida °
**Algiers** ■
Blida °
Bejaia °
Skikda °
Constantine °
Setif °
Djemila
Bordj Bou
Arreridj °
Batna °
Tebessa °
El Oued °
Djelfa °
Ghardaia °
Ouargla °
Touggourt °

*Atlas Mountains*

*Great
Western Erg*

*Great
Eastern Erg*

**ALGERIA**

Er Rachidia °
Erfoud °
Bechar °
Adrar °

*Chech Erg*

*Tademait
Plateau*

*Ahaggar
Mountains*
**Mount Tahat**
2,918m
(9,573ft) ▲
Illizi °
Tamanrasset °

Tropic of Cancer

25°

**WESTERN
SAHARA**
(Morocco)

Laayoune ■
Boujdour °
Ad Dakhla °

Tan-Tan °
Es Semara °

Zouerat °

Atar °

Akjoujt °

Nouadhibou °
Cape Blanc

Tindouf °

**MAURITANIA**

*S A H A R A*

Tropic of Cancer

20°

30°W 35°

**NIGER**

Maradi
Tahoua
Katsina
Gusau
Sokoto
Zaria
Birnin-Kebbi
Minna
Kaduna
Bida
Abuja
Kandi
**NIGERIA**
Ilorin
Ogbomoso
Saki
Ibadan
Enugu
Onitsha
Benin City
Owo
Warri
Port Harcourt
Abeokuta
Lagos
Niger Delta
*Kainji Reservoir*

**Niamey**
Dosso
Tillaberi
**BENIN**
Natitingou
Djougou
Parakou
Fada-Ngourma
Sokode
Abomey
**TOGO**
Cotonou
**Porto-Novo**
**Lome**
**Accra**
*Bight of Benin*
Cape Coast
Sekondi-Takoradi

*Gulf of Guinea*

Tenkodogo
Bawku
**Ouagadougou**
**BURKINA FASO**
Dori
Ouahigouya
Koudougou
Bobo Dioulasso
*White Volta*
Wenchi
**GHANA**
Tamale
Damongo
Wa
Koforidua
Kumasi
Tarkwa
*Lake Volta*

**SAO TOME
AND PRINCIPE**
*Principe*
**Sao Tome**
*Equator*

*5°E*

**NIGER** ... 

Mopti
Niono
Segou
San
Tougan
**Bamako**
Koutiala
Sikasso
Bougouni
Banfora
*Black Volta*
*Niger*
Odienne
Korhogo
Bouna
Bondoukou
Katiola
**IVORY COAST**
Bouake
**Yamoussoukro**
Man
Daloa
Bouake
Adzope
Abidjan
Divo
Gagnoa
Gagnoa
San Pedro
*Cape Palmas*
*Cape Three Points*

Kita
Kayes
Nioro du Sahel
Kedougou
Siguiri
Kankan
**GUINEA**
Gueckedou
Nzerekore
1,752m
(5,748ft)
Zorzor
**LIBERIA**
Tubmanburg
Harper
Kenema
**Monrovia**

St. Louis
Louga
Dara
Thies
**Dakar**
**SENEGAL**
Kaolack
Tambacounda
Kolda
Bignona
Ziguinchor
**Banjul**
**THE GAMBIA**
**GUINEA-BISSAU**
**Bissau**
*Bissagos Archipelago*
Boke
Boffa
Labe
Kindia
Makeni
Sefadu
Bo
**Conakry**
**Freetown**
**SIERRA LEONE**
Kaedi
Selibabi
Atrous

*ATLANTIC OCEAN*

Kaolack
Kedougou
Mamou

## Cape Verde inset

*ATLANTIC OCEAN*
**M**
*25°W*
*Santo Antao*
*Sao Nicolau*
*Boa Vista*
*Sal*
**CAPE VERDE**
Mindelo
*Sao Tiago*
*Maio*
**Praia**
*Fogo*
**11**
**12**
*15° N*
*0°*

## Map key

# Northwest Africa

Wetland
Mountain
Tundra
Ice
Cultivation
Urban

■ National capital
● Internal capital
◎ Major city or town
○ Other town

See also main key
on page 15.

1:12,000,000

0   100   200   300 miles
0   200   400km

Boreal forest
Temperate forest
Tropical forest
Temperate grassland
Savanna
Semi-desert and scrub
Hot desert

▬ International boundary
▬ Internal boundary
▲ Height above or below sea level
2,490m
(7,988ft)

Copyright © Usborne Publishing Ltd.

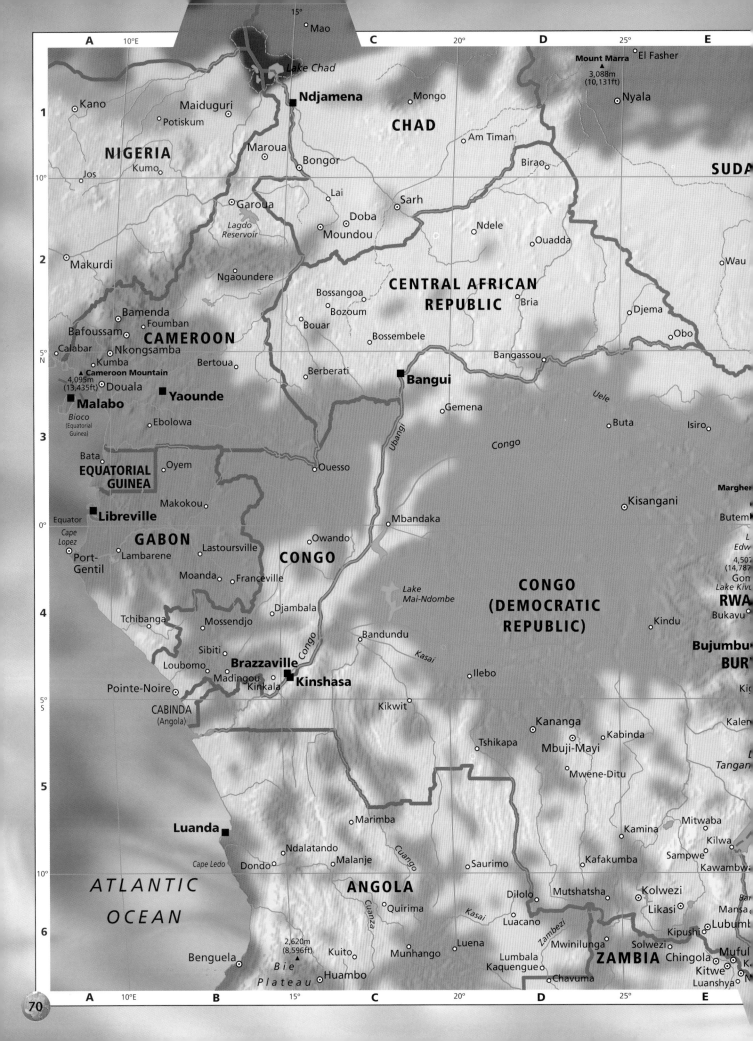

F 35° G 40° H 45° J 50° K

Kosti
Ras Dashen
4,620m
(15,157ft)
Mekele
Assab
Bab al Mandab
Taizz
YEMEN
Aden
Gulf of Aden
Cape Guardafui

Gonder
Lake Tana
DJIBOUTI
Dikhil
Djibouti
Boosaaso

1

Bahir Dar
Dese
Berbera

Malakal
Ethiopian
Highlands
Dire Dawa
Hargeysa

10°

Nekemte
Addis Ababa
Harer
SOMALIA

Gambela
Debre Zeyit
Nazret
Eyl

White Nile
Jima
ETHIOPIA

2

Awasa
Blue Nile

Lake
Abaya
Gode

Juba
Beledweyne
5°
N

White Nile
Moyale
Mandera

Gulu
Lake
Turkana
Juba
Baydhabo

UGANDA
Soroti
Mount Elgon
4,321m
(14,176ft)
Mbale
Kitale
Eldoret
Baardheere
Mogadishu

3

Lake
Albert
Lake
Kyoga
Kisumu
Meru
Garissa
Marka

ampala
Jinja
Nakuru
Kirinyaga
(Mount Kenya)
5,199m
(17,057ft)
KENYA

Masaka
Nyeri
Thika

barara
Kisii
Nairobi
Machakos
Kismaayo

0°

Lake Victoria
Great Rift Valley
Kilimanjaro
5,895m
(19,340ft)
Moshi
Malindi

ali
Mwanza
Arusha
Mombasa

4

Tabora
Tanga
Pemba Island
INDIAN

5°
S

Dodoma
Zanzibar
Zanzibar Island
OCEAN

TANZANIA
Morogoro
Dar es Salaam

Lake Rukwa
Iringa
Mafia
Island

5

ft Valley
Mbeya
Makumbako
Ilonga
Njinjo

Tunduma
Karonga
Liwale
Lindi

Kasama
Isoka
Songea
Mtwara
COMOROS

10°

Mpika
Mzuzu
Lake Nyasa
(Lake Malawi)
Tunduru
Masasi
Palma
Cape Delgado
Grand Comoro
(Njazidja)
Moroni

6

MBIA
Lundazi
Lupilichi
Mecula
Mueda
Mutsamudu
Anjouan
Island
(Nzwani)

MALAWI
MOZAMBIQUE
Nungo
Pemba
Fomboni
Mamoudzou

Chipata
Kasungu
Lichinga
Ruvuma
Mohilla Island
(Mwali)
Mayotte
(France)

Petauke
Lilongwe
Cuamba

Luangwa
35° G 40° H 45° J 50° K

## Central Africa

| | |
|---|---|
| | Boreal forest |
| | Temperate forest |
| | Tropical forest |
| | Temperate grassland |
| | Savanna |
| | Semi-desert and scrub |
| | Hot desert |
| | Wetland |
| | Mountain |
| | Tundra |
| | Ice |
| | Cultivation |
| | Urban |
| ■ | National capital |
| ● | Internal capital |
| ⊙ | Major city or town |
| ○ | Other town |
| | International boundary |
| | Internal boundary |
| ▲ 2,490m (7,988ft) | Height above or below sea level |

See also main key on page 15.

1:12,000,000

0   200   400km

0  100  200  300 miles

71

Copyright © Usborne Publishing Ltd.

ATLANTIC

OCEAN

**Luanda** ■
Ndalatando ○
Dondo ○
Cape Ledo

Marimba ○
Cuango

Kafakumba ○

Saurimo ○

Kamina ○
Mitwaba ○
Pweto ○

Kilwa ○
Sampwe ○

Mbala

Lake
Mweru

Kawambwa ○

Mpika

CONGO
(DEMOCRATIC
REPUBLIC)

Malanje ○

Quirima ○
Cuanza

Kasai

ANGOLA

Munhango ○

Luena ○

Kuito ○

Cangombe ○

Mumbue ○

Menongue ○

Luacano ○
Zambezi

Dilolo ○

Mutshatsha ○

Kolwezi ○
Likasi ○

Mwinilunga ○

Solwezi ○

Lubumbashi ○
Kipushi ○
Mufulira ○
Chingola ○
Kitwe ○
Ndola ○
Luanshya ○

Mansa ○

Kabunda ○

Mkushi ○

Lumbala
Kaquengue ○

Chavuma ○

Zambezi ○

Lukulu ○

ZAMBIA

Kabwe ○

**Lusaka** ■

Rufunsa ○

Petau

Cabo
Res

Benguela ○

Lucira ○
Cape St. Martha

2,620m
(8,596ft) ▲
Huambo ○
*Bie*
*Plateau*

Matala ○

Menongue ○

Lumbala
Nguimbo ○

Mavinga ○

Mongu ○

Kataba ○
Ngoma ○

Kafue ○
Zambezi

Zumb

Namibe ○
Albino Point

Lubango ○

Caiundo ○

Luiana ○

Sesheke ○

Lake
Kariba

Zimba ○

Kariba ○

Chinhoyi ○

Bindu

Xangongo ○
Cunene

Foz do
Cunene ○

Cuangar ○

Rundu ○
Andara ○

Livingstone ○
*Victoria Falls*

Binga ○

Kamativi ○

Kadoma ○

**Harare** ■

*Caprivi Strip*

Hwange ○

Okavango

Opuwo ○

Ondangwa ○
Etosha
Pan

Tsumeb ○

*Okavango
Swamp*

Nokaneng ○

Maun ○

Bulawayo ○

Gweru ○

ZIMBABWE

Mas

Zvishav
Chired

*Namib Desert*

Okaukuejo ○
Kamanjab ○

Otavi ○

Otjiwarongo ○

Tsau ○
*Lake
Ngami*

*Makgadikgadi
Pans
(Makarikari)*

Francistown ○

Plumtree ○

Rakops ○

Orapa ○

Selebi-
Phikwe ○

Messina ○

Sukses ○

**NAMIBIA**

Karibib ○
Okahandja ○

Mamuno ○

Gobabis ○

Tshwane ○

**BOTSWANA**

Serowe ○

Mahalapye ○

Warmbad ○

Pietersburg ○

Swakopmund ○
■ **Windhoek**
Walvis Bay ○

Rehoboth ○

Leonardville ○

Kang ○

Molepolole ○

**Gaborone** ■
Mochudi ○

Nelspruit ○

Gra

*Tropic of Capricorn*

Kalkrand ○

Tshane ○

Kanye ○

*Kalahari
Desert*

Werda ○

**Pretoria** ■
Krugersdorp ○
Benoni ○
Johannesburg ○
Springs ○

**Mbab**

**Lobamba**
**SWAZILA**

Mariental ○

Gochas ○

Terra Firma ○

Mmabatho ○

Orkneyo ○

Standerton ○

Tses ○

Keetmanshoop ○

Tshabong ○

Hotazel ○

Kroonstad ○
Welkom ○ Bethlehem ○

Harrismith ○

Luderitz ○

Seeheim ○

Grunau ○

Molopo

Upington ○
*Orange*

Kenhardt ○

Kimberley ○

Douglas ○

**Bloemfontein** ■

*Tugela Falls*

Ladysmith ○

**Maseru** ■

**LESOTHO**
Mafeteng ○

Pietermaritz

Du

Alexander Bay ○

Prieska ○

**SOUTH AFRICA**
De Aar ○

*Orange*

2,770m
(9,088ft) ▲
*Drakensberg*

Bitterfontein ○

Carnarvon ○

Graaff-
Reinet ○
Cradock ○

Bisho ○

East London ○

Umtata ○

Cape Columbine

*Great Karoo*

Beaufort West ○

Groot

Grahamstown ○

Uitenhage ○

Paarl ○
**Cape Town** ■
Worcester ○
Stellenbosch ○
Oudtshoorn ○

Port Elizabeth ○

Cape of Good Hope
Cape Agulhas

Cape St. Francis

35° **G** 40° **H** 45° **J** 50° **K**

1

ьbeya
Makumbako
Njinjo
oIlonga

ma
Karonga
Liwale
Lindi
Mtwara

**TANZANIA**
Masasi
oPalma
Cape Delgado

⊙Mzuzu
Songea
Tunduru
Mueda
Mecula
Lupilichi
*Lake Nyasa
(Lake Malawi)*
oMecula

asungu
Lichinga
Nungo

**SEYCHELLES**

Aldabra Group
Providence

St. Pierre
Bancs
Providence
Assumption
Cosmoledo Group
Astove
Farquhar
Group

10°
S

Grand
Comoro
(Njazidja)
**COMOROS**

**Moroni** ■
Anjouan Island
(Nzwani)

Glorioso Islands
(Reunion)

Cape Amber

Fomboni o
Mohilla Island
(Mwali)
oMutsamudu

Antsiranana

■**Lilongwe**
**MALAWI**
Cuamba
Mamoudzou
Mayotte
(France)
Nosy Be
oAmbilobe
Ambanja

Zomba
Lake
Chilwa
Cape Melamo
⊙Nacala
oMozambique
Analalava
Bealanana
Antalaha

2

Blantyre o
Milange
oMozambique
Maroantsetra
Mandritsara

Zambezi
oMocuba
Angoche
Cape St. Andrew
Besalampy
Mahajanga
Maevatanana

Quelimane
Juan de Nova
(Reunion)
Ikopa
Nosy
Boraha

ani
t)
e

**MOZAMBIQUE**

Antsalova
Tsiroanomandidy
⊙Toamasina

15°

animani
Beira
Belo-
Tsiribihina
■**Antananarivo**

ngabera
Mania
oAntsirabe

Nova
Mambone
Malaimbandy
Ambositra

angena
Bassas da India
(Reunion)
**MADAGASCAR**

Chigubo
Europa
Island
(Reunion)
Morombe
Manja
Beroroha
oFianarantsoa

20°

Massinga
Barra Falsa Point
Ihosy
▲2,658m
(8,720ft)
Manakara

St. Denis
*Reunion*
(France)

Barra Point
Inhambane
Toliara
Betroka

3

oBekily

Xai-Xai
Tropic of Capricorn

uto

Androka
Tolanaro

**INDIAN**
Cape St. Mary

**OCEAN**

4

ucia

**Mozambique Channel**

25°

20°

5

**K** 55°E **L**

*INDIAN OCEAN*

3
3

**MAURITIUS**
**Port Louis**

20°S
20°S

St. Denis
oReunion
(France)

4
4

**Same scale as main map**

**K** 55°E **L**

30°

## Southern Africa

| | |
|---|---|
| ■ Boreal forest | Wetland |
| Temperate forest | Mountain |
| Tropical forest | Tundra |
| Temperate grassland | Ice |
| Savanna | Cultivation |
| Semi-desert and scrub | Urban |
| Hot desert | |

■ National capital
● Internal capital
⊙ Major city or town
o Other town

*See also main key
on page 15.*

— International boundary
— Internal boundary

▲2,490m
(7,988ft)
Height above or below sea level

1:12,000,000

0   200   400km

0   100   200   300 miles

5

6

35° **G** 40° **H** 45° **J** 50° **K** 55° **L**

73

Copyright © Usborne Publishing Ltd.

# THE ARCTIC

The Arctic is not a continent. It is a region north of the Arctic Circle line of latitude, around the North Pole. The Arctic consists of the Arctic Ocean, islands such as Greenland and the most northerly parts of mainland Europe, North America and Asia. The Arctic region is covered in ice and snow almost all year round.

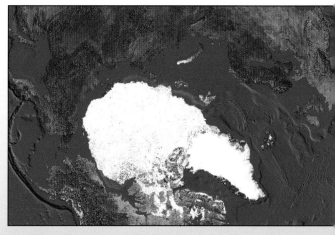

*The large white area in this satellite image is ice covering the Arctic Ocean and Greenland. At the top left of the image is the edge of Russia and at the top right is part of Europe.*

*These Inuit people are wearing thick, animal-skin coats, boots and gloves to keep warm.*

## Internet link

For a link to a website where you can discover more about the Arctic, including its wildlife, climate and native peoples, go to **www.usborne-quicklinks.com**

## Facts

**Size of Arctic Ocean**
14,056,000 sq km (5,426,000 sq miles)
**Highest point** Gunnbjorns Mountain, Greenland *3,700m (12,139ft)*
**Lowest point** Fram Basin, Arctic Ocean *-4,665m (-15,305ft)*
**Lowest recorded temperature** -67.8°C (-90°F)

**Main mineral deposits**
Diamonds, gold
**Main fuel deposits**
Oil, natural gas

*Seals living in Arctic regions have a thick layer of fat under their skin to keep them warm in the freezing weather.*

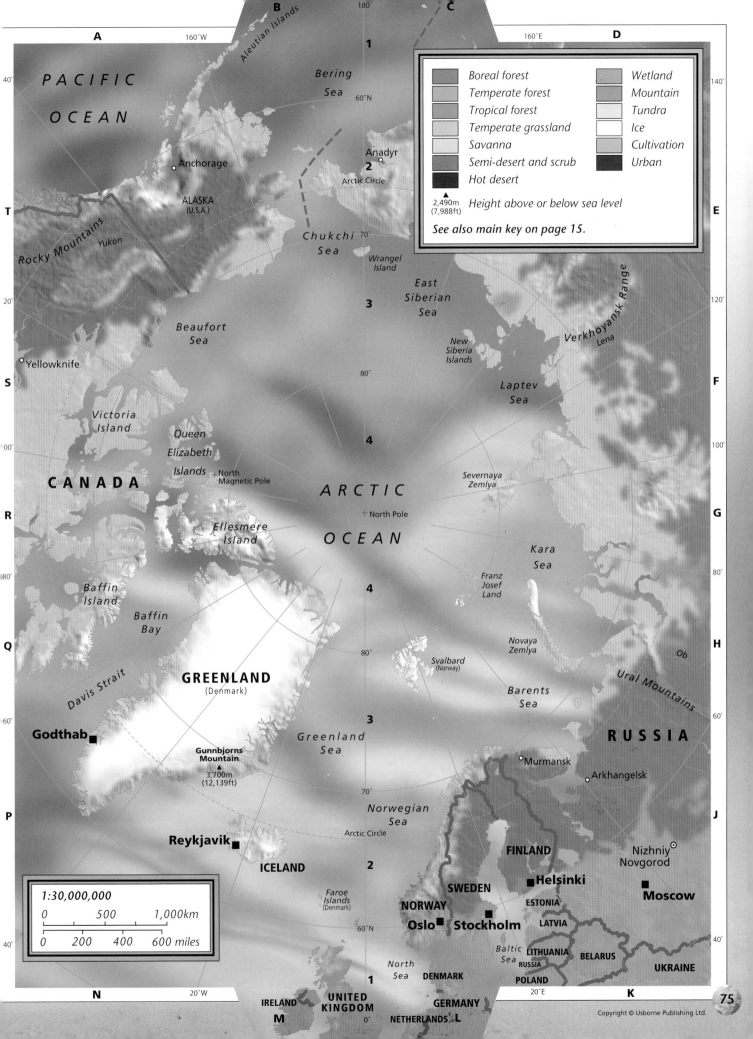

**A** 160°W **B** 180° **C** 160°E **D**

PACIFIC OCEAN

Aleutian Islands

Bering Sea

60°N

Anadyr

ALASKA (U.S.A.)

Arctic Circle

Chukchi Sea 70°

Wrangel Island

East Siberian Sea

Anchorage

Rocky Mountains

Yukon

Beaufort Sea

80°

New Siberia Islands

Verkhoyansk Range

Lena

Laptev Sea

Yellowknife

Victoria Island

Queen Elizabeth Islands

North Magnetic Pole

ARCTIC

Severnaya Zemlya

CANADA

North Pole

OCEAN

Ellesmere Island

Kara Sea

Franz Josef Land

Baffin Island

80°

Novaya Zemlya

Ob

Baffin Bay

Svalbard (Norway)

Ural Mountains

Davis Strait

GREENLAND (Denmark)

Barents Sea

80°

RUSSIA

Godthab

60°

Gunnbjorns Mountain 3,700m (12,139ft)

Greenland Sea

Murmansk

Arkhangelsk

70°

Norwegian Sea

Arctic Circle

Reykjavik

Nizhniy Novgorod

FINLAND

ICELAND

Helsinki

SWEDEN

Moscow

Faroe Islands (Denmark)

ESTONIA

NORWAY

LATVIA

Oslo   Stockholm

Baltic Sea

LITHUANIA

BELARUS

North Sea

RUSSIA

UKRAINE

DENMARK

POLAND

IRELAND   UNITED KINGDOM   GERMANY

NETHERLANDS

**Key:**
- Boreal forest
- Temperate forest
- Tropical forest
- Temperate grassland
- Savanna
- Semi-desert and scrub
- Hot desert
- Wetland
- Mountain
- Tundra
- Ice
- Cultivation
- Urban

2,490m (7,988ft) Height above or below sea level

*See also main key on page 15.*

1:30,000,000

0   500   1,000km

0   200   400   600 miles

Copyright © Usborne Publishing Ltd.

# ANTARCTICA

Antarctica is a huge, frozen continent within the Antarctic Circle. It is almost completely covered by an enormous ice sheet, which is more than 3km (2 miles) deep in some places. Nobody lives permanently in Antarctica, though many scientists visit to study the area. No plants grow in the ice, and the only land animals are tiny mites. But many animals, including penguins, seals, whales and fish, live in the seas around Antarctica.

*This ship takes tourists on Antarctic expeditions. Visitors can see animals such as these gentoo penguins, which come onto land to breed.*

### Internet link

For a link to a website where you can find out more about Antarctica and the creatures that live in the seas around it, go to **www.usborne-quicklinks.com**

## Facts

**Total land area**  14,000,000 sq km (5,405,442 sq miles), of which 13,720,000 sq km (5,297,333 sq miles) are covered in ice
**Highest point**  Vinson Massif *5,140m (16,863ft)*
**Lowest point**  Bentley Subglacial Trench  *-2,555m (-8,382ft)*
**Lowest recorded temperature** -89.2°C (-128.6°F)

**Main mineral deposits**  Iron ore, chromium, copper, gold, nickel, platinum

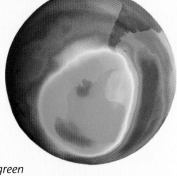

*The green area in this satellite photograph is a hole in the ozone layer over Antarctica. The hole is caused by atmospheric pollution.*

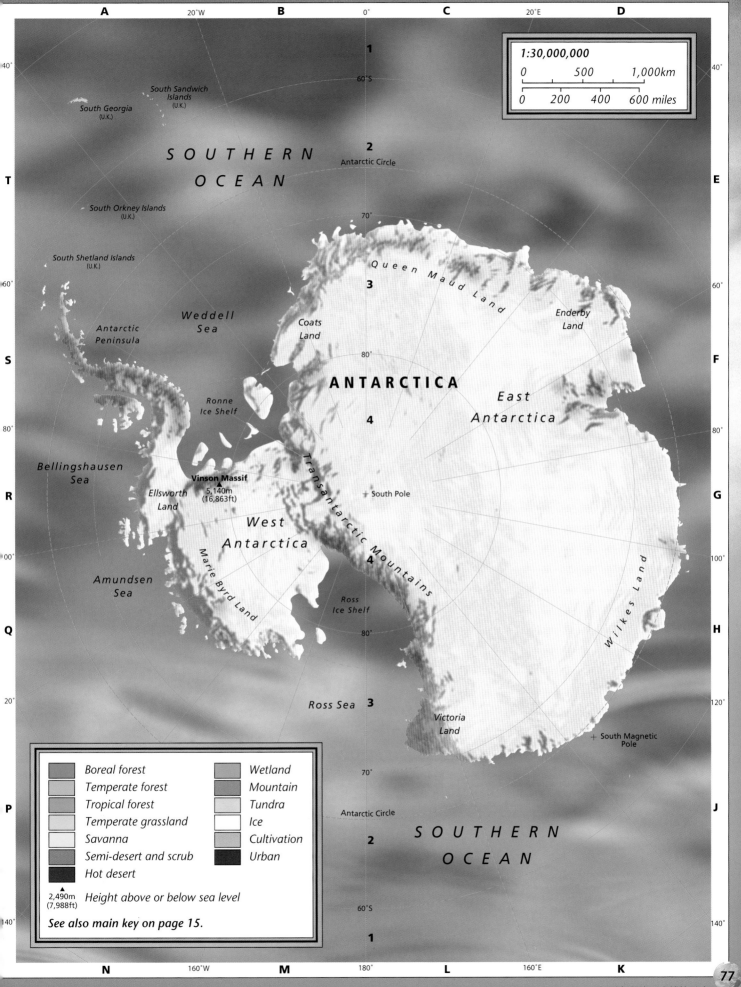

A    20°W    B    0°    C    20°E    D

**1:30,000,000**

| 0 | | 500 | | 1,000km |
|---|---|---|---|---|

| 0 | 200 | 400 | 600 miles |
|---|---|---|---|

**1**

40°

60°S

Antarctic Circle

**2**

70°

T

E

*South Georgia*
(U.K.)

*South Sandwich Islands*
(U.K.)

S O U T H E R N
O C E A N

*South Orkney Islands*
(U.K.)

*South Shetland Islands*
(U.K.)

**3**

60°

*Queen Maud Land*

*Enderby Land*

*Weddell Sea*

*Coats Land*

*Antarctic Peninsula*

S

F

80°

**ANTARCTICA**

*East Antarctica*

*Ronne Ice Shelf*

**4**

*Bellingshausen Sea*

R

G

**Vinson Massif**
▲
5,140m
(16,863ft)

+ South Pole

*Ellsworth Land*

*West Antarctica*

100°

80°

*Transantarctic Mountains*

*Wilkes Land*

**4**

*Amundsen Sea*

*Marie Byrd Land*

*Ross Ice Shelf*

Q

H

80°

*Ross Sea*

**3**

120°

20°

*Victoria Land*

+ South Magnetic Pole

70°

P

J

Antarctic Circle

**2**

S O U T H E R N
O C E A N

60°S

**1**

140°

| | Boreal forest | | Wetland |
|---|---|---|---|
| | Temperate forest | | Mountain |
| | Tropical forest | | Tundra |
| | Temperate grassland | | Ice |
| | Savanna | | Cultivation |
| | Semi-desert and scrub | | Urban |
| | Hot desert | | |

▲ 2,490m
(7,988ft)   *Height above or below sea level*

**See also main key on page 15.**

N    160°W    M    180°    L    160°E    K

Copyright © Usborne Publishing Ltd.

# WORLD RECORDS

Here are some of the Earth's longest rivers, highest mountains and other amazing world records. But the world is always changing; mountains wear down, rivers change shape, and new buildings are constructed. Ways of measuring things can also change. That's why you may find slightly different figures in different books.

| Highest mountains | |
|---|---|
| Everest, Nepal/China | 8,850m (29,035ft) |
| K2, Pakistan/China | 8,611m (28,251ft) |
| Kanchenjunga, India/Nepal | 8,597m (28,208ft) |
| Lhotse I, Nepal/China | 8,511m (27,923ft) |
| Makalu I, Nepal/China | 8,481m (27,824ft) |
| Lhotse II, Nepal/China | 8,400m (27,560ft) |
| Dhaulagiri, Nepal | 8,172m (26,810ft) |
| Manaslu I, Nepal | 8,156m (26,760ft) |
| Cho Oyu, Nepal/China | 8,153m (26,750ft) |
| Nanga Parbat, Pakistan | 8,126m (26,660ft) |

| Longest rivers | |
|---|---|
| Nile, Africa | 6,671km (4,145 miles) |
| Amazon, South America | 6,440km (4,000 miles) |
| Chang Jiang (Yangtze), China | 6,380km (3,964 miles) |
| Mississippi/Missouri, U.S.A. | 6,019km (3,741 miles) |
| Yenisey/Angara, Russia | 5,540km (3,442 miles) |
| Huang He (Yellow), China | 5,464km (3,395 miles) |
| Ob/Irtysh/Black Irtysh, Asia | 5,411km (3,362 miles) |
| Amur/Shilka/Onon, Asia | 4,416km (2,744 miles) |
| Lena, Russia | 4,400km (2,734 miles) |
| Congo, Africa | 4,374km (2,718 miles) |

| Biggest natural lakes | |
|---|---|
| Caspian Sea | 370,999 sq km (143,243 sq miles) |
| Lake Superior | 82,414 sq km (31,820 sq miles) |
| Lake Victoria | 69,215 sq km (26,724 sq miles) |
| Lake Huron | 59,596 sq km (23,010 sq miles) |
| Lake Michigan | 58,016 sq km (22,400 sq miles) |
| Lake Tanganyika | 32,764 sq km (12,650 sq miles) |
| Lake Baikal | 31,500 sq km (12,162 sq miles) |
| Great Bear Lake | 31,328 sq km (12,096 sq miles) |
| Lake Nyasa | 29,928 sq km (11,555 sq miles) |
| Aral Sea | 28,600 sq km (11,042 sq miles) |

| Deepest ocean |
|---|
| The Mariana Trench, part of the Pacific Ocean, is the deepest part of the sea at 10,911m (35,797ft) deep. |

| Deepest lake |
|---|
| Lake Baikal in Russia is the deepest lake in the world. At its deepest point it is 1,637m (5,370ft) deep. |

| Biggest islands | |
|---|---|
| Greenland | 2,175,600 sq km (840,000 sq miles) |
| New Guinea | 800,000 sq km (309,000 sq miles) |
| Borneo | 751,100 sq km (290,000 sq miles) |
| Madagascar | 587,040 sq km (226,656 sq miles) |
| Baffin Island | 507,451 sq km (195,928 sq miles) |
| Sumatra | 437,607 sq km (184,706 sq miles) |
| Great Britain | 234,410 sq km (90,506 sq miles) |
| Honshu | 227,920 sq km (88,000 sq miles) |
| Victoria Island | 217,290 sq km (83,896 sq miles) |
| Ellesmere Island | 196,236 sq km (75,767 sq miles) |

| Tallest inhabited buildings | |
|---|---|
| Petronas Towers, Malaysia | 452m (1,483ft) |
| Sears Tower, U.S.A. | 443m (1,454ft) |
| Jin Mao Building, China | 420m (1,378ft) |
| CITIC Plaza, China | 391m (1,283ft) |
| Shun Hing Square, China | 384m (1,260ft) |
| Plaza Rakyat, Malaysia | 382m (1,254ft) |
| Empire State Building, U.S.A. | 381m (1,250ft) |
| Central Plaza, China | 373m (1,227ft) |
| Bank of China, China | 368m (1,209ft) |
| Emirates Tower, U.A.E. | 350m (1,148ft) |

| Biggest cities/urban areas | |
|---|---|
| Tokyo, Japan | 26.4 million |
| Mexico City, Mexico | 18.1 million |
| Bombay, India | 18.1 million |
| Sao Paulo, Brazil | 17.8 million |
| New York, U.S.A. | 16.6 million |
| Lagos, Nigeria | 13.4 million |
| Los Angeles, U.S.A. | 13.1 million |
| Calcutta, India | 12.9 million |
| Shanghai, China | 12.9 million |
| Buenos Aires, Argentina | 12.6 million |

| Famous waterfalls | Height |
|---|---|
| Angel Falls, Venezuela | 979m (3,212ft) |
| Sutherland Falls, New Zealand | 580m (1,904ft) |
| Mardalfossen, Norway | 517m (1,696ft) |
| Jog Falls, India | 253m (830ft) |
| Victoria Falls, Zimbabwe/Zambia | 108m (355ft) |
| Iguacu Falls, Brazil/Argentina | 82m (269ft) |
| Niagara Falls, Canada/U.S.A. | 57m (187ft) |

# Natural disasters

Natural disasters can be measured in different ways. For example, some earthquakes score highly on the Richter scale, while others cause more destruction. The earthquakes, volcanic eruptions, floods, hurricanes and tornadoes listed here are among the most famous and destructive disasters in history.

| Earthquakes | Richter scale | Disastrous effects |
|---|---|---|
| San Francisco, U.S.A., 1906 | 7.9 | 3,000 died in resulting fire |
| Messina, Italy, 1908 | 7.5 | More than 70,000 people died |
| Tokyo-Kanto, Japan, 1923 | 8.3 | Great Tokyo Fire; 142,807 died |
| Quetta, Pakistan, 1935 | 7.5 | 30–60,000 died; city destroyed |
| Concepcion, Chile, 1960 | 8.7 | 2,000 died; strongest quake ever |
| Alaska, U.S.A., 1964 | 8.6 | 125 died; strongest U.S. quake ever |
| Tangshan, China, 1976 | 7.9 | More than 655,000 people died |
| Manjil-Rudbar, Iran, 1990 | 7.7 | 50,000 died; cities destroyed |
| Kobe, Japan, 1995 | 6.8 | 6,400 died; over $147bn damage |
| Gujarat, India, 2001 | 8.0 | 20,085 died; 2$^{nd}$ strongest Indian quake |

| Volcanic eruptions | Disastrous effects |
|---|---|
| Mount Vesuvius, Italy, AD79 | Pompeii flattened; up to 20,000 died |
| Tambora, Indonesia, 1815 | 92,000 people starved to death |
| Krakatau, Indonesia, 1883 | 36,500 drowned in resulting tsunami |
| Mount Pelee, Martinique, 1902 | Nearly 30,000 people buried in ash flows |
| Kelut, Indonesia, 1919 | Over 5,000 people drowned in mud |
| Agung, Indonesia, 1963 | 1,200 people suffocated in hot ash |
| Mount St. Helens, U.S.A., 1980 | Only 61 died but a large area was destroyed |
| Ruiz, Colombia, 1985 | 25,000 people died in giant mud flows |
| Mt. Pinatubo, Philippines, 1991 | 800 killed by collapsing roofs and disease |
| Island of Montserrat, 1995 | Volcano left most of the island uninhabitable |

| Floods | Disastrous effects |
|---|---|
| Holland, 1228 | 100,000 drowned by a sea flood |
| Kaifeng, China, 1642 | 300,000 died after rebels destroyed a dyke |
| Johnstown, U.S.A., 1889 | 2,200 killed in a flood caused by rain |
| Italy, 1963 | Vaoint Dam overflowed; 2–3,000 killed |
| East Pakistan, 1970 | Giant wave caused by cyclone killed 250,000 |
| Bangladesh, 1988 | 1,300 died, 30m homeless in monsoon flood |
| Southern U.S.A., 1993 | $12bn of damage after Mississippi flooded |
| China, 1998 | Chang Jiang overflow left 14m homeless |
| Papua New Guinea, 1998 | Tsunamis killed 2,000 people |
| Venezuela, 1999 | Floods and mudslides killed 5,000–20,000 |

| Storms | Disastrous effects |
|---|---|
| Caribbean "Great Hurricane", 1780 | Biggest ever hurricane killed over 20,000 |
| Hong Kong typhoon, China, 1906 | 10,000 people died in this giant hurricane |
| Killer tornado, U.S.A., 1925 | Up to 700 people died in Ellington, Missouri |
| Tropical Storm Agnes, U.S.A., 1972 | $3.5bn damage, 129 dead |
| Hurricane Fifi, Honduras, 1974 | 8,000 people died and 100,000 left homeless |
| Hurricane Georges, U.S.A., 1998 | Caribbean and U.S.A. hit; $5bn of damage |
| Hurricane Mitch, C. America, 1998 | Over 9,000 killed across Central America |

## Amazing Earth facts

The Earth is 12,103km (7,520 miles) across. Its circumference (the distance around the Equator) is 38,022km (23,627 miles) and it is 149,503,000 km (92,897,000 miles) away from the Sun.

To make one complete orbit around the Sun, the Earth has to travel 938,900,000km (583,400,000 miles). To do this in just a year, it has to travel very fast. Because of the atmosphere surrounding the Earth, you can't feel it moving. But in fact you are zooming through space faster than any rocket.

• **Orbit speed** The Earth travels around the Sun at a speed of about 106,000kph (65,868mph).

• **Spinning speed** The Earth also spins around an axis, but the speed you are spinning at depends on where you live. Places on the Equator move at 1,600kph (995mph). New York moves at around 1,100kph (684mph). Near the poles, the spinning is not very fast at all. (You can see how this works by looking at a spinning globe.)

• **Solar System speed** The whole Solar System, including the Sun, the Earth and its moon, and the other planets and their moons, is moving at 72,400kph (45,000 mph) through the galaxy.

• **Galaxy speed** Our galaxy, the Milky Way, whizzes through the universe at a speed of 2,172,150kph (1,350,000mph).

# TIME ZONES

The Earth is divided into different time zones. Within each zone, people usually set their clocks to the same time. If you fly between two zones, you change your watch to the time in the new zone.

## Dividing up time

There are 25 time zones. They are separated by one-hour intervals and there is a time zone every 15 degrees of longitude. There are 12 one-hour zones both ahead of and behind Greenwich Mean Time (GMT), the time at the Prime Meridian Line.

For convenience, whole countries usually keep the same local time instead of sticking to the zones exactly. For example, China could be divided into several time zones, but instead the whole country has the same time. A few places, such as India, use non-standard half hour deviations.

## Summer time

Some places adjust their clocks in summer. For example, in the U.K. all clocks go forward one hour. It is a way of getting more out of the days by having an extra hour of light.

## Changing dates

The International Date Line runs mostly through the Pacific Ocean and bends to avoid the land. Places to the west of it are 24 hours ahead of places to the east. This means that if you travel east across it you lose a day and if you travel west across it you gain a day.

*This map shows the time zones. The times at the top of the map tell you the time in the different zones when it is noon at the Prime Meridian Line. There are two midnight zones, one for each day on either side of the International Date Line. The numbers in circles tell you how many hours ahead of or behind Greenwich Mean Time an area is.*

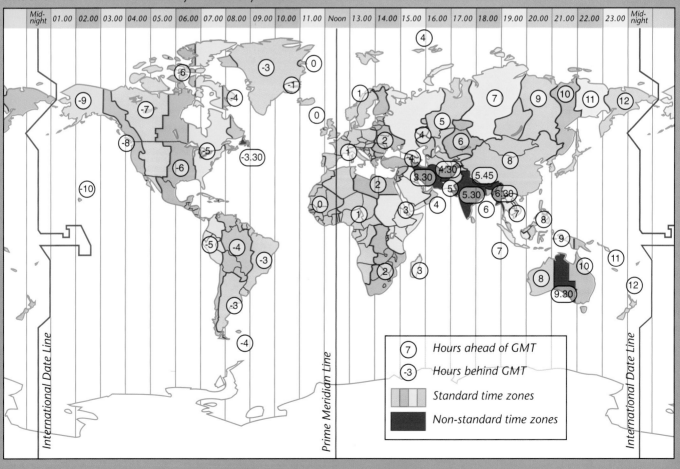

# TYPES OF GOVERNMENTS

Most states have one main leader along with a parliament or assembly of politicians. The main types of governments are listed and explained below. A state can have a combination of more than one of these types of governments. For example, the United States of America is a federal republic.

## Anarchy
Anarchy means a situation where there is no government. This can happen after a civil war, when a government has been destroyed and rival groups are battling to take its place.

## Capitalist state
In a Capitalist or free-market state, people can own their own businesses and property, and buy services such as healthcare privately. However, most Capitalist governments also provide national health, education and welfare services.

## Commonwealth
This word is sometimes used to mean a democratic republic, in which all the state's citizens are seen as having an equal interest in the functioning of the state.

## Communist state
Under Communism, the state owns things like factories, farms and businesses, and provides healthcare, welfare and education for its people.

## Democracy
In a democracy, the government is elected by the people, using a voting system.

## Dictatorship
This is a state run by a single, unelected leader, who may use force to keep control. In a military dictatorship, the army is in power.

## Federal government
In a federal system, such as that of the U.S.A., a central government shares power with a number of smaller regional governments.

## Monarchy
A monarchy is a state with a king or queen. In some traditional monarchies, the monarch has complete power. A constitutional monarchy, however, also has a separate, usually democratic, government and the monarch's powers are limited.

## Regional or local government
A government that controls a smaller area within a state. Some regional governments have very limited powers, and are largely directed by the central government. Others, such as the regional governments in the U.S.A., have much more power and can make their own laws.

## Republic
A republic is a state with no monarch. The head of state is usually an elected president.

## Revolutionary government
After a revolution, when a government is overthrown by force, the new regime is sometimes called a revolutionary government.

## Totalitarian state
This is a state with only one political party, in which individuals are forced to obey the government and may also be prevented from leaving the country.

## Transitional government
A government that is changing from one system to another is known as a transitional government. For example, a dictatorship may become a democracy after the dictator dies, but the transition between the systems can take several years.

# GAZETTEER OF STATES

**Afghanistan**

**Albania**

**Algeria**

**Andorra**

**Angola**

**Antigua and Barbuda**

• **Argentina**

This gazetteer lists the world's 193 independent states, along with key facts about each one. In the lists of languages, the language that is most widely spoken is given first, even if it is not the official language. In the lists of religions, the one followed by the most people is also placed first. Every state has a national flag, which is usually used to represent the country abroad. A few states also have a state flag which they prefer to use instead. The state flags appear here with a dot • beside them.

**AFGHANISTAN (Asia)**
**Area:** 647,500 sq km (249,935 sq miles)
**Population:** 27,755,775
**Capital city:** Kabul
**Main languages:** Dari, Pashto
**Main religion:** Muslim
**Government:** transitional
**Currency:** 1 afghani = 100 puls

**ALBANIA (Europe)**
**Area:** 28,750 sq km (11,100 sq miles)
**Population:** 3,544,841
**Capital city:** Tirana
**Main language:** Albanian
**Main religions:** Muslim, Albanian Orthodox
**Government:** emerging democracy
**Currency:** 1 lek = 100 qintars

**ALGERIA (Africa)**
**Area:** 2,381,740 sq km (919,589 sq miles)
**Population:** 32,277,942
**Capital city:** Algiers
**Main languages:** Arabic, French, Berber dialects
**Main religion:** Sunni Muslim
**Government:** republic
**Currency:** 1 Algerian dinar = 100 centimes

**ANDORRA (Europe)**
**Area:** 468 sq km (181 sq miles)
**Population:** 68,403
**Capital city:** Andorra la Vella
**Main languages:** Catalan, Spanish
**Main religion:** Roman Catholic
**Government:** parliamentary democracy
**Currency:** 1 euro = 100 cents

**ANGOLA (Africa)**
**Area:** 1,246,700 sq km (481,351 sq miles)
**Population:** 10,593,171
**Capital city:** Luanda
**Main languages:** Kilongo, Kimbundu, other Bantu languages, Portuguese
**Main religions:** indigenous, Roman Catholic, Protestant
**Government:** transitional
**Currency:** 1 kwanza = 100 lwei

**ANTIGUA AND BARBUDA (North America)**
**Area:** 442 sq km (171 sq miles)
**Population:** 67,448
**Capital city:** Saint John's
**Main languages:** Caribbean Creole, English
**Main religion:** Protestant
**Government:** constitutional monarchy
**Currency:** 1 East Caribbean dollar = 100 cents

**ARGENTINA (South America)**
**Area:** 2,766,890 sq km (1,068,305 sq miles)
**Population:** 37,812,817
**Capital city:** Buenos Aires
**Main language:** Spanish
**Main religion:** Roman Catholic
**Government:** republic
**Currency:** 1 peso = 100 centavos

**ARMENIA (Asia)**
**Area:** 29,800 sq km (11,506 sq miles)
**Population:** 3,336,100
**Capital city:** Yerevan
**Main language:** Armenian
**Main religion:** Armenian Orthodox
**Government:** republic
**Currency:** 1 dram = 100 luma

**AUSTRALIA (Australasia/Oceania)**
**Area:** 7,686,850 sq km (2,967,124 sq miles)
**Population:** 19,546,792
**Capital city:** Canberra
**Main language:** English
**Main religion:** Christian
**Government:** federal democratic monarchy
**Currency:** 1 Australian dollar = 100 cents

**AUSTRIA (Europe)**
**Area:** 83,858 sq km (32,378 sq miles)
**Population:** 8,169,929
**Capital city:** Vienna
**Main language:** German
**Main religion:** Roman Catholic
**Government:** federal republic
**Currency:** 1 euro = 100 cents

**Armenia**

**Australia**

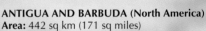

**Austria**

**Azerbaijan**

**Bahamas, The**

**Bahrain**

**Bangladesh**

**Barbados**

**Belarus**

**Belgium**

**Belize**

**Benin**

**Bhutan**

• **Bolivia**

**AZERBAIJAN (Asia)**
**Area:** 86,600 sq km (33,436 sq miles)
**Population:** 7,798,497
**Capital city:** Baku
**Main language:** Azeri
**Main religion:** Muslim
**Government:** republic
**Currency:** 1 manat = 100 gopiks

**BAHAMAS, THE (North America)**
**Area:** 13,940 sq km (5,382 sq miles)
**Population:** 300,529
**Capital city:** Nassau
**Main languages:** Bahamian Creole, English
**Main religion:** Christian
**Government:** parliamentary democracy
**Currency:** 1 Bahamian dollar = 100 cents

**BAHRAIN (Asia)**
**Area:** 665 sq km (257 sq miles)
**Population:** 656,397
**Capital city:** Manama
**Main languages:** Arabic, English
**Main religion:** Muslim
**Government:** traditional monarchy
**Currency:** 1 Bahraini dinar = 1,000 fils

**BANGLADESH (Asia)**
**Area:** 144,000 sq km (55,598 sq miles)
**Population:** 133,376,684
**Capital city:** Dhaka
**Main languages:** Bengali, English
**Main religions:** Muslim, Hindu
**Government:** republic
**Currency:** 1 taka = 100 poisha

**BARBADOS (North America)**
**Area:** 430 sq km (166 sq miles)
**Population:** 276,607
**Capital city:** Bridgetown
**Main languages:** Bajan, English
**Main religion:** Christian
**Government:** parliamentary democracy
**Currency:** 1 Barbadian dollar = 100 cents

**BELARUS (Europe)**
**Area:** 207,600 sq km (80,154 sq miles)
**Population:** 10,335,382
**Capital city:** Minsk
**Main language:** Belarusian
**Main religion:** Eastern Orthodox
**Government:** republic
**Currency:** 1 Belarusian ruble = 100 kopecks

**BELGIUM (Europe)**
**Area:** 30,510 sq km (11,780 sq miles)
**Population:** 10,274,595
**Capital city:** Brussels
**Main languages:** Dutch, French
**Main religions:** Roman Catholic, Protestant
**Government:** constitutional monarchy
**Currency:** 1 euro = 100 cents

**BELIZE (North America)**
**Area:** 22,960 sq km (8,865 sq miles)
**Population:** 262,999
**Capital city:** Belmopan
**Main languages:** Spanish, Belize Creole, English, Garifuna, Maya

**Main religions:** Roman Catholic, Protestant
**Government:** parliamentary democracy
**Currency:** 1 Belizean dollar = 100 cents

**BENIN (Africa)**
**Area:** 112,620 sq km (43,483 sq miles)
**Population:** 6,787,625
**Capital city:** Porto-Novo
**Main languages:** Fon, French, Yoruba
**Main religions:** indigenous, Christian, Muslim
**Government:** republic
**Currency:** 1 CFA* franc = 100 centimes

**BHUTAN (Asia)**
**Area:** 47,000 sq km (18,146 sq miles)
**Population:** 2,094,176
**Capital city:** Thimphu
**Main languages:** Dzongkha, Nepali
**Main religions:** Buddhist, Hindu
**Government:** monarchy
**Currency:** 1 ngultrum = 100 chetrum

**BOLIVIA (South America)**
**Area:** 1,098,580 sq km (424,162 sq miles)
**Population:** 8,445,134
**Capital cities:** La Paz, Sucre
**Main languages:** Spanish, Quechua, Aymara
**Main religion:** Roman Catholic
**Government:** republic
**Currency:** 1 boliviano = 100 centavos

**BOSNIA AND HERZEGOVINA (Europe)**
**Area:** 51,129 sq km (19,741 sq miles)
**Population:** 3,964,388
**Capital city:** Sarajevo
**Main languages:** Bosnian, Serbian, Croatian
**Main religions:** Muslim, Orthodox, Roman Catholic
**Government:** emerging federal democracy
**Currency:** 1 marka = 100 pfenninga

**BOTSWANA (Africa)**
**Area:** 600,372 sq km (231,743 sq miles)
**Population:** 1,591,232
**Capital city:** Gaborone
**Main languages:** Setswana, Kalanga, English
**Main religions:** indigenous, Christian
**Government:** parliamentary republic
**Currency:** 1 pula = 100 thebe

**BRAZIL (South America)**
**Area:** 8,547,400 sq km (3,300,151 sq miles)
**Population:** 176,029,560
**Capital city:** Brasilia
**Main language:** Portuguese
**Main religion:** Roman Catholic
**Government:** federal republic
**Currency:** 1 real = 100 centavos

**BRUNEI (Asia)**
**Area:** 5,770 sq km (2,228 sq miles)
**Population:** 350,898
**Capital city:** Bandar Seri Begawan
**Main languages:** Malay, English, Chinese
**Main religions:** Muslim, Buddhist
**Government:** constitutional sultanate (a type of monarchy)
**Currency:** 1 Bruneian dollar = 100 cents

**Bosnia and Herzegovina**

**Botswana**

**Brazil**

**Brunei**

**Bulgaria**

**Burkina Faso**

**Burma (Myanmar)**

*CFA = Communaute Financiere Africaine*

**Burundi**

**Cambodia**

**Cameroon**

**Canada**

**Cape Verde**

**Central African Republic**

**Chad**

**BULGARIA (Europe)**
**Area:** 110,910 sq km (42,822 sq miles)
**Population:** 7,621,337
**Capital city:** Sofia
**Main language:** Bulgarian
**Main religions:** Bulgarian Orthodox, Muslim
**Government:** parliamentary democracy
**Currency:** 1 lev = 100 stotinki

**BURKINA FASO (Africa)**
**Area:** 274,200 sq km (105,869 sq miles)
**Population:** 12,603,185
**Capital city:** Ouagadougou
**Main languages:** Moore, Jula, French
**Main religions:** Muslim, indigenous
**Government:** republic
**Currency:** 1 CFA* franc = 100 centimes

**BURMA (MYANMAR) (Asia)**
**Area:** 678,500 sq km (261,969 sq miles)
**Population:** 42,238,224
**Capital city:** Rangoon
**Main language:** Burmese
**Main religion:** Buddhist
**Government:** military dictatorship
**Currency:** 1 kyat = 100 pyas

**BURUNDI (Africa)**
**Area:** 27,830 sq km (10,745 sq miles)
**Population:** 6,373,002
**Capital city:** Bujumbura
**Main languages:** Kirundi, French, Swahili
**Main religions:** Christian, indigenous
**Government:** republic
**Currency:** 1 Burundi franc = 100 centimes

**CAMBODIA (Asia)**
**Area:** 181,040 sq km (69,900 sq miles)
**Population:** 12,775,324
**Capital city:** Phnom Penh
**Main language:** Khmer
**Main religion:** Buddhist
**Government:** constitutional monarchy
**Currency:** 1 new riel = 100 sen

**CAMEROON (Africa)**
**Area:** 475,440 sq km (183,567 sq miles)
**Population:** 16,184,748
**Capital city:** Yaounde
**Main languages:** Cameroon Pidgin English, Ewondo, Fula, French, English
**Main religions:** indigenous, Christian, Muslim
**Government:** republic
**Currency:** 1 CFA* franc = 100 centimes

**CANADA (North America)**
**Area:** 9,970,610 sq km (3,849,653 sq miles)
**Population:** 31,902,268
**Capital city:** Ottawa
**Main languages:** English, French
**Main religions:** Roman Catholic, Protestant
**Government:** federal democracy
**Currency:** 1 Canadian dollar = 100 cents

**CAPE VERDE (Africa)**
**Area:** 4,033 sq km (1,557 sq miles)
**Population:** 408,760
**Capital city:** Praia
**Main languages:** Crioulo*, Portuguese

**Main religions:** Roman Catholic, Protestant
**Government:** republic
**Currency:** 1 Cape Verdean escudo = 100 centavos

**CENTRAL AFRICAN REPUBLIC (Africa)**
**Area:** 622,984 sq km (240,536 sq miles)
**Population:** 3,642,739
**Capital city:** Bangui
**Main languages:** Sangho, French
**Main religions:** indigenous, Christian, Muslim
**Government:** republic
**Currency:** 1 CFA* franc = 100 centimes

**CHAD (Africa)**
**Area:** 1,284,000 sq km (495,752 sq miles)
**Population:** 8,997,237
**Capital city:** Ndjamena
**Main languages:** Arabic, Sara, French
**Main religions:** Muslim, Christian, indigenous
**Government:** republic
**Currency:** 1 CFA* franc = 100 centimes

**CHILE (South America)**
**Area:** 756,626 sq km (292,133 sq miles)
**Population:** 15,498,930
**Capital city:** Santiago
**Main language:** Spanish
**Main religions:** Roman Catholic, Protestant
**Government:** republic
**Currency:** 1 Chilean peso = 100 centavos

**CHINA (Asia)**
**Area:** 9,596,960 sq km (3,705,386 sq miles)
**Population:** 1,284,303,705
**Capital city:** Beijing
**Main languages:** Mandarin Chinese, Yue, Wu
**Main religions:** Taoist, Buddhist
**Government:** Communist state
**Currency:** 1 yuan = 10 jiao

**COLOMBIA (South America)**
**Area:** 1,138,910 sq km (439,733 sq miles)
**Population:** 41,008,227
**Capital city:** Bogota
**Main language:** Spanish
**Main religion:** Roman Catholic
**Government:** republic
**Currency:** 1 Colombian peso = 100 centavos

**COMOROS (Africa)**
**Area:** 2,170 sq km (838 sq miles)
**Population:** 614,382
**Capital city:** Moroni
**Main languages:** Comorian*, French, Arabic
**Main religion:** Sunni Muslim
**Government:** republic
**Currency:** 1 Comoran franc = 100 centimes

**CONGO (Africa)**
**Area:** 342,000 sq km (132,046 sq miles)
**Population:** 2,958,448
**Capital city:** Brazzaville
**Main languages:** Munukutuba, Lingala, French
**Main religions:** Christian, animist
**Government:** republic
**Currency:** 1 CFA* franc = 100 centimes

**Chile**

**China**

**Colombia**

**Comoros**

**Congo**

**Congo (Democratic Republic)**

**Costa Rica**

*CFA = Communaute Financiere Africaine; Comorian = a blend of Swahili and Arabic; Crioulo = a blend of Portuguese and West African

**Croatia**

**Cuba**

**Cyprus**

**Czech Republic**

**Denmark**

Djibouti image

**Djibouti**

Dominica image

**Dominica**

**CONGO (DEMOCRATIC REPUBLIC) (Africa)**
**Area:** 2,345,410 sq km (905,563 sq miles)
**Population:** 55,225,478
**Capital city:** Kinshasa
**Main languages:** Lingala, Swahili, Kikongo, Tshiluba, French
**Main religions:** Roman Catholic, Protestant, Kimbanguist, Muslim
**Government:** transitional
**Currency:** 1 Congolese franc = 100 centimes

**COSTA RICA (North America)**
**Area:** 51,100 sq km (19,730 sq miles)
**Population:** 3,834,934
**Capital city:** San Jose
**Main language:** Spanish
**Main religions:** Roman Catholic, Evangelical
**Government:** democratic republic
**Currency:** 1 Costa Rican colon = 100 centimos

**CROATIA (Europe)**
**Area:** 56,538 sq km (21,829 sq miles)
**Population:** 4,390,751
**Capital city:** Zagreb
**Main language:** Croatian
**Main religions:** Roman Catholic, Orthodox
**Government:** parliamentary democracy
**Currency:** 1 kuna = 100 lipas

**CUBA (North America)**
**Area:** 110,860 sq km (42,803 sq miles)
**Population:** 11,224,321
**Capital city:** Havana
**Main language:** Spanish
**Main religion:** Roman Catholic
**Government:** Communist state
**Currency:** 1 Cuban peso = 100 centavos

**CYPRUS (Europe)**
**Area:** 9,250 sq km (3,571 sq miles)
**Population:** 767,314
**Capital city:** Nicosia
**Main languages:** Greek, Turkish
**Main religions:** Greek Orthodox, Muslim
**Government:** republic with a self-proclaimed independent Turkish area
**Currency:** Greek Cypriot area: 1 Cypriot pound = 100 cents; Turkish Cypriot area: 1 Turkish lira = 100 kurus

**CZECH REPUBLIC (Europe)**
**Area:** 78,866 sq km (30,450 sq miles)
**Population:** 10,256,760
**Capital city:** Prague
**Main language:** Czech
**Main religion:** Roman Catholic
**Government:** parliamentary democracy
**Currency:** 1 koruna = 100 haleru

**DENMARK (Europe)**
**Area:** 43,094 sq km (16,639 sq miles)
**Population:** 5,368,854
**Capital city:** Copenhagen
**Main language:** Danish
**Main religion:** Evangelical Lutheran
**Government:** constitutional monarchy
**Currency:** 1 Danish krone = 100 oere

**DJIBOUTI (Africa)**
**Area:** 23,200 sq km (8,957 sq miles)
**Population:** 472,810
**Capital city:** Djibouti
**Main languages:** Afar, Somali, Arabic, French
**Main religion:** Muslim
**Government:** republic
**Currency:** 1 Djiboutian franc = 100 centimes

**DOMINICA (North America)**
**Area:** 751 sq km (290 sq miles)
**Population:** 70,158
**Capital city:** Roseau
**Main languages:** English, French patois
**Main religions:** Roman Catholic, Protestant
**Government:** democratic republic
**Currency:** 1 East Caribbean dollar = 100 cents

**DOMINICAN REPUBLIC (North America)**
**Area:** 48,730 sq km (18,815 sq miles)
**Population:** 8,721,594
**Capital city:** Santo Domingo
**Main language:** Spanish
**Main religion:** Roman Catholic
**Government:** democratic republic
**Currency:** 1 Dominican peso = 100 centavos

**EAST TIMOR (Asia)**
**Area:** 15,007 sq km (5,794 sq miles)
**Population:** 952,618
**Capital city:** Dili
**Main languages:** Tetum, Portuguese, Indonesian
**Main religions:** Roman Catholic, animist
**Government:** republic
**Currency:** 1 U.S. dollar = 100 cents

**ECUADOR (South America)**
**Area:** 283,560 sq km (109,483 sq miles)
**Population:** 13,447,494
**Capital city:** Quito
**Main languages:** Spanish, Quechua
**Main religion:** Roman Catholic
**Government:** republic
**Currency:** 1 sucre = 100 centavos

**EGYPT (Africa)**
**Area:** 1,001,450 sq km (386,660 sq miles)
**Population:** 70,712,345
**Capital city:** Cairo
**Main language:** Arabic
**Main religion:** Sunni Muslim
**Government:** republic
**Currency:** 1 Egyptian pound = 100 piasters

**EL SALVADOR (North America)**
**Area:** 21,040 sq km (8,124 sq miles)
**Population:** 6,353,681
**Capital city:** San Salvador
**Main language:** Spanish
**Main religion:** Roman Catholic
**Government:** republic
**Currency:** 1 Salvadoran colon = 100 centavos

**EQUATORIAL GUINEA (Africa)**
**Area:** 28,050 sq km (10,830 sq miles)
**Population:** 498,144
**Capital city:** Malabo

• **Dominican Republic**

**East Timor**

• **Ecuador**

**Egypt**

• **El Salvador**

**Equatorial Guinea**

**Eritrea**

**Estonia**

Main languages: Fang, Bubi, other Bantu languages, Spanish, French, Pidgin English
Main religion: Christian
Government: republic
Currency: 1 CFA* franc = 100 centimes

**ERITREA (Africa)**
Area: 121,320 sq km (46,842 sq miles)
Population: 4,465,651
Capital city: Asmara
Main languages: Tigrinya, Afar, Arabic
Main religions: Muslim, Coptic Christian, Roman Catholic, Protestant
Government: transitional
Currency: 1 nafka = 100 cents

**Ethiopia**

**ESTONIA (Europe)**
Area: 45,226 sq km (17,462 sq miles)
Population: 1,415,681
Capital city: Tallinn
Main languages: Estonian, Russian
Main religions: Evangelical Lutheran, Russian and Estonian Orthodox, other Christian
Government: parliamentary democracy
Currency: 1 Estonian kroon = 100 senti

**ETHIOPIA (Africa)**
Area: 1,127,127 sq km (435,184 sq miles)
Population: 67,673,031
Capital city: Addis Ababa
Main languages: Amharic, Tigrinya, Arabic
Main religions: Muslim, Ethiopian Orthodox, animist
Government: federal republic
Currency: 1 birr = 100 cents

**Federated States of Micronesia**

**FEDERATED STATES OF MICRONESIA (Australasia/Oceania)**
Area: 702 sq km (271 sq miles)
Population: 135,869
Capital city: Palikir
Main languages: Chuuk, Ponapean, English
Main religions: Roman Catholic, Protestant
Government: democracy
Currency: 1 U.S. dollar = 100 cents

**Fiji**

**FIJI (Australasia/Oceania)**
Area: 18,270 sq km (7,054 sq miles)
Population: 856,346
Capital city: Suva
Main languages: Fijian, Hindustani, English
Main religions: Christian, Hindu
Government: republic
Currency: 1 Fijian dollar = 100 cents

**Finland**

**FINLAND (Europe)**
Area: 337,030 sq km (130,127 sq miles)
Population: 5,183,545
Capital city: Helsinki
Main language: Finnish
Main religion: Evangelical Lutheran
Government: republic
Currency: 1 euro = 100 cents

**France**

**FRANCE (Europe)**
Area: 547,030 sq km (211,208 sq miles)
Population: 59,765,983
Capital city: Paris
Main language: French

**Gabon**

Main religion: Roman Catholic
Government: republic
Currency: 1 euro = 100 cents

**GABON (Africa)**
Area: 267,670 sq km (103,347 sq miles)
Population: 1,233,353
Capital city: Libreville
Main languages: Fang, Myene, French
Main religions: Christian, animist
Government: republic
Currency: 1 CFA* franc = 100 centimes

**GAMBIA, THE (Africa)**
Area: 11,300 sq km (4,363 sq miles)
Population: 1,455,842
Capital city: Banjul
Main languages: Mandinka, Fula, Wolof, English
Main religion: Muslim
Government: democratic republic
Currency: 1 dalasi = 100 butut

**GEORGIA (Asia)**
Area: 69,700 sq km (26,911 sq miles)
Population: 4,960,951
Capital city: Tbilisi
Main languages: Georgian, Russian
Main religions: Georgian Orthodox, Muslim, Russian Orthodox
Government: republic
Currency: 1 lari = 100 tetri

**GERMANY (Europe)**
Area: 357,021 sq km (137,846 sq miles)
Population: 83,251,851
Capital city: Berlin
Main language: German
Main religions: Protestant, Roman Catholic
Government: federal republic
Currency: 1 euro = 100 cents

**GHANA (Africa)**
Area: 239,460 sq km (92,456 sq miles)
Population: 20,244,154
Capital city: Accra
Main languages: Twi, Fante, Ga, Hausa, Dagbani, Ewe, Nzemi, English
Main religions: indigenous, Muslim, Christian
Government: democratic republic
Currency: 1 new cedi = 100 pesewas

**GREECE (Europe)**
Area: 131,940 sq km (50,942 sq miles)
Population: 10,645,343
Capital city: Athens
Main language: Greek
Main religion: Greek Orthodox
Government: parliamentary republic
Currency: 1 euro = 100 cents

**GRENADA (North America)**
Area: 340 sq km (131 sq miles)
Population: 89,211
Capital city: Saint George's
Main languages: English, French patois
Main religions: Roman Catholic, Protestant
Government: constitutional monarchy
Currency: 1 East Caribbean dollar = 100 cents

**Gambia, The**

**Georgia**

**Germany**

**Ghana**

**Greece**

**Grenada**

**Guatemala**

*CFA = Communaute Financiere Africaine

**Guinea**

**Guinea-Bissau**

**Guyana**

**• Haiti**

**Honduras**

**Hungary**

**Iceland**

**GUATEMALA (North America)**
**Area:** 108,890 sq km (42,042 sq miles)
**Population:** 13,314,079
**Capital city:** Guatemala City
**Main languages:** Spanish, Amerindian languages including Quiche, Kekchi, Cakchiquel, Mam
**Main religions:** Roman Catholic, Protestant, indigenous Mayan beliefs
**Government:** democratic republic
**Currency:** 1 quetzal = 100 centavos

**GUINEA (Africa)**
**Area:** 245,860 sq km (94,927 sq miles)
**Population:** 7,775,065
**Capital city:** Conakry
**Main languages:** Fuuta Jalon, Mallinke, Susu, French
**Main religion:** Muslim
**Government:** republic
**Currency:** 1 Guinean franc = 100 centimes

**GUINEA-BISSAU (Africa)**
**Area:** 36,120 sq km (13,946 sq miles)
**Population:** 1,345,479
**Capital city:** Bissau
**Main languages:** Crioulo*, Balante, Pulaar, Mandjak, Mandinka, Portuguese
**Main religions:** indigenous, Muslim
**Government:** republic
**Currency:** 1 CFA* franc = 100 centimes

**GUYANA (South America)**
**Area:** 214,970 sq km (83,000 sq miles)
**Population:** 698,209
**Capital city:** Georgetown
**Main languages:** Guyanese Creole, English, Amerindian languages, Caribbean Hindi
**Main religions:** Christian, Hindu
**Government:** republic
**Currency:** 1 Guyanese dollar = 100 cents

**HAITI (North America)**
**Area:** 27,750 sq km (10,714 sq miles)
**Population:** 7,063,722
**Capital city:** Port-au-Prince
**Main languages:** Haitian Creole, French
**Main religions:** Roman Catholic, Protestant, Voodoo
**Government:** republic
**Currency:** 1 gourde = 100 centimes

**HONDURAS (North America)**
**Area:** 112,090 sq km (43,278 sq miles)
**Population:** 6,560,608
**Capital city:** Tegucigalpa
**Main language:** Spanish
**Main religion:** Roman Catholic
**Government:** republic
**Currency:** 1 lempira = 100 centavos

**HUNGARY (Europe)**
**Area:** 93,030 sq km (35,919 sq miles)
**Population:** 10,075,034
**Capital city:** Budapest
**Main language:** Hungarian
**Main religions:** Roman Catholic, Calvinist
**Government:** parliamentary democracy
**Currency:** 1 forint = 100 filler

**ICELAND (Europe)**
**Area:** 103,000 sq km (39,768 sq miles)
**Population:** 279,384
**Capital city:** Reykjavik
**Main language:** Icelandic
**Main religion:** Evangelical Lutheran
**Government:** republic
**Currency:** 1 Icelandic krona = 100 aurar

**INDIA (Asia)**
**Area:** 3,287,590 sq km (1,269,339 sq miles)
**Population:** 1,045,845,226
**Capital city:** New Delhi
**Main languages:** Hindi, English, Bengali, Urdu, over 1,600 other languages and dialects
**Main religions:** Hindu, Muslim
**Government:** federal republic
**Currency:** 1 Indian rupee = 100 paise

**INDONESIA (Asia)**
**Area:** 1,919,440 sq km (741,096 sq miles)
**Population:** 231,328,092
**Capital city:** Jakarta
**Main languages:** Bahasa Indonesia, English, Dutch, Javanese
**Main religion:** Muslim
**Government:** republic
**Currency:** 1 Indonesian rupiah = 100 sen

**IRAN (Asia)**
**Area:** 1,648,000 sq km (636,293 sq miles)
**Population:** 66,622,704
**Capital city:** Tehran
**Main languages:** Farsi and other Persian dialects, Azeri
**Main religions:** Shi'a Muslim, Sunni Muslim
**Government:** Islamic republic
**Currency:** 10 Iranian rials = 1 toman

**IRAQ (Asia)**
**Area:** 437,072 sq km (168,754 sq miles)
**Population:** 24,001,816
**Capital city:** Baghdad
**Main languages:** Arabic, Kurdish
**Main religion:** Muslim
**Government:** republic under a military regime
**Currency:** 1 Iraqi dinar = 1,000 fils

**IRELAND (Europe)**
**Area:** 70,280 sq km (27,135 sq miles)
**Population:** 3,883,159
**Capital city:** Dublin
**Main languages:** English, Irish (Gaelic)
**Main religion:** Roman Catholic
**Government:** republic
**Currency:** 1 euro = 100 cents

**ISRAEL (Asia)**
**Area:** 20,770 sq km (8,019 sq miles)
**Population:** 6,029,529
**Capital city:** Jerusalem
**Main languages:** Hebrew, Arabic
**Main religions:** Jewish, Muslim
**Government:** parliamentary democracy
**Currency:** 1 Israeli shekel = 100 agorot

**India**

**Indonesia**

**Iran**

**Iraq**

**Ireland**

**Israel**

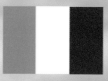

**Italy**

*CFA = Communaute Financiere Africaine;
Crioulo = a blend of Portuguese and West African

**Ivory Coast**

**ITALY (Europe)**
**Area:** 301,230 sq km (116,305 sq miles)
**Population:** 57,715,625
**Capital city:** Rome
**Main language:** Italian
**Main religion:** Roman Catholic
**Government:** republic
**Currency:** 1 euro = 100 cents

**IVORY COAST (Africa)**
**Area:** 322,460 sq km (124,502 sq miles)
**Population:** 16,804,784
**Capital city:** Yamoussoukro
**Main languages:** Baoule, Dioula, French
**Main religions:** Christian, Muslim, animist
**Government:** republic
**Currency:** 1 CFA* = 100 centimes

**Jamaica**

**JAMAICA (North America)**
**Area:** 10,990 sq km (4,243 sq miles)
**Population:** 2,680,029
**Capital city:** Kingston
**Main languages:** Southwestern Caribbean Creole, English
**Main religion:** Protestant
**Government:** parliamentary democracy
**Currency:** 1 Jamaican dollar = 100 cents

**Japan**

**JAPAN (Asia)**
**Area:** 377,835 sq km (145,882 sq miles)
**Population:** 126,974,628
**Capital city:** Tokyo
**Main language:** Japanese
**Main religions:** Shinto, Buddhist
**Government:** constitutional monarchy
**Currency:** 1 yen = 100 sen

**Jordan**

**JORDAN (Asia)**
**Area:** 92,300 sq km (35,637 sq miles)
**Population:** 5,307,470
**Capital city:** Amman
**Main languages:** Arabic, English
**Main religion:** Sunni Muslim
**Government:** constitutional monarchy
**Currency:** 1 Jordanian dinar = 1,000 fils

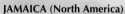
**Kazakhstan**

**KAZAKHSTAN (Asia)**
**Area:** 2,717,300 sq km (1,049,150 sq miles)
**Population:** 16,741,519
**Capital city:** Astana
**Main languages:** Kazakh, Russian
**Main religions:** Muslim, Russian Orthodox
**Government:** republic
**Currency:** 1 Kazakhstani tenge = 100 tiyn

**Kenya**

**KENYA (Africa)**
**Area:** 582,650 sq km (224,961 sq miles)
**Population:** 31,138,735
**Capital city:** Nairobi
**Main languages:** Swahili, English, Bantu languages
**Main religions:** Christian, indigenous
**Government:** republic
**Currency:** 1 Kenyan shilling = 100 cents

**Kiribati**

**KIRIBATI (Australasia/Oceania)**
**Area:** 811 sq km (313 sq miles)
**Population:** 96,335
**Capital city:** Bairiki (on Tarawa island)

**Main languages:** Gilbertese, English
**Main religions:** Roman Catholic, Protestant
**Government:** republic
**Currency:** 1 Australian dollar = 100 cents

**KUWAIT (Asia)**
**Area:** 17,820 sq km (6,880 sq miles)
**Population:** 2,111,561
**Capital city:** Kuwait City
**Main languages:** Arabic, English
**Main religion:** Muslim
**Government:** monarchy
**Currency:** 1 Kuwaiti dinar = 1,000 fils

**KYRGYZSTAN (Asia)**
**Area:** 198,500 sq km (76,641 sq miles)
**Population:** 4,822,166
**Capital city:** Bishkek
**Main languages:** Kyrgyz, Russian
**Main religions:** Muslim, Russian Orthodox
**Government:** republic
**Currency:** 1 Kyrgyzstani som = 100 tyiyn

**LAOS (Asia)**
**Area:** 236,800 sq km (91,428 sq miles)
**Population:** 5,777,180
**Capital city:** Vientiane
**Main languages:** Lao, French, English
**Main religions:** Buddhist, animist
**Government:** Communist state
**Currency:** 1 new kip = 100 at

**LATVIA (Europe)**
**Area:** 64,589 sq km (24,938 sq miles)
**Population:** 2,366,515
**Capital city:** Riga
**Main languages:** Latvian, Russian
**Main religions:** Lutheran, Roman Catholic, Russian Orthodox
**Government:** parliamentary democracy
**Currency:** 1 Latvian lat = 100 santims

**LEBANON (Asia)**
**Area:** 10,400 sq km (4,015 sq miles)
**Population:** 3,677,780
**Capital city:** Beirut
**Main languages:** Arabic, French, English
**Main religions:** Muslim, Christian
**Government:** republic
**Currency:** 1 Lebanese pound = 100 piasters

**LESOTHO (Africa)**
**Area:** 30,350 sq km (11,718 sq miles)
**Population:** 2,207,954
**Capital cities:** Maseru, Lobamba
**Main languages:** Sesotho, English, Zulu, Xhosa
**Main religions:** Christian, indigenous
**Government:** constitutional monarchy
**Currency:** 1 loti = 100 lisente

**LIBERIA (Africa)**
**Area:** 111,370 sq km (43,000 sq miles)
**Population:** 3,288,198
**Capital city:** Monrovia
**Main languages:** Kpelle, English, Bassa
**Main religions:** indigenous, Christian, Muslim
**Government:** republic
**Currency:** 1 Liberian dollar = 100 cents

**Kuwait**

**Kyrgyzstan**

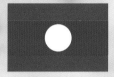
**Laos**

**Latvia**

**Lebanon**

**Lesotho**

**Liberia**

*CFA = Communaute Financiere Africaine

**Libya**

**LIBYA (Africa)**
**Area:** 1,759,540 sq km (679,358 sq miles)
**Population:** 5,368,585
**Capital city:** Tripoli
**Main languages:** Arabic, Italian, English
**Main religion:** Sunni Muslim
**Government:** military rule
**Currency:** 1 Libyan dinar = 1,000 dirhams

**Liechtenstein**

**LIECHTENSTEIN (Europe)**
**Area:** 160 sq km (62 sq miles)
**Population:** 32,842
**Capital city:** Vaduz
**Main languages:** German, Alemannic
**Main religion:** Roman Catholic
**Government:** constitutional monarchy
**Currency:** 1 Swiss franc = 100 centimes

**Lithuania**

**LITHUANIA (Europe)**
**Area:** 65,200 sq km (25,174 sq miles)
**Population:** 3,601,138
**Capital city:** Vilnius
**Main languages:** Lithuanian, Polish, Russian
**Main religions:** Roman Catholic, Lutheran, Russian Orthodox
**Government:** democracy
**Currency:** 1 Lithuanian litas = 100 centas

**Luxembourg**

**LUXEMBOURG (Europe)**
**Area:** 2,586 sq km (998 sq miles)
**Population:** 448,569
**Capital city:** Luxembourg
**Main languages:** Luxemburgish, German, French
**Main religion:** Roman Catholic
**Government:** constitutional monarchy
**Currency:** 1 euro = 100 cents

**Macedonia**

**MACEDONIA (Europe)**
**Area:** 25,333 sq km (9,781 sq miles)
**Population:** 2,054,800
**Capital city:** Skopje
**Main languages:** Macedonian, Albanian
**Main religions:** Macedonian Orthodox, Muslim
**Government:** emerging democracy
**Currency:** 1 Macedonian denar = 100 deni

**Madagascar**

**MADAGASCAR (Africa)**
**Area:** 587,040 sq km (226,656 sq miles)
**Population:** 16,473,477
**Capital city:** Antananarivo
**Main languages:** Malagasy, French
**Main religions:** indigenous beliefs, Christian
**Government:** republic
**Currency:** 1 Malagasy franc = 100 centimes

**Malawi**

**MALAWI (Africa)**
**Area:** 118,480 sq km (45,745 sq miles)
**Population:** 10,701,824
**Capital city:** Lilongwe
**Main languages:** Chichewa, English
**Main religions:** Protestant, Roman Catholic, Muslim
**Government:** parliamentary democracy
**Currency:** 1 Malawian kwacha = 100 tambala

**MALAYSIA (Asia)**
**Area:** 329,750 sq km (127,316 sq miles)
**Population:** 22,662,365
**Capital city:** Kuala Lumpur
**Main languages:** Bahasa Melayu, English, Chinese dialects, Tamil
**Main religions:** Muslim, Buddhist, Daoist
**Government:** constitutional monarchy
**Currency:** 1 ringgit = 100 sen

**Malaysia**

**MALDIVES (Asia)**
**Area:** 300 sq km (116 sq miles)
**Population:** 320,165
**Capital city:** Male
**Main languages:** Maldivian, English
**Main religion:** Sunni Muslim
**Government:** republic
**Currency:** 1 rufiyaa = 100 laari

**Maldives**

**MALI (Africa)**
**Area:** 1,240,000 sq km (478,764 sq miles)
**Population:** 11,340,480
**Capital city:** Bamako
**Main languages:** Bambara, Fulani, Songhai, French
**Main religion:** Muslim
**Government:** republic
**Currency:** 1 CFA* franc = 100 centimes

**Mali**

**MALTA (Europe)**
**Area:** 316 sq km (122 sq miles)
**Population:** 397,499
**Capital city:** Valletta
**Main languages:** Maltese, English
**Main religion:** Roman Catholic
**Government:** republic
**Currency:** 1 Maltese lira = 100 cents

**Malta**

**MARSHALL ISLANDS (Australasia/Oceania)**
**Area:** 181 sq km (70 sq miles)
**Population:** 73,630
**Capital city:** Majuro
**Main languages:** Marshallese, English
**Main religion:** Protestant
**Government:** republic
**Currency:** 1 U.S. dollar = 100 cents

**Marshall Islands**

**MAURITANIA (Africa)**
**Area:** 1,030,700 sq km (397,953 sq miles)
**Population:** 2,828,858
**Capital city:** Nouakchott
**Main languages:** Arabic, Wolof, French
**Main religion:** Muslim
**Government:** republic
**Currency:** 1 ouguiya = 5 khoums

**Mauritania**

**MAURITIUS (Africa)**
**Area:** 2,040 sq km (788 sq miles)
**Population:** 1,200,206
**Capital city:** Port Louis
**Main languages:** Mauritius Creole French, French, Hindi, Bhojpuri, Urdu, Tamil, English
**Main religions:** Hindu, Christian, Muslim
**Government:** parliamentary democracy
**Currency:** 1 Mauritian rupee = 100 cents

**Mauritius**

**MEXICO (North America)**
**Area:** 1,972,550 sq km (761,602 sq miles)
**Population:** 103,400,165
**Capital city:** Mexico City
**Main languages:** Spanish, Mayan, Nahuatl

*CFA = Communaute Financiere Africaine

**Mexico**

**Main religion:** Roman Catholic
**Government:** federal republic
**Currency:** 1 Mexican peso = 100 centavos

**MOLDOVA (Europe)**
**Area:** 33,843 sq km (13,067 sq miles)
**Population:** 4,434,547
**Capital city:** Chisinau
**Main languages:** Moldovan, Russian, Gagauz
**Main religion:** Eastern Orthodox
**Government:** republic
**Currency:** 1 Moldovan leu = 100 bani

**Moldova**

**MONACO (Europe)**
**Area:** 1.95 sq km (0.75 sq miles)
**Population:** 31,987
**Capital city:** Monaco
**Main languages:** French, Monegasque, Italian
**Main religion:** Roman Catholic
**Government:** constitutional monarchy
**Currency:** 1 euro = 100 cents

**Monaco**

**MONGOLIA (Asia)**
**Area:** 1,565,000 sq km (604,247 sq miles)
**Population:** 2,694,432
**Capital city:** Ulan Bator
**Main language:** Khalkha Mongol
**Main religion:** Tibetan Buddist Lamaist
**Government:** republic
**Currency:** 1 tugrik = 100 mongos

**Mongolia**

**MOROCCO (Africa)**
**Area:** 446,550 sq km (172,413 sq miles)
**Population:** 31,167,783
**Capital city:** Rabat
**Main languages:** Arabic, Berber, French
**Main religion:** Muslim
**Government:** constitutional monarchy
**Currency:** 1 Moroccan dirham = 100 centimes

**Morocco**

**MOZAMBIQUE (Africa)**
**Area:** 801,590 sq km (309,494 sq miles)
**Population:** 19,607,519
**Capital city:** Maputo
**Main languages:** Makua, Tsonga, Portuguese
**Main religions:** indigenous, Christian, Muslim
**Government:** republic
**Currency:** 1 metical = 100 centavos

**Mozambique**

**NAMIBIA (Africa)**
**Area:** 825,418 sq km (318,694 sq miles)
**Population:** 1,820,916
**Capital city:** Windhoek
**Main languages:** Afrikaans, German, English
**Main religions:** Christian, indigenous
**Government:** republic
**Currency:** 1 Namibian dollar = 100 cents

**Namibia**

**NAURU (Australasia/Oceania)**
**Area:** 21 sq km (8 sq miles)
**Population:** 12,329
**Capital city:** Yaren
**Main languages:** Nauruan, English
**Main religion:** Christian
**Government:** republic
**Currency:** 1 Australian dollar = 100 cents

**NEPAL (Asia)**
**Area:** 140,800 sq km (54,363 sq miles)
**Population:** 25,873,917
**Capital city:** Kathmandu
**Main languages:** Nepali, Maithili
**Main religions:** Hindu, Buddhist
**Government:** constitutional monarchy
**Currency:** 1 Nepalese rupee = 100 paisa

**NETHERLANDS (Europe)**
**Area:** 41,532 sq km (16,036 sq miles)
**Population:** 16,067,754
**Capital cities:** Amsterdam, The Hague
**Main language:** Dutch
**Main religion:** Christian
**Government:** constitutional monarchy
**Currency:** 1 euro = 100 cents

**NEW ZEALAND (Australasia/Oceania)**
**Area:** 268,680 sq km (103,737 sq miles)
**Population:** 3,908,037
**Capital city:** Wellington
**Main languages:** English, Maori
**Main religion:** Christian
**Government:** parliamentary democracy
**Currency:** 1 New Zealand dollar = 100 cents

**NICARAGUA (North America)**
**Area:** 129,494 sq km (49,998 sq miles)
**Population:** 5,023,818
**Capital city:** Managua
**Main language:** Spanish
**Main religion:** Roman Catholic
**Government:** republic
**Currency:** 1 gold cordoba = 100 centavos

**NIGER (Africa)**
**Area:** 1,267,000 sq km (489,189 sq miles)
**Population:** 10,639,744
**Capital city:** Niamey
**Main languages:** Hausa, Djerma, French
**Main religion:** Muslim
**Government:** republic
**Currency:** 1 CFA* franc = 100 centimes

**NIGERIA (Africa)**
**Area:** 923,768 sq km (356,667 sq miles)
**Population:** 129,934,911
**Capital city:** Abuja
**Main languages:** Hausa, Yoruba, Igbo, English
**Main religions:** Muslim, Christian, indigenous
**Government:** republic
**Currency:** 1 naira = 100 kobo

**NORTH KOREA (Asia)**
**Area:** 120,540 sq km (46,540 sq miles)
**Population:** 22,224,195
**Capital city:** Pyongyang
**Main language:** Korean
**Main religions:** Buddhist, Confucianist
**Government:** authoritarian socialist
**Currency:** 1 North Korean won = 100 chon

**NORWAY (Europe)**
**Area:** 324,220 sq km (125,181 sq miles)
**Population:** 4,525,116
**Capital city:** Oslo
**Main language:** Norwegian

**Nauru**

**Nepal**

**Netherlands**

**New Zealand**

**Nicaragua**

**Niger**

**Nigeria**

*CFA = Communaute Financiere Africaine

**North Korea**

**Norway**

**Oman**

**Pakistan**

**Palau**

**Panama**

**Papua
New Guinea**

**Main religion:** Evangelical Lutheran
**Government:** constitutional monarchy
**Currency:** 1 Norwegian krone = 100 oere

**OMAN (Asia)**
**Area:** 212,460 sq km (82,031 sq miles)
**Population:** 2,713,462
**Capital city:** Muscat
**Main languages:** Arabic, English, Baluchi
**Main religion:** Muslim
**Government:** monarchy
**Currency:** 1 Omani rial = 1,000 baiza

**PAKISTAN (Asia)**
**Area:** 803,940 sq km (310,401 sq miles)
**Population:** 147,663,429
**Capital city:** Islamabad
**Main languages:** Punjabi, Sindhi, Urdu,
English
**Main religion:** Muslim
**Government:** federal republic
**Currency:** 1 Pakistani rupee = 100 paisa

**PALAU (Australasia/Oceania)**
**Area:** 459 sq km (177 sq miles)
**Population:** 19,409
**Capital city:** Koror
**Main languages:** Palauan, English
**Main religions:** Christian, Modekngei
**Government:** democratic republic
**Currency:** 1 U.S. dollar = 100 cents

**PANAMA (North America)**
**Area:** 78,200 sq km (30,193 sq miles)
**Population:** 2,882,329
**Capital city:** Panama City
**Main languages:** Spanish, English
**Main religions:** Roman Catholic, Protestant
**Government:** democracy
**Currency:** 1 balboa = 100 centesimos

**PAPUA NEW GUINEA
(Australasia/Oceania)**
**Area:** 462,840 sq km (178,703 sq miles)
**Population:** 5,172,033
**Capital city:** Port Moresby
**Main languages:** Tok Pisin, Hiri Motu, English
**Main religions:** Christian, indigenous
**Government:** parliamentary democracy
**Currency:** 1 kina = 100 toea

**PARAGUAY (South America)**
**Area:** 406,750 sq km (157,046 sq miles)
**Population:** 5,884,491
**Capital city:** Asuncion
**Main languages:** Guarani, Spanish
**Main religion:** Roman Catholic
**Government:** republic
**Currency:** 1 guarani = 100 centimos

**PERU (South America)**
**Area:** 1,285,220 sq km (496,223 sq miles)
**Population:** 27,949,639
**Capital city:** Lima
**Main languages:** Spanish, Quechua,
Aymara
**Main religion:** Roman Catholic
**Government:** republic
**Currency:** 1 nuevo sol = 100 centimos

**PHILIPPINES (Asia)**
**Area:** 300,000 sq km (115,830 sq miles)
**Population:** 84,525,639
**Capital city:** Manila
**Main languages:** Tagalog, English, Ilocano
**Main religion:** Roman Catholic
**Government:** republic
**Currency:** 1 Philippine peso = 100 centavos

**POLAND (Europe)**
**Area:** 312,685 sq km (120,727 sq miles)
**Population:** 38,625,478
**Capital city:** Warsaw
**Main language:** Polish
**Main religion:** Roman Catholic
**Government:** democratic republic
**Currency:** 1 zloty = 100 groszy

**PORTUGAL (Europe)**
**Area:** 92,391 sq km (35,672 sq miles)
**Population:** 10,084,245
**Capital city:** Lisbon
**Main language:** Portuguese
**Main religion:** Roman Catholic
**Government:** parliamentary democracy
**Currency:** 1 euro = 100 cents

**QATAR (Asia)**
**Area:** 11,437 sq km (4,416 sq miles)
**Population:** 793,341
**Capital city:** Doha
**Main languages:** Arabic, English
**Main religion:** Muslim
**Government:** monarchy
**Currency:** 1 Qatari riyal = 100 dirhams

**ROMANIA (Europe)**
**Area:** 237,500 sq km (91,699 sq miles)
**Population:** 22,317,730
**Capital city:** Bucharest
**Main languages:** Romanian, Hungarian, German
**Main religion:** Romanian Orthodox
**Government:** republic
**Currency:** 1 leu = 100 bani

**RUSSIA (Europe and Asia)**
**Area:** 17,075,200 sq km (6,592,735 sq miles)
**Population:** 144,978,573
**Capital city:** Moscow
**Main language:** Russian
**Main religions:** Russian Orthodox, Muslim
**Government:** federal government
**Currency:** 1 ruble = 100 kopeks

**RWANDA (Africa)**
**Area:** 26,338 sq km (10,169 sq miles)
**Population:** 7,398,074
**Capital city:** Kigali
**Main languages:** Kinyarwanda, French,
English, Swahili
**Main religions:** Roman Catholic, Protestant,
Adventist
**Government:** republic
**Currency:** 1 Rwandan franc = 100 centimes

**SAINT KITTS AND NEVIS
(North America)**
**Area:** 261 sq km (101 sq miles)
**Population:** 38,736

**Paraguay**

**• Peru**

**Philippines**

**Poland**

**Portugal**

**Qatar**

**Romania**

**Russia**

Capital city: Basseterre
Main language: English
Main religions: Protestant, Roman Catholic
Government: constitutional monarchy
Currency: 1 East Caribbean dollar = 100 cents

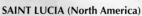

**Rwanda**

**SAINT LUCIA (North America)**
Area: 620 sq km (239 sq miles)
Population: 160,145
Capital city: Castries
Main languages: French patois, English
Main religion: Roman Catholic
Government: parliamentary democracy
Currency: 1 East Caribbean dollar = 100 cents

**SAINT VINCENT AND THE GRENADINES
(North America)**
Area: 389 sq km (150 sq miles)
Population: 116,394
Capital city: Kingstown
Main languages: English, French patois
Main religions: Protestant, Roman Catholic
Government: parliamentary democracy
Currency: 1 East Caribbean dollar = 100 cents

**Saint Kitts
and Nevis**

**SAMOA (Australasia/Oceania)**
Area: 2,860 sq km (1,104 sq miles)
Population: 178,631
Capital city: Apia
Main languages: Samoan, English
Main religion: Christian
Government: constitutional monarchy
Currency: 1 tala = 100 sene

**Saint Lucia**

**SAN MARINO (Europe)**
Area: 61 sq km (24 sq miles)
Population: 27,730
Capital city: San Marino
Main language: Italian
Main religion: Roman Catholic
Government: republic
Currency: 1 euro = 100 cents

**SAO TOME AND PRINCIPE (Africa)**
Area: 1,001 sq km (386 sq miles)
Population: 170,372
Capital city: Sao Tome
Main languages: Crioulo* dialects, Portuguese
Main religion: Christian
Government: republic
Currency: 1 dobra = 100 centimos

**Saint Vincent and
the Grenadines**

**SAUDI ARABIA (Asia)**
Area: 1,960,582 sq km (756,987 sq miles)
Population: 23,513,330
Capital city: Riyadh
Main language: Arabic
Main religion: Muslim
Government: monarchy
Currency: 1 Saudi riyal = 100 halalah

**Samoa**

**SENEGAL (Africa)**
Area: 196,190 sq km (75,749 sq miles)
Population: 10,589,571
Capital city: Dakar
Main languages: Wolof, French, Pulaar
Main religion: Muslim
Government: democratic republic
Currency: 1 CFA* franc = 100 centimes

**• San Marino**

**SERBIA AND MONTENEGRO (Europe)**
Area: 102,350 sq km (39,517 sq miles)
Population: 10,656,929
Capital city: Belgrade
Main language: Serbian
Main religions: Orthodox, Muslim
Government: republic
Currency: 1 Yugoslavian new dinar = 100 paras

**SEYCHELLES (Africa)**
Area: 455 sq km (176 sq miles)
Population: 80,098
Capital city: Victoria
Main languages: Seselwa, English, French
Main religion: Roman Catholic
Government: republic
Currency: 1 Seychelles rupee = 100 cents

**SIERRA LEONE (Africa)**
Area: 71,740 sq km (27,699 sq miles)
Population: 5,614,743
Capital city: Freetown
Main languages: Mende, Temne, Krio, English
Main religions: Muslim, indigenous, Christian
Government: constitutional democracy
Currency: 1 leone = 100 cents

**SINGAPORE (Asia)**
Area: 692 sq km (267 sq miles)
Population: 4,452,732
Capital city: Singapore
Main languages: Chinese, Malay, English, Tamil
Main religions: Buddhist, Muslim
Government: parliamentary republic
Currency: 1 Singapore dollar = 100 cents

**SLOVAKIA (Europe)**
Area: 48,845 sq km (18,859 sq miles)
Population: 5,422,366
Capital city: Bratislava
Main languages: Slovak, Hungarian
Main religion: Roman Catholic
Government: parliamentary democracy
Currency: 1 koruna = 100 halierov

**SLOVENIA (Europe)**
Area: 20,273 sq km (7,827 sq miles)
Population: 1,932,917
Capital city: Ljubljana
Main language: Slovenian
Main religion: Roman Catholic
Government: democratic republic
Currency: 1 tolar = 100 stotins

**SOLOMON ISLANDS (Australasia/Oceania)**
Area: 28,450 sq km (10,985 sq miles)
Population: 494,786
Capital city: Honiara
Main languages: Solomon pidgin, Kwara'ae,
To'abaita, English
Main religion: Christian
Government: parliamentary democracy
Currency: 1 Solomon Islands dollar = 100 cents

**SOMALIA (Africa)**
Area: 637,657 sq km (246,199 sq miles)
Population: 7,753,310
Capital city: Mogadishu
Main languages: Somali, Arabic, Oromo

**Sao Tome
and Principe**

**Saudi Arabia**

**Senegal**

**Serbia and
Montenegro**

**Seychelles**

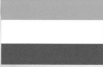

**Sierra Leone**

**Singapore**

*CFA = Communaute Financiere Africaine; Crioulo = a
blend of Portuguese and West African

**Slovakia**

• **Slovenia**

**Solomon Islands**

**Somalia**

**South Africa**

**South Korea**

• **Spain**

**Sri Lanka**

**Sudan**

**Surinam**

**Swaziland**

**Sweden**

**Switzerland**

**Syria**

**Main religion:** Sunni Muslim
**Government:** currently has no government
**Currency:** 1 Somali shilling = 100 cents

**SOUTH AFRICA (Africa)**
**Area:** 1,219,912 sq km (471,008 sq miles)
**Population:** 43,647,658
**Capital cities:** Pretoria, Cape Town, Bloemfontein
**Main languages:** Zulu, Xhosa, Afrikaans, Pedi, English, Tswana, Sotho, Tsonga, Swati, Venda, Ndebele
**Main religions:** Christian, indigenous
**Government:** republic
**Currency:** 1 rand = 100 cents

**SOUTH KOREA (Asia)**
**Area:** 98,480 sq km (38,023 sq miles)
**Population:** 48,324,000
**Capital city:** Seoul
**Main language:** Korean
**Main religions:** Christian, Buddhist
**Government:** republic
**Currency:** 1 South Korean won = 100 chun

**SPAIN (Europe)**
**Area:** 504,782 sq km (194,898 sq miles)
**Population:** 40,077,100
**Capital city:** Madrid
**Main languages:** Castilian Spanish, Catalan
**Main religion:** Roman Catholic
**Government:** constitutional monarchy
**Currency:** 1 euro = 100 cents

**SRI LANKA (Asia)**
**Area:** 65,610 sq km (25,332 sq miles)
**Population:** 19,576,783
**Capital cities:** Colombo, Sri Jayewardenepura Kotte
**Main languages:** Sinhala, Tamil, English
**Main religions:** Buddhist, Hindu
**Government:** republic
**Currency:** 1 Sri Lankan rupee = 100 cents

**SUDAN (Africa)**
**Area:** 2,505,810 sq km (967,493 sq miles)
**Population:** 37,090,298
**Capital city:** Khartoum
**Main languages:** Arabic, English
**Main religions:** Sunni Muslim, indigenous
**Government:** Islamic republic
**Currency:** 1 Sudanese dinar = 100 piastres

**SURINAM (South America)**
**Area:** 163,270 sq km (63,039 sq miles)
**Population:** 436,494
**Capital city:** Paramaribo
**Main languages:** Sranang Tongo, Dutch, English
**Main religions:** Christian, Hindu, Muslim
**Government:** constitutional democracy
**Currency:** 1 Surinamese guilder = 100 cents

**SWAZILAND (Africa)**
**Area:** 17,363 sq km (6,704 sq miles)
**Population:** 1,123,605
**Capital cities:** Mbabane, Lobamba

**Main languages:** Swati, English
**Main religions:** Christian, indigenous, Muslim
**Government:** monarchy
**Currency:** 1 lilangeni = 100 cents

**SWEDEN (Europe)**
**Area:** 449,964 sq km (173,731 sq miles)
**Population:** 8,876,744
**Capital city:** Stockholm
**Main language:** Swedish
**Main religion:** Lutheran
**Government:** constitutional monarchy
**Currency:** 1 Swedish krona = 100 oere

**SWITZERLAND (Europe)**
**Area:** 41,290 sq km (15,942 sq miles)
**Population:** 7,301,994
**Capital city:** Bern
**Main languages:** German, French, Italian
**Main religions:** Roman Catholic, Protestant
**Government:** federal republic
**Currency:** 1 Swiss franc = 100 centimes

**SYRIA (Asia)**
**Area:** 185,180 sq km (71,498 sq miles)
**Population:** 17,155,814
**Capital city:** Damascus
**Main languages:** Arabic, Kurdish
**Main religions:** Muslim, Christian
**Government:** republic under military regime
**Currency:** 1 Syrian pound = 100 piastres

**TAIWAN (Asia)**
**Area:** 35,980 sq km (13,892 sq miles)
**Population:** 22,548,009
**Capital city:** Taipei
**Main languages:** Taiwanese, Mandarin Chinese, Hakka Chinese
**Main religions:** Buddhist, Confucian, Daoist
**Government:** democracy
**Currency:** 1 New Taiwan dollar = 100 cents

**TAJIKISTAN (Asia)**
**Area:** 143,100 sq km (55,251 sq miles)
**Population:** 6,719,567
**Capital city:** Dushanbe
**Main languages:** Tajik, Russian
**Main religion:** Sunni Muslim
**Government:** republic
**Currency:** 1 somoni = 100 dirams

**TANZANIA (Africa)**
**Area:** 945,087 sq km (364,898 sq miles)
**Population:** 37,187,939
**Capital cities:** Dar es Salaam, Dodoma
**Main languages:** Swahili, English, Sukuma
**Main religions:** Christian, Muslim, indigenous
**Government:** republic
**Currency:** 1 Tanzanian shilling = 100 cents

**THAILAND (Asia)**
**Area:** 514,000 sq km (198,455 sq miles)
**Population:** 62,354,402
**Capital city:** Bangkok
**Main languages:** Thai, English, Chaochow
**Main religion:** Buddhist
**Government:** constitutional monarchy
**Currency:** 1 baht = 100 satang

**Taiwan**

**TOGO (Africa)**
**Area:** 56,785 sq km (21,925 sq miles)
**Population:** 5,285,501
**Capital city:** Lome
**Main languages:** Mina, Ewe, Kabye, French
**Main religions:** indigenous, Christian, Muslim
**Government:** republic
**Currency:** 1 CFA* franc = 100 centimes

**TONGA (Australasia/Oceania)**
**Area**: 748 sq km (289 sq miles)
**Population:** 106,137
**Capital city:** Nukualofa
**Main languages:** Tongan, English
**Main religion:** Christian
**Government:** constitutional monarchy
**Currency:** 1 pa'anga = 100 seniti

**Tajikistan**

**TRINIDAD AND TOBAGO (North America)**
**Area:** 5,128 sq km (1,980 sq miles)
**Population:** 1,163,724
**Capital city:** Port-of-Spain
**Main languages:** English, French, Spanish, Hindi
**Main religions:** Christian, Hindu
**Government:** parliamentary democracy
**Currency:** 1 Trinidad and Tobago dollar =
100 cents

**TUNISIA (Africa)**
**Area:** 163,610 sq km (63,170 sq miles)
**Population:** 9,815,644
**Capital city:** Tunis
**Main languages:** Arabic, French
**Main religion:** Muslim
**Government:** republic
**Currency:** 1 Tunisian dinar = 1,000
millimes

**Tanzania**

**Thailand**

**TURKEY (Europe and Asia)**
**Area:** 780,580 sq km (301,382 sq miles)
**Population:** 67,308,928
**Capital city:** Ankara
**Main language:** Turkish
**Main religion:** Muslim
**Government:** democratic republic
**Currency:** 1 Turkish lira = 100 kurus

**TURKMENISTAN (Asia)**
**Area:** 488,100 sq km (188,455 sq miles)
**Population:** 4,688,963
**Capital city:** Ashgabat (Ashkhabad)
**Main languages:** Turkmen, Russian
**Main religion**: Muslim
**Government:** republic
**Currency:** 1 Turkmen manat = 100 tenesi

**Togo**

**TUVALU (Australasia/Oceania)**
**Area:** 26 sq km (10 sq miles)
**Population:** 11,146
**Capital city:** Funafuti
**Main languages:** Tuvaluan, English
**Main religion:** Congregationalist
**Government:** constitutional monarchy
**Currency:** 1 Tuvaluan dollar or 1 Australian
dollar = 100 cents

**Tonga**

**UGANDA (Africa)**
**Area:** 236,040 sq km (91,135 sq miles)
**Population:** 24,699,073

**Capital city:** Kampala
**Main languages:** Luganda, English, Swahili
**Main religion:** Christian, Muslim, indigenous
**Government:** republic
**Currency:** 1 Ugandan shilling = 100 cents

**UKRAINE (Europe)**
**Area:** 603,700 sq km (233,089 sq miles)
**Population:** 48,396,470
**Capital city:** Kiev
**Main languages:** Ukrainian, Russian
**Main religion:** Ukrainian Orthodox
**Government:** republic
**Currency:** 1 hryvnia = 100 kopiykas

**UNITED ARAB EMIRATES (Asia)**
**Area:** 82,880 sq km (32,000 sq miles)
**Population:** 2,445,989
**Capital city:** Abu Dhabi
**Main languages:** Arabic, English
**Main religion:** Muslim
**Government:** federation
**Currency:** 1 Emirati dirham = 100 fils

**UNITED KINGDOM (Europe)**
**Area:** 244,820 sq km (94,525 sq miles)
**Population:** 59,778,002
**Capital city:** London
**Main language:** English
**Main religions:** Anglican, Roman Catholic
**Government:** constitutional monarchy
**Currency:** 1 British pound = 100 pence

**UNITED STATES OF AMERICA**
**(North America)**
**Area:** 9,629,091 sq km (3,717,792 sq miles)
**Population:** 280,562,489
**Capital city:** Washington D.C.
**Main language:** English
**Main religions:** Protestant, Roman Catholic
**Government:** federal republic
**Currency:** 1 U.S. dollar = 100 cents

**URUGUAY (South America)**
**Area:** 176,220 sq km (68,039 sq miles)
**Population:** 3,386,575
**Capital city:** Montevideo
**Main language:** Spanish
**Main religion:** Roman Catholic
**Government:** republic
**Currency:** 1 Uruguayan peso = 100 centesimos

**UZBEKISTAN (Asia)**
**Area:** 447,400 sq km (172,741 sq miles)
**Population:** 25,563,441
**Capital city:** Tashkent
**Main languages:** Uzbek, Russian
**Main religions:** Muslim, Eastern Orthodox
**Government:** republic
**Currency:** 1 Uzbekistani sum = 100 tyyn

**VANUATU (Australasia/Oceania)**
**Area:** 12,189 sq km (4,706 sq miles)
**Population:** 196,178
**Capital city:** Port-Vila
**Main languages:** Bislama, French, English
**Main religion:** Christian
**Government:** republic
**Currency:** 1 vatu = 100 centimes

**Trinidad and Tobago**

**Tunisia**

**Turkey**

**Turkmenistan**

**Tuvalu**

**Uganda**

*CFA = Communaute Financiere Africaine

Ukraine

United
Arab Emirates

United Kingdom

United States
of America

Uruguay

Uzbekistan

**VATICAN CITY (Europe)**
**Area:** 0.44 sq km (0.17 sq miles)
**Population:** 900
**Capital city:** Vatican City
**Main languages:** Italian, Latin
**Main religion:** Roman Catholic
**Government:** led by the Pope
**Currency:** 1 euro = 100 cents

**VENEZUELA (South America)**
**Area:** 912,050 sq km (352,143 sq miles)
**Population:** 24,287,670
**Capital city:** Caracas
**Main language:** Spanish
**Main religion:** Roman Catholic
**Government:** federal republic
**Currency:** 1 bolivar = 100 centimos

**VIETNAM (Asia)**
**Area:** 329,560 sq km (127,243 sq miles)
**Population:** 81,098,416
**Capital city:** Hanoi
**Main languages:** Vietnamese, French,
English, Khmer, Chinese
**Main religion:** Buddhist
**Government:** Communist state
**Currency:** 1 new dong = 100 xu

**YEMEN (Asia)**
**Area:** 527,970 sq km (203,849 sq miles)
**Population:** 18,701,257
**Capital city:** Sana
**Main language:** Arabic
**Main religion:** Muslim
**Government:** republic
**Currency:** 1 Yemeni rial = 100 fils

**ZAMBIA (Africa)**
**Area:** 752,614 sq km (290,584 sq miles)
**Population:** 9,959,037
**Capital city:** Lusaka
**Main languages:** Bemba, Tonga, Nyanja,
English
**Main religions:** Christian, Muslim, Hindu
**Government:** republic
**Currency:** 1 Zambian kwacha = 100 ngwee

**ZIMBABWE (Africa)**
**Area:** 390,580 sq km (150,803 sq miles)
**Population:** 11,376,676
**Capital city:** Harare
**Main languages:** Shona, Ndebele, English
**Main religions:** Christian, indigenous
**Government:** republic
**Currency:** 1 Zimbabwean dollar = 100 cents

# The United Nations

The United Nations (U.N.) is
an organization which aims
to bring countries together
to work for peace and
development. Of the world's
193 states, 191 belong to the
U.N. Those that
don't belong
are Taiwan
and the
Vatican City.

## Internet link

For a link to a website where you
can match countries and their flags
in a great game, go to
**www.usborne-quicklinks.com**

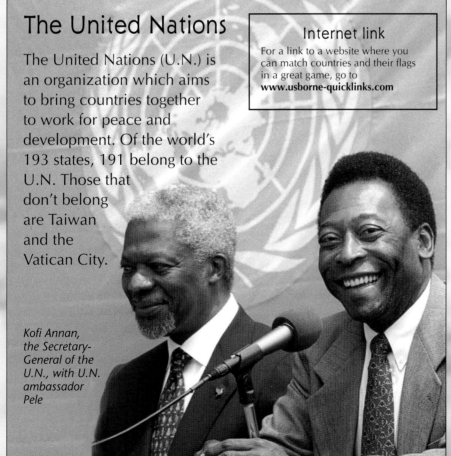

*Kofi Annan,
the Secretary-
General of the
U.N., with U.N.
ambassador
Pele*

Vanuatu

Vatican City

Venezuela

Vietnam

Yemen

Zambia

Zimbabwe

# USEFUL WEBSITES

On these pages, there are descriptions of websites that have information, photographs and games on the theme of maps and geography. For links to these sites, go to the Usborne Quicklinks website at **www.usborne-quicklinks.com** and enter the keywords "essential atlas". There you will find links to take you to all the sites.

## Map resources

**Website 1**
Find street maps of any town or city in the world.

**Website 2**
See maps that show which parts of the Earth are in daylight or darkness at this very moment, plus up-to-date weather conditions across the globe.

**Website 3**
Download clip art of world, continent, country and state maps, as well as flags and globes.

**Website 4**
Find maps of any country in the world, plus information about their geography, people, government, economy and more.

*This is part of Kluane National Park, in Yukon Territory, Canada. A huge mass of ice known as a glacier flows slowly downhill, cutting valleys through the mountains.*

## World wildlife

**Website 1**
Discover some of the weird and wonderful creatures that live in the world's oceans and seas.

**Website 2**
Learn about the world's endangered animals and find out what can be done to stop them from becoming extinct.

**Website 3**
Find out about amazing animals and watch videos of them in the wild.

**Website 4**
Learn about the unusual animals that live in the Galapagos Islands, including iguanas and giant tortoises.

**Website 5**
Read about animals that live in the Arctic, such as walruses, snowy owls, polar bears and arctic foxes.

# Amazing Earth

### Website 1
Read fascinating facts about some of the world's most interesting locations, including the Amazon Rainforest, Greenland and Madagascar. This site also has short films to watch and quiz questions to answer.

### Website 2
Find out about natural disasters such as earthquakes and tsunamis and see animated diagrams of how each forms.

### Website 3
Take an interactive tour of Everest, the highest mountain in the world.

### Website 4
Read up-to-date information about all the current volcanic eruptions around the world.

### Website 5
Explore the vast Sahara Desert and learn about its landscape and peoples.

### Website 6
Discover all kinds of underground caves and find out how they were formed.

*A birdwing butterfly feeds from a tropical flower. Birdwings are the world's largest butterflies and live in the rainforests of Asia and Australasia.*

## Quizzes and games

### Website 1
See if you can identify and name countries and capital cities.

### Website 2
Try all kinds of geography quizzes and have a go at some online crosswords.

### Website 3
Take a safari quiz and find out if you have what it takes to survive in the wild.

### Website 4
Test your knowledge of the world's deserts.

# MAP INDEX

This is an index of the places and features named on the maps. Each entry consists of the following parts: the name (given in bold type), the country or region within which it is located (given in italics), the page on which the name can be found (given in bold type), and the grid reference (also given in bold type). For some names, there is also a description explaining what kind of place it is – for example a country, internal administrative area (state or province), national capital or internal capital. To find a place on a map, first find the map indicated by the page reference. Then use the grid reference to find the square containing the name or town symbol. See page 9 for help with using the grid.

## a

**Abaco,** *The Bahamas,* **25 L5**
**Abadan,** *Iran,* **51 E5**
**Abakan,** *Russia,* **52 E3**
**Abaya, Lake,** *Ethiopia,* **71 G2**
**Abeche,** *Chad,* **66 F6**
**Abeokuta,** *Nigeria,* **69 F7**
**Aberdeen,** *United Kingdom,* **60 D2**
**Aberystwyth,** *United Kingdom,* **60 C3**
**Abha,** *Saudi Arabia,* **51 D8**
**Abidjan,** *Ivory Coast,* **69 E7**
**Abilene,** *U.S.A.,* **24 G4**
**Abomey,** *Benin,* **69 F7**
**Abu Dhabi,** *United Arab Emirates, national capital,* **51 F7**
**Abuja,** *Nigeria, national capital,* **69 G7**
**Abu Kamal,** *Syria,* **50 D5**
**Abu Simbel,** *Egypt,* **67 H4**
**Acapulco,** *Mexico,* **26 E4**
**Accra,** *Ghana, national capital,* **69 E7**
**Acklins Island,** *The Bahamas,* **25 L6**
**Aconcagua,** *Argentina,* **32 E6**
**Adana,** *Turkey,* **50 C4**
**Adapazari,** *Turkey,* **63 J3**
**Ad Dakhla,** *Western Sahara,* **68 B4**
**Ad Dammam,** *Saudi Arabia,* **51 F6**
**Addis Ababa,** *Ethiopia, national capital,* **71 G2**
**Adelaide,** *Australia, internal capital,* **38 G6**
**Aden,** *Yemen,* **51 E9**
**Aden, Gulf of,** *Africa/Asia,* **51 E9**
**Admiralty Islands,** *Papua New Guinea,* **43 L4**
**Adrar,** *Algeria,* **68 E3**
**Adriatic Sea,** *Europe,* **62 E3**
**Adzope,** *Ivory Coast,* **69 E7**
**Aegean Sea,** *Europe,* **63 H4**
**Afghanistan,** *Asia, country,* **48 A4**
**Africa,** **19**
**Agadez,** *Niger,* **66 C5**
**Agadir,** *Morocco,* **68 D2**
**Agra,** *India,* **48 D5**
**Agrigento,** *Italy,* **62 E4**
**Agua Prieta,** *Mexico,* **26 C1**
**Aguascalientes,** *Mexico,* **26 D3**
**Agulhas, Cape,** *South Africa,* **72 C6**
**Agulhas Negras, Mount,** *Brazil,* **32 K4**
**Ahaggar Mountains,** *Algeria,* **68 G4**
**Ahmadabad,** *India,* **49 C6**
**Ahvaz,** *Iran,* **51 E5**
**Aix-en-Provence,** *France,* **61 F6**
**Aizawl,** *India,* **49 G6**
**Ajaccio,** *France,* **61 G6**
**Ajdabiya,** *Libya,* **66 F2**
**Ajmer,** *India,* **48 C5**
**Akhisar,** *Turkey,* **63 H4**
**Akita,** *Japan,* **47 P3**
**Akjoujt,** *Mauritania,* **68 C5**
**Akola,** *India,* **49 D6**
**Aksaray,** *Turkey,* **63 K4**
**Aksu,** *China,* **48 E2**
**Alabama,** *U.S.A., internal admin. area,* **25 J4**
**Al Amarah,** *Iraq,* **51 E5**
**Aland Islands,** *Finland,* **58 F3**
**Alanya,** *Turkey,* **63 J4**
**Al Aqabah,** *Jordan,* **51 C6**
**Alaska,** *U.S.A., internal admin. area,* **22 D2**

**Alaska, Gulf of,** *North America,* **22 E3**
**Alaska Peninsula,** *U.S.A.,* **22 D3**
**Alaska Range,** *U.S.A.,* **22 D2**
**Alavus,** *Finland,* **58 G3**
**Al Ayn,** *United Arab Emirates,* **51 G7**
**Albacete,** *Spain,* **61 D7**
**Albania,** *Europe, country,* **63 F3**
**Albany,** *Australia,* **38 C7**
**Albany,** *Georgia, U.S.A.,* **25 K4**
**Albany,** *New York, U.S.A., internal capital,* **25 M2**
**Al Bayda,** *Libya,* **66 F2**
**Alberta,** *Canada, internal admin. area,* **22 H3**
**Albert, Lake,** *Africa,* **71 F3**
**Albino Point,** *Angola,* **72 B3**
**Alboran Island,** *Spain,* **61 D7**
**Alborg,** *Denmark,* **59 D4**
**Albuquerque,** *U.S.A.,* **24 E3**
**Aldabra Group,** *Seychelles,* **73 J1**
**Aleppo,** *Syria,* **50 C4**
**Alesund,** *Norway,* **58 C3**
**Aleutian Islands,** *U.S.A.,* **23 A3**
**Alexander Archipelago,** *Canada,* **22 F3**
**Alexander Bay,** *South Africa,* **72 C5**
**Alexandria,** *Egypt,* **67 G2**
**Algeciras,** *Spain,* **61 C7**
**Algeria,** *Africa, country,* **68 F3**
**Algiers,** *Algeria, national capital,* **68 F1**
**Al Hillah,** *Iraq,* **50 D5**
**Al Hoceima,** *Morocco,* **68 E1**
**Al Hudaydah,** *Yemen,* **51 D9**
**Ali Bayramli,** *Azerbaijan,* **50 E4**
**Alicante,** *Spain,* **61 D7**
**Alice Springs,** *Australia,* **38 F4**
**Aligarh,** *India,* **48 D5**
**Al Jawf,** *Libya,* **66 F4**
**Al Khums,** *Libya,* **66 D2**
**Al Kut,** *Iraq,* **51 E5**
**Allahabad,** *India,* **48 E5**
**Almaty,** *Kazakhstan,* **48 D2**
**Almeria,** *Spain,* **61 D7**
**Almetyevsk,** *Russia,* **57 G3**
**Almirante,** *Panama,* **27 H6**
**Al Mubarrez,** *Saudi Arabia,* **51 E6**
**Al Mukalla,** *Yemen,* **51 E9**
**Alor Setar,** *Malaysia,* **42 B2**
**Alps,** *Europe,* **62 D2**
**Al Qamishli,** *Syria,* **50 D4**
**Alta,** *Norway,* **58 G1**
**Altai Mountains,** *Asia,* **46 D1**
**Altamira,** *Brazil,* **31 H4**
**Altay,** *China,* **48 F1**
**Altay,** *Mongolia,* **46 E1**
**Altun Mountains,** *China,* **48 G3**
**Aluksne,** *Latvia,* **59 H4**
**Alytus,** *Lithuania,* **59 H5**
**Amadjuak Lake,** *Canada,* **23 M2**
**Amami,** *Japan,* **47 L5**
**Amarillo,** *U.S.A.,* **24 F3**
**Amazon,** *South America,* **30 H4**
**Amazon Delta,** *Brazil,* **31 J3**
**Ambanja,** *Madagascar,* **73 J2**
**Ambato,** *Ecuador,* **30 C4**
**Amber, Cape,** *Madagascar,* **73 J2**
**Ambilobe,** *Madagascar,* **73 J2**
**Ambon,** *Indonesia,* **43 G4**
**Ambositra,** *Madagascar,* **73 J4**

**American Samoa,** *Oceania, dependency,* **36 F6**
**America, United States of,** *North America, country,* **24 F3**
**Amiens,** *France,* **60 E4**
**Amman,** *Jordan, national capital,* **51 C5**
**Amravati,** *India,* **49 D6**
**Amritsar,** *India,* **48 C4**
**Amsterdam,** *Netherlands, national capital,* **60 F3**
**Am Timan,** *Chad,* **66 F6**
**Amu Darya,** *Asia,* **50 H4**
**Amundsen Gulf,** *Canada,* **22 G1**
**Amundsen Sea,** *Antarctica,* **77 Q3**
**Amur,** *Asia,* **53 G3**
**Anadyr,** *Russia,* **53 J2**
**Anadyr, Gulf of,** *Asia,* **53 K2**
**Analalava,** *Madagascar,* **73 J2**
**Anambas Islands,** *Indonesia,* **42 C3**
**Anchorage,** *U.S.A.,* **22 E2**
**Ancona,** *Italy,* **62 E3**
**Andaman Islands,** *India,* **49 G8**
**Andaman Sea,** *Asia,* **44 C5**
**Andara,** *Namibia,* **72 D3**
**Andes,** *South America,* **32 E5**
**Andorra,** *Europe, country,* **61 E6**
**Andorra la Vella,** *Andorra, national capital,* **61 E6**
**Andreanof Islands,** *U.S.A.,* **23 B3**
**Androka,** *Madagascar,* **73 H5**
**Andros,** *The Bahamas,* **25 L6**
**Aneto, Pico de,** *Spain,* **61 E6**
**Angel Falls,** *Venezuela,* **30 F2**
**Angers,** *France,* **60 D5**
**Angkor,** *Cambodia,* **44 D5**
**Angoche,** *Mozambique,* **73 G3**
**Angola,** *Africa, country,* **72 C2**
**Angra do Heroismo,** *Azores,* **68 K10**
**Angren,** *Uzbekistan,* **48 C2**
**Anguilla,** *North America,* **26 M4**
**Anjouan Island,** *Comoros,* **73 H2**
**Ankara,** *Turkey, national capital,* **63 K3**
**Annaba,** *Algeria,* **68 G1**
**An Najaf,** *Iraq,* **51 D5**
**Annapolis,** *U.S.A., internal capital,* **25 L3**
**An Nasiriyah,** *Iraq,* **51 E5**
**Anqing,** *China,* **47 J4**
**Anshan,** *China,* **47 K2**
**Antalaha,** *Madagascar,* **73 K2**
**Antalya,** *Turkey,* **63 J4**
**Antalya, Gulf of,** *Turkey,* **63 J4**
**Antananarivo,** *Madagascar, national capital,* **73 J3**
**Antarctica,** **77 B4**
**Antarctic Peninsula,** *Antarctica,* **77 T2**
**Anticosti Island,** *Canada,* **23 N4**
**Antigua and Barbuda,** *North America, country,* **26 M4**
**Antofagasta,** *Chile,* **32 D4**
**Antsalova,** *Madagascar,* **73 H3**
**Antsirabe,** *Madagascar,* **73 J3**
**Antsiranana,** *Madagascar,* **73 J2**
**Antwerp,** *Belgium,* **60 F4**
**Aomori,** *Japan,* **47 P2**
**Aoraki,** *New Zealand,* **39 P8**
**Apalachee Bay,** *U.S.A.,* **25 K5**
**Aparri,** *Philippines,* **45 H4**
**Apatity,** *Russia,* **58 K2**

**Apennines,** *Italy,* **62 E3**
**Apia,** *Samoa, national capital,* **36 F6**
**Appalachian Mountains,** *U.S.A.,* **25 K3**
**Aqsay,** *Kazakhstan,* **57 G3**
**Aqtau,** *Kazakhstan,* **50 F3**
**Aqtobe,** *Kazakhstan,* **57 H3**
**Arabian Desert,** *Africa,* **67 H3**
**Arabian Peninsula,** *Asia,* **51 E7**
**Arabian Sea,** *Asia,* **51 G8**
**Aracaju,** *Brazil,* **31 L6**
**Arad,** *Romania,* **63 G2**
**Arafura Sea,** *Asia/Australasia,* **43 H5**
**Araguaia,** *Brazil,* **31 H6**
**Araguaina,** *Brazil,* **31 J5**
**Arak,** *Iran,* **50 E5**
**Aral,** *Kazakhstan,* **50 H2**
**Aral Sea,** *Asia,* **50 G2**
**Arapiraca,** *Brazil,* **31 L5**
**Araraquara,** *Brazil,* **32 J4**
**Araure,** *Venezuela,* **30 E2**
**Arbil,** *Iraq,* **50 D4**
**Arctic Ocean,** **75 A4**
**Ardabil,** *Iran,* **50 E4**
**Arendal,** *Norway,* **58 D4**
**Arequipa,** *Peru,* **30 D7**
**Argentina,** *South America, country,* **33 E7**
**Argentino, Lake,** *Argentina,* **33 D10**
**Arhus,** *Denmark,* **59 D4**
**Arica,** *Chile,* **32 D3**
**Arica, Gulf of,** *South America,* **30 D7**
**Arizona,** *U.S.A., internal admin. area,* **24 D4**
**Arkansas,** *U.S.A.,* **25 G3**
**Arkansas,** *U.S.A., internal admin. area,* **25 H4**
**Arkhangelsk,** *Russia,* **52 C2**
**Armenia,** *Asia, country,* **50 D3**
**Armidale,** *Australia,* **39 K6**
**Arnhem,** *Netherlands,* **60 F4**
**Arnhem Land,** *Australia,* **38 F2**
**Arqalyq,** *Kazakhstan,* **50 J1**
**Ar Ramadi,** *Iraq,* **50 D5**
**Ar Raqqah,** *Syria,* **50 C4**
**Aruba,** *North America,* **27 K5**
**Aru Islands,** *Indonesia,* **43 J5**
**Arusha,** *Tanzania,* **71 G4**
**Arzamas,** *Russia,* **56 E2**
**Asahikawa,** *Japan,* **47 P2**
**Asansol,** *India,* **49 F6**
**Ashgabat,** *Turkmenistan, national capital,* **50 G4**
**Ashkhabad,** *Turkmenistan, national capital,* **50 G4**
**Asia,** **19**
**Asir,** *Saudi Arabia,* **51 D7**
**Asmara,** *Eritrea, national capital,* **67 J5**
**Assab,** *Eritrea,* **67 K6**
**As Sulaymaniyah,** *Iraq,* **50 E4**
**Assumption,** *Seychelles,* **73 J1**
**Astana,** *Kazakhstan, national capital,* **52 D3**
**Astove,** *Seychelles,* **73 J2**
**Astrakhan,** *Russia,* **57 F4**
**Asuncion,** *Paraguay, national capital,* **32 G5**
**Aswan,** *Egypt,* **67 H4**
**Aswan High Dam,** *Egypt,* **67 H4**
**Asyut,** *Egypt,* **67 H3**
**Atacama Desert,** *Chile,* **32 E3**

Florencia, *Colombia,* 30 C3
Flores, *Azores,* 68 J10
Flores, *Indonesia,* 43 F5
Flores Sea, *Indonesia,* 43 F5
Floresta, *Brazil,* 31 L5
Floriano, *Brazil,* 31 K5
Florianopolis, *Brazil,* 32 J5
Florida, *U.S.A., internal admin. area,* 25 K5
Florida Keys, *U.S.A.,* 25 K6
Florida, Straits of, *North America,* 25 K6
Focsani, *Romania,* 63 H2
Foggia, *Italy,* 62 E3
Fogo, *Cape Verde,* 69 M12
Fomboni, *Comoros,* 73 H2
Formosa, *Argentina,* 32 G5
Fort Albany, *Canada,* 23 L3
Fortaleza, *Brazil,* 31 L4
Fort Chipewyan, *Canada,* 22 H3
Fort-de-France, *Martinique,* 26 M5
Fort Lauderdale, *U.S.A.,* 25 K5
Fort McMurray, *Canada,* 22 H3
Fort Nelson, *Canada,* 22 G3
Fort Peck Lake, *U.S.A.,* 24 E1
Fort Providence, *Canada,* 22 H2
Fort St. John, *Canada,* 22 G3
Fort Severn, *Canada,* 23 L3
Fort Vermilion, *Canada,* 22 H3
Fort Wayne, *U.S.A.,* 25 J2
Fort Worth, *U.S.A.,* 24 G4
Foumban, *Cameroon,* 70 B2
Foxe Basin, *Canada,* 23 M2
Foxe Peninsula, *Canada,* 23 M2
Fox Islands, *U.S.A.,* 23 C3
Foz do Cunene, *Angola,* 72 B3
Foz do Iguacu, *Brazil,* 32 H5
France, *Europe, country,* 61 E5
Franceville, *Gabon,* 70 B4
Francistown, *Botswana,* 72 E4
Frankfort, *U.S.A., internal capital,* 25 K3
Frankfurt, *Germany,* 60 G4
Franz Josef Land, *Russia,* 52 C1
Fraser Island, *Australia,* 39 K5
Fredericton, *Canada, internal capital,* 23 N4
Fredrikstad, *Norway,* 58 D4
Freeport City, *The Bahamas,* 25 L5
Freetown, *Sierra Leone, national capital,* 69 C7
Freiburg, *Germany,* 60 F4
French Guiana, *South America, dependency,* 31 H3
French Polynesia, *Oceania, dependency,* 37 J6
Fresno, *U.S.A.,* 24 C3
Frisian Islands, *Europe,* 60 F3
Froya, *Norway,* 58 D3
Fuerteventura, *Canary Islands,* 68 B3
Fuji, Mount, *Japan,* 47 N3
Fukui, *Japan,* 47 N3
Fukuoka, *Japan,* 47 M4
Fukushima, *Japan,* 47 P3
Funafuti, *Tuvalu, national capital,* 36 E5
Funchal, *Madeira,* 68 B2
Furnas Reservoir, *Brazil,* 32 J4
Fushun, *China,* 47 K2
Fuxin, *China,* 47 K2
Fyn, *Denmark,* 59 D5

## g
Gabes, *Tunisia,* 66 D2
Gabes, Gulf of, *Africa,* 66 D2
Gabon, *Africa, country,* 70 B4
Gaborone, *Botswana, national capital,* 72 E4
Gafsa, *Tunisia,* 66 C2
Gagnoa, *Ivory Coast,* 69 D7
Gairdner, Lake, *Australia,* 38 F6
Galapagos Islands, *Ecuador,* 30 N9
Galati, *Romania,* 63 J2
Galdhopiggen, *Norway,* 58 D3
Galle, *Sri Lanka,* 49 E9
Gallinas, Cape, *Colombia,* 30 D1
Galveston, *U.S.A.,* 25 H5
Galway, *Ireland,* 60 B3
Gambela, *Ethiopia,* 71 F2

Gambia, The, *Africa, country,* 69 B6
Ganca, *Azerbaijan,* 50 E3
Gander, *Canada,* 23 P4
Ganges, *Asia,* 48 E5
Ganges, Mouths of the, *Asia,* 49 F6
Ganzhou, *China,* 47 H5
Gao, *Mali,* 69 F5
Garda, Lake, *Italy,* 62 D2
Garissa, *Kenya,* 71 G4
Garonne, *France,* 61 E5
Garoua, *Cameroon,* 70 B2
Gaspe, *Canada,* 23 N4
Gatchina, *Russia,* 58 J4
Gavle, *Sweden,* 58 F3
Gaza, *Israel,* 51 B5
Gaziantep, *Turkey,* 50 C4
Gdansk, *Poland,* 59 F5
Gdansk, Gulf of, *Poland,* 59 F5
Gdynia, *Poland,* 59 F5
Gedaref, *Sudan,* 67 J6
Geelong, *Australia,* 38 H7
Gejiu, *China,* 46 F6
Gemena, *Democratic Republic of Congo,* 70 C3
General Roca, *Argentina,* 33 E7
General Santos, *Philippines,* 45 J6
General Villegas, *Argentina,* 32 F7
Geneva, *Switzerland,* 62 C2
Geneva, Lake, *Europe,* 62 C2
Genoa, *Italy,* 62 D2
Genoa, Gulf of, *Italy,* 62 D2
Gent, *Belgium,* 60 E4
Georgetown, *Guyana, national capital,* 31 G2
George Town, *Malaysia,* 42 B2
Georgia, *Asia, country,* 50 D3
Georgia, *U.S.A., internal admin. area,* 25 K4
Gera, *Germany,* 60 H4
Geraldton, *Australia,* 38 B5
Gerlachovsky stit, *Slovakia,* 59 G6
Germany, *Europe, country,* 60 G4
Gerona, *Spain,* 61 G6
Ghadamis, *Libya,* 66 C2
Ghana, *Africa, country,* 69 E7
Ghardaia, *Algeria,* 68 F2
Gharyan, *Libya,* 66 D2
Ghat, *Libya,* 66 D3
Gibraltar, *Europe,* 61 C7
Gibson Desert, *Australia,* 38 E4
Gijon, *Spain,* 61 C6
Gilbert Islands, *Kiribati,* 36 E5
Gilgit, *Pakistan,* 48 C3
Girardeau, Cape, *U.S.A.,* 25 J3
Giza, Pyramids of, *Egypt,* 67 H3
Gladstone, *Australia,* 39 K4
Glama, *Norway,* 58 D3
Glasgow, *United Kingdom,* 60 C3
Glazov, *Russia,* 57 G2
Glorioso Islands, *Africa,* 73 J2
Gloucester, *United Kingdom,* 60 D4
Gobabis, *Namibia,* 72 C4
Gobi Desert, *Asia,* 46 F2
Gochas, *Namibia,* 72 C4
Godavari, *India,* 49 D7
Gode, *Ethiopia,* 71 H2
Goiania, *Brazil,* 32 J3
Gold Coast, *Australia,* 39 K5
Golmud, *China,* 48 G3
Goma, *Democratic Republic of Congo,* 70 E4
Gonaives, *Haiti,* 27 K4
Gonder, *Ethiopia,* 71 G1
Gongga Shan, *China,* 46 F5
Good Hope, Cape of, *South Africa,* 72 C6
Goose Lake, *U.S.A.,* 24 B2
Gorakhpur, *India,* 49 E5
Gorgan, *Iran,* 50 F4
Gori, *Georgia,* 50 D3
Gorki Reservoir, *Russia,* 56 E2
Gorontalo, *Indonesia,* 43 F3
Gorzow Wielkopolski, *Poland,* 59 E5
Gothenburg, *Sweden,* 59 E4
Gotland, *Sweden,* 59 F4
Gottingen, *Germany,* 60 G4

Gouin Reservoir, *Canada,* 25 L1
Goundam, *Mali,* 69 E5
Governador Valadares, *Brazil,* 32 K3
Graaff-Reinet, *South Africa,* 72 D6
Grafton, *Australia,* 39 K5
Grahamstown, *South Africa,* 72 E6
Granada, *Spain,* 61 D7
Gran Canaria, *Canary Islands,* 68 B3
Gran Chaco, *South America,* 32 F4
Grand Bahama, *The Bahamas,* 25 L5
Grand Canal, *China,* 47 J4
Grand Canyon, *U.S.A.,* 24 D3
Grand Comoro, *Comoros,* 73 H2
Grande Bay, *Argentina,* 33 E10
Grande Prairie, *Canada,* 22 H3
Grand Forks, *U.S.A.,* 25 G1
Grand Island, *U.S.A.,* 24 G2
Grand Junction, *U.S.A.,* 24 E3
Grand Rapids, *Canada,* 23 K3
Grand Rapids, *U.S.A.,* 25 J2
Grand Teton, *U.S.A.,* 24 D2
Graskop, *South Africa,* 72 F5
Graz, *Austria,* 62 E2
Great Australian Bight, *Australia,* 38 F6
Great Barrier Reef, *Australia,* 38 J3
Great Basin, *U.S.A.,* 24 C2
Great Bear Lake, *Canada,* 22 G2
Great Dividing Range, *Australia,* 39 J6
Greater Antilles, *North America,* 27 J4
Greater Khingan Range, *China,* 47 J1
Greater Sunda Islands, *Asia,* 42 C4
Great Eastern Erg, *Algeria,* 68 G3
Great Falls, *U.S.A.,* 24 D1
Great Inagua, *The Bahamas,* 27 K3
Great Karoo, *South Africa,* 72 D6
Great Plains, *U.S.A.,* 24 F2
Great Rift Valley, *Africa,* 71 F5
Great Salt Desert, *Iran,* 50 F5
Great Salt Lake, *U.S.A.,* 24 D2
Great Salt Lake Desert, *U.S.A.,* 24 D2
Great Sandy Desert, *Australia,* 38 D4
Great Slave Lake, *Canada,* 22 H2
Great Victoria Desert, *Australia,* 38 D5
Great Wall of China, *China,* 46 F3
Great Western Erg, *Algeria,* 68 E2
Greece, *Europe, country,* 63 G4
Green Bay, *U.S.A.,* 25 J2
Greenland, *North America, dependency,* 75 P3
Greenland Sea, *Atlantic Ocean,* 75 M3
Greensboro, *U.S.A.,* 25 L3
Greenville, *U.S.A.,* 25 H4
Grenada, *North America, country,* 26 M5
Grenoble, *France,* 61 F5
Griffith, *Australia,* 38 J6
Groningen, *Netherlands,* 60 F3
Groot, *South Africa,* 72 D6
Groote Eylandt, *Australia,* 38 G2
Grossglockner, *Austria,* 62 E2
Groznyy, *Russia,* 50 E3
Grudziadz, *Poland,* 59 F5
Grunau, *Namibia,* 72 C5
Grytviken, *South Georgia,* 33 L10
Guadalajara, *Mexico,* 26 D4
Guadalquivir, *Spain,* 61 C7
Guadalupe Island, *Mexico,* 26 A2
Guadeloupe, *North America,* 26 M4
Guadiana, *Europe,* 61 C7
Gualeguaychu, *Argentina,* 32 G6
Guam, *Oceania,* 36 B3
Guangzhou, *China,* 47 H6
Guantanamo, *Cuba,* 27 J3
Guarapuava, *Brazil,* 32 H5
Guardafui, Cape, *Somalia,* 71 K1
Guatemala, *North America, country,* 26 F4
Guatemala City, *Guatemala, national capital,* 26 F5
Guaviare, *Colombia,* 30 E3
Guayaquil, *Ecuador,* 30 C4
Guayaquil, Gulf of, *Ecuador,* 30 B4
Gueckedou, *Guinea,* 69 C7
Guelma, *Algeria,* 62 C4
Guiana Highlands, *Venezuela,* 30 E2
Guilin, *China,* 46 H5
Guinea, *Africa, country,* 69 C6

Guinea-Bissau, *Africa, country,* 69 B6
Guinea, Gulf of, *Africa,* 69 F8
Guiria, *Venezuela,* 30 F1
Guiyang, *China,* 46 G5
Gujranwala, *Pakistan,* 48 C4
Gujrat, *Pakistan,* 48 C4
Gulbarga, *India,* 49 D7
Gulf, The, *Asia,* 51 F6
Gulu, *Uganda,* 71 F3
Gunnbjorns Mountain, *Greenland,* 75 N2
Gunung Kerinci, *Indonesia,* 42 B4
Gunung Tahan, *Malaysia,* 42 B3
Gurupi, *Brazil,* 32 J2
Gusau, *Nigeria,* 69 G6
Guwahati, *India,* 48 G5
Guyana, *South America, country,* 31 G2
Gwalior, *India,* 48 D5
Gweru, *Zimbabwe,* 72 E3
Gympie, *Australia,* 39 K5
Gyor, *Hungary,* 59 F7

## h
Haapsalu, *Estonia,* 58 G4
Haarlem, *Netherlands,* 60 F3
Hadhramaut, *Yemen,* 51 E9
Ha Giang, *Vietnam,* 44 E3
Hague, The, *Netherlands, national capital,* 60 F3
Haifa, *Israel,* 50 B5
Haikou, *China,* 46 H6
Hail, *Saudi Arabia,* 51 D6
Hailar, *China,* 47 J1
Hainan, *China,* 46 H7
Hai Phong, *Vietnam,* 44 E3
Haiti, *North America, country,* 27 K4
Hakodate, *Japan,* 47 P2
Halifax, *Canada, internal capital,* 23 N4
Halmahera, *Indonesia,* 43 G3
Halmstad, *Sweden,* 59 E4
Hamadan, *Iran,* 50 E5
Hamah, *Syria,* 50 C4
Hamamatsu, *Japan,* 47 N4
Hamburg, *Germany,* 60 G3
Hameenlinna, *Finland,* 58 H3
Hamhung, *North Korea,* 47 L3
Hami, *China,* 48 G2
Hamilton, *Canada,* 23 M4
Hamilton, *New Zealand,* 39 Q7
Hammerfest, *Norway,* 58 G1
Handan, *China,* 47 H3
Hangzhou, *China,* 47 K4
Hannover, *Germany,* 60 G3
Hanoi, *Vietnam, national capital,* 44 E3
Happy Valley-Goose Bay, *Canada,* 23 N3
Haradh, *Saudi Arabia,* 51 E7
Harare, *Zimbabwe, national capital,* 72 F3
Harbin, *China,* 47 L1
Harer, *Ethiopia,* 71 H2
Hargeysa, *Somalia,* 71 H2
Harney Basin, *U.S.A.,* 24 C2
Harper, *Liberia,* 69 D8
Harrisburg, *U.S.A., internal capital,* 25 L2
Harrismith, *South Africa,* 72 E5
Hartford, *U.S.A., internal capital,* 25 M2
Hatteras, Cape, *U.S.A.,* 25 L3
Hattiesburg, *U.S.A.,* 25 J4
Hat Yai, *Thailand,* 44 D6
Hauki Lake, *Finland,* 58 J3
Havana, *Cuba, national capital,* 27 H3
Hawaii, *Pacific Ocean, internal admin. area,* 25 P7
Hawaiian Islands, *Pacific Ocean,* 25 P7
Hebrides, *United Kingdom,* 60 C2
Hefei, *China,* 47 J4
Hegang, *China,* 47 M1
Hejaz, *Saudi Arabia,* 51 C6
Helena, *U.S.A., internal capital,* 24 D1
Helmand, *Asia,* 48 B4
Helsingborg, *Sweden,* 59 E4
Helsinki, *Finland, national capital,* 58 H3
Hengyang, *China,* 46 H5
Henzada, *Burma,* 44 C4
Herat, *Afghanistan,* 48 A4
Hermosillo, *Mexico,* 26 B2
Hiiumaa, *Estonia,* 58 G4
Hilo, *U.S.A.,* 25 P8

Himalayas, *Asia*, 48 E4
Hindu Kush, *Asia*, 48 B3
Hinton, *Canada*, 22 H3
Hiroshima, *Japan*, 47 M4
Hispaniola, *North America*, 27 K4
Hitra, *Norway*, 58 D3
Hobart, *Australia, internal capital*, 38 J8
Ho Chi Minh City, *Vietnam*, 44 E5
Hohhot, *China*, 46 H2
Hokkaido, *Japan*, 47 P2
Holguin, *Cuba*, 27 J3
Homs, *Syria*, 50 C5
Homyel, *Belarus*, 59 J5
Honduras, *North America, country*, 27 G4
Honduras, Gulf of, *North America*, 27 G4
Honefoss, *Norway*, 58 D3
Hong Kong, *China*, 47 H6
Honiara, *Solomon Islands, national capital*, 36 D5
Honolulu, *U.S.A., internal capital*, 25 P7
Honshu, *Japan*, 47 N3
Horlivka, *Ukraine*, 56 D4
Hormuz, Strait of, *Asia*, 51 G6
Horn, Cape, *Chile*, 33 D11
Horn Lake, *Sweden*, 58 F2
Hotan, *China*, 48 D3
Hotazel, *South Africa*, 72 D5
Houston, *U.S.A.*, 25 G5
Hradec Kralove, *Czech Republic*, 62 E1
Hrodna, *Belarus*, 59 G5
Huacrachuco, *Peru*, 30 C5
Huaihua, *China*, 46 H5
Huang He, *China*, 47 H3
Huambo, *Angola*, 72 C2
Huancayo, *Peru*, 30 C6
Huanuco, *Peru*, 30 C5
Huascaran, Mount, *Peru*, 30 C5
Hubli, *India*, 49 D7
Hudiksvall, *Sweden*, 58 F3
Hudson Bay, *Canada*, 23 L3
Hudson Strait, *Canada*, 23 M2
Hue, *Vietnam*, 44 E4
Huelva, *Spain*, 61 C7
Hull, *United Kingdom*, 60 D3
Hulun Lake, *China*, 47 J1
Hungary, *Europe, country*, 59 F7
Huntsville, *Canada*, 23 M4
Huntsville, *U.S.A.*, 25 J4
Hurghada, *Egypt*, 67 H3
Huron, Lake, *U.S.A.*, 25 K2
Hvannadalshnukur, *Iceland*, 58 P2
Hwange, *Zimbabwe*, 72 E3
Hyderabad, *India*, 49 D7
Hyderabad, *Pakistan*, 48 B5
Hyesan, *North Korea*, 47 L2

## i

Iasi, *Romania*, 63 H2
Ibadan, *Nigeria*, 69 F7
Ibague, *Colombia*, 30 C3
Ibarra, *Ecuador*, 30 C3
Ibb, *Yemen*, 51 D9
Iberian Mountains, *Spain*, 61 D6
Ibiza, *Spain*, 61 E7
Ica, *Peru*, 30 C6
Iceland, *Europe, country*, 58 P2
Idaho, *U.S.A., internal admin. area*, 24 C2
Idaho Falls, *U.S.A.*, 24 D2
Ierapetra, *Greece*, 63 H5
Iguacu Falls, *South America*, 32 H5
Ihosy, *Madagascar*, 73 J4
Ikopa, *Madagascar*, 73 J3
Ilagan, *Philippines*, 45 H4
Ilebo, *Democratic Republic of Congo*, 70 D4
Ilheus, *Brazil*, 32 L2
Iliamna Lake, *U.S.A.*, 22 D2
Iligan, *Philippines*, 45 H6
Illapel, *Chile*, 32 D6
Illimani, Mount, *Bolivia*, 32 E3
Illinois, *U.S.A., internal admin. area*, 25 J2
Illizi, *Algeria*, 68 G3
Ilmen, Lake, *Russia*, 58 J4
Iloilo, *Philippines*, 45 H5
Ilonga, *Tanzania*, 71 G5
Ilorin, *Nigeria*, 69 F7

Imperatriz, *Brazil*, 31 J5
Imphal, *India*, 49 G6
Inari, Lake, *Finland*, 58 H1
Inchon, *South Korea*, 47 L3
Indals, *Sweden*, 58 E3
Inderbor, *Kazakhstan*, 57 G4
India, *Asia, country*, 49 D6
Indiana, *U.S.A., internal admin. area*, 25 J2
Indianapolis, *U.S.A., internal capital*, 25 J3
Indian Ocean, 19
Indonesia, *Asia, country*, 42 C5
Indore, *India*, 49 D6
Indus, *Asia*, 48 B5
Ingolstadt, *Germany*, 60 G4
Inhambane, *Mozambique*, 73 G4
Inner Mongolia, *China*, 47 H2
Innsbruck, *Austria*, 62 D2
Inukjuak, *Canada*, 23 M3
Inuvik, *Canada*, 22 F2
Invercargill, *New Zealand*, 39 N9
Inyangani, *Zimbabwe*, 73 F3
Ioannina, *Greece*, 63 G4
Ionian Sea, *Europe*, 63 F4
Iowa, *U.S.A., internal admin. area*, 25 H2
Ipiales, *Colombia*, 30 C3
Ipoh, *Malaysia*, 42 B3
Ipswich, *United Kingdom*, 60 E3
Iqaluit, *Canada, internal capital*, 23 N2
Iquique, *Chile*, 32 D5
Iquitos, *Peru*, 30 D4
Irakleio, *Greece*, 63 H5
Iran, *Asia, country*, 50 F5
Iranshahr, *Iran*, 51 H6
Iraq, *Asia, country*, 50 D5
Irbid, *Jordan*, 50 C5
Ireland, *Europe, country*, 60 B3
Iringa, *Tanzania*, 71 G5
Irish Sea, *Europe*, 60 C3
Irkutsk, *Russia*, 53 F3
Irrawaddy, *Burma*, 44 C4
Irrawaddy, Mouths of the, *Burma*, 44 B4
Irtysh, *Asia*, 52 D3
Isabela, *Ecuador*, 30 N10
Isafjordhur, *Iceland*, 58 N2
Isiro, *Democratic Republic of Congo*, 70 E3
Islamabad, *Pakistan, national capital*, 48 C4
Isle of Man, *Europe*, 60 C3
Isle of Wight, *United Kingdom*, 60 D4
Ismailia, *Egypt*, 67 H2
Isoka, *Zambia*, 73 F2
Isparta, *Turkey*, 63 J4
Israel, *Asia, country*, 51 B5
Issyk, Lake, *Kyrgyzstan*, 48 D2
Istanbul, *Turkey*, 63 J3
Itaituba, *Brazil*, 31 G4
Itajai, *Brazil*, 32 J5
Italy, *Europe, country*, 62 D2
Itapetininga, *Brazil*, 32 J4
Ivano-Frankivsk, *Ukraine*, 59 H6
Ivanovo, *Russia*, 56 E2
Ivdel, *Russia*, 57 J1
Ivory Coast, *Africa, country*, 69 D7
Ivujivik, *Canada*, 23 M2
Izhevsk, *Russia*, 57 G2
Izmir, *Turkey*, 63 H4

## j

Jabalpur, *India*, 49 D6
Jackson, *Mississippi, U.S.A., internal capital*, 25 H4
Jackson, *Tennessee, U.S.A.*, 25 J3
Jacksonville, *U.S.A.*, 25 K4
Jaen, *Spain*, 61 D7
Jaffna, *Sri Lanka*, 49 E9
Jaipur, *India*, 48 D5
Jakarta, *Indonesia, national capital*, 42 C5
Jalalabad, *Afghanistan*, 48 C4
Jalal-Abad, *Kyrgyzstan*, 48 C2
Jamaica, *North America, country*, 27 J4
Jambi, *Indonesia*, 42 B4
James Bay, *Canada*, 23 L3
Jamestown, *U.S.A.*, 25 L2

Jammu, *India*, 48 C4
Jammu and Kashmir, *Asia*, 48 D4
Jamnagar, *India*, 49 C6
Jamshedpur, *India*, 49 F6
Japan, *Asia, country*, 47 N3
Japan, Sea of, *Asia*, 47 M2
Japura, *Brazil*, 30 E4
Jatai, *Brazil*, 32 H3
Java, *Indonesia*, 42 C5
Java Sea, *Indonesia*, 42 C5
Jayapura, *Indonesia*, 43 K4
Jedda, *Saudi Arabia*, 51 C7
Jefferson City, *U.S.A., internal capital*, 25 H3
Jekabpils, *Latvia*, 59 H4
Jelgava, *Latvia*, 59 G4
Jember, *Indonesia*, 42 D5
Jerba, *Tunisia*, 66 D2
Jerez de la Frontera, *Spain*, 61 C7
Jerusalem, *Israel, national capital*, 51 C5
Jhansi, *India*, 48 D5
Jiamusi, *China*, 47 M1
Jilin, *China*, 47 L2
Jinhua, *China*, 47 J5
Jining, *China*, 47 J3
Jinja, *Uganda*, 71 F3
Jinzhou, *China*, 47 K2
Jixi, *China*, 47 M1
Jizzax, *Uzbekistan*, 48 B2
Joao Pessoa, *Brazil*, 31 M5
Jodhpur, *India*, 48 C5
Johannesburg, *South Africa*, 72 E5
Johnston Atoll, *Oceania*, 36 G3
Johor Bahru, *Malaysia*, 42 B3
Jolo, *Philippines*, 45 H6
Jonesboro, *U.S.A.*, 25 H3
Jonkoping, *Sweden*, 59 E4
Jordan, *Asia, country*, 51 C5
Jorhat, *India*, 48 G5
Jos, *Nigeria*, 70 A2
Juan de Nova, *Africa*, 73 H3
Juazeiro, *Brazil*, 31 K5
Juazeiro do Norte, *Brazil*, 31 L5
Juba, *Africa*, 71 H3
Juba, *Sudan*, 71 F3
Juchitan, *Mexico*, 26 E4
Juiz de Fora, *Brazil*, 32 K4
Juliaca, *Peru*, 30 D7
Juneau, *U.S.A., internal capital*, 22 F3
Jurmala, *Latvia*, 59 G4
Jurua, *Brazil*, 30 E5
Jutland, *Europe*, 59 D4
Jyvaskyla, *Finland*, 58 H3

## k

K2, *Asia*, 48 D3
Kaamanen, *Finland*, 58 H1
Kabinda, *Democratic Republic of Congo*, 70 D5
Kabul, *Afghanistan, national capital*, 48 B4
Kabunda, *Democratic Republic of Congo*, 70 E6
Kabwe, *Zambia*, 72 E2
Kadoma, *Zimbabwe*, 72 E3
Kaduna, *Nigeria*, 69 G6
Kaedi, *Mauritania*, 69 C5
Kafakumba, *Democratic Republic of Congo*, 70 D5
Kafue, *Zambia*, 72 E3
Kagoshima, *Japan*, 47 M4
Kahramanmaras, *Turkey*, 50 C4
Kahului, *U.S.A.*, 25 P7
Kainji Reservoir, *Nigeria*, 69 F6
Kairouan, *Tunisia*, 66 D1
Kajaani, *Finland*, 58 H2
Kakhovske Reservoir, *Ukraine*, 56 C4
Kalahari Desert, *Africa*, 72 D4
Kalamata, *Greece*, 63 G4
Kalemie, *Democratic Republic of Congo*, 70 E5
Kalgoorlie, *Australia*, 38 D6
Kaliningrad, *Russia*, 59 G5
Kalisz, *Poland*, 59 F6
Kalkrand, *Namibia*, 72 C4

Kalmar, *Sweden*, 59 F4
Kaluga, *Russia*, 56 D3
Kamanjab, *Namibia*, 72 B3
Kama Reservoir, *Russia*, 57 H2
Kamativi, *Zimbabwe*, 72 E3
Kamchatka Peninsula, *Russia*, 53 H3
Kamenka, *Russia*, 56 E3
Kamina, *Democratic Republic of Congo*, 70 E5
Kamloops, *Canada*, 22 G3
Kampala, *Uganda, national capital*, 71 F3
Kampong Cham, *Cambodia*, 44 E5
Kampong Chhnang, *Cambodia*, 44 D5
Kampong Saom, *Cambodia*, 44 D5
Kamyanets-Podilskyy, *Ukraine*, 59 H6
Kamyshin, *Russia*, 56 F3
Kananga, *Democratic Republic of Congo*, 70 D5
Kanazawa, *Japan*, 47 N3
Kandahar, *Afghanistan*, 48 B4
Kandalaksha, *Russia*, 58 K2
Kandi, *Benin*, 69 F6
Kandy, *Sri Lanka*, 49 E9
Kang, *Botswana*, 72 D4
Kangaroo Island, *Australia*, 38 G7
Kanggye, *North Korea*, 47 L2
Kankan, *Guinea*, 69 D6
Kano, *Nigeria*, 66 C6
Kanpur, *India*, 48 E5
Kansas, *U.S.A., internal admin. area*, 24 G3
Kansas City, *U.S.A.*, 25 H3
Kanye, *Botswana*, 72 E4
Kaohsiung, *Taiwan*, 47 K6
Kaolack, *Senegal*, 69 B6
Kara-Balta, *Kyrgyzstan*, 48 C2
Karabuk, *Turkey*, 63 K3
Karachi, *Pakistan*, 49 B6
Karaj, *Iran*, 50 F4
Karakol, *Kyrgyzstan*, 48 D2
Karakorum Range, *Asia*, 48 D3
Kara Kum Desert, *Turkmenistan*, 50 G3
Karaman, *Turkey*, 63 K4
Karamay, *China*, 48 E1
Kara Sea, *Russia*, 52 D2
Kariba, *Zimbabwe*, 72 E3
Kariba, Lake, *Africa*, 72 E3
Karibib, *Namibia*, 72 C4
Karimata Strait, *Indonesia*, 42 C4
Karlovac, *Croatia*, 62 E2
Karlovy Vary, *Czech Republic*, 62 E1
Karlshamn, *Sweden*, 59 E4
Karlsruhe, *Germany*, 60 G4
Karlstad, *Sweden*, 58 E4
Karmoy, *Norway*, 58 C4
Karonga, *Malawi*, 73 F1
Karora, *Eritrea*, 67 J5
Karpathos, *Greece*, 63 H5
Karratha, *Australia*, 38 C4
Kasai, *Africa*, 70 C4
Kasama, *Zambia*, 72 F2
Kashi, *China*, 48 D3
Kassala, *Sudan*, 67 J5
Kassel, *Germany*, 60 G4
Kasungu, *Malawi*, 73 F2
Kataba, *Zambia*, 72 E3
Kathmandu, *Nepal, national capital*, 48 F5
Katiola, *Ivory Coast*, 69 D7
Katowice, *Poland*, 59 F6
Katsina, *Nigeria*, 69 G6
Kattegat, *Europe*, 59 D4
Kauai, *U.S.A.*, 25 P7
Kaukau Veld, *Africa*, 72 C4
Kaunas, *Lithuania*, 59 G5
Kavala, *Greece*, 63 H3
Kawambwa, *Zambia*, 72 E1
Kayes, *Mali*, 69 C6
Kayseri, *Turkey*, 50 C4
Kazakhstan, *Asia, country*, 52 C3
Kazan, *Russia*, 57 F2
Kaztalovka, *Kazakhstan*, 57 F4
Kebnekaise, *Sweden*, 58 F2
Kecskemet, *Hungary*, 59 F7
Kedougou, *Senegal*, 69 C6
Keetmanshoop, *Namibia*, 72 C5

Liverpool, *United Kingdom*, 60 D3
Livingstone, *Zambia*, 72 E3
Livorno, *Italy*, 62 D3
Liwale, *Tanzania*, 71 G5
Ljubljana, *Slovenia, national capital*, 62 E2
Llanos, *South America*, 30 D2
Lloydminster, *Canada*, 22 J3
Lobamba, *Lesotho, national capital*, 72 F5
Lodz, *Poland*, 59 F6
Lofoten, *Norway*, 58 E1
Logan, Mount, *Canada*, 22 F2
Logrono, *Spain*, 61 D6
Loire, *France*, 60 E5
Loja, *Ecuador*, 30 C4
Lokan Reservoir, *Finland*, 58 H2
Lolland, *Denmark*, 59 D5
Lombok, *Indonesia*, 42 E5
Lome, *Togo, national capital*, 69 F7
London, *Canada*, 23 L4
London, *United Kingdom, national capital*, 60 D4
Londonderry, *United Kingdom*, 60 C3
Londrina, *Brazil*, 32 H4
Long Island, *The Bahamas*, 25 L6
Long Xuyen, *Vietnam*, 44 E5
Lopez, Cape, *Gabon*, 70 A4
Lop Lake, *China*, 48 G2
Lord Howe Island, *Australia*, 39 L6
Los Angeles, *Chile*, 33 D7
Los Angeles, *U.S.A.*, 24 C4
Los Mochis, *Mexico*, 26 C2
Louangphrabang, *Laos*, 44 D4
Loubomo, *Congo*, 70 B4
Louga, *Senegal*, 69 B5
Louisiana, *U.S.A., internal admin. area*, 25 H4
Lower California, *Mexico*, 26 B2
Loyalty Islands, *New Caledonia*, 39 N4
Luacano, *Angola*, 72 D2
Luanda, *Angola, national capital*, 72 B1
Luangwa, *Africa*, 72 F2
Luanshya, *Zambia*, 72 E2
Lubango, *Angola*, 72 B2
Lubbock, *U.S.A.*, 24 F4
Lublin, *Poland*, 59 G6
Lubny, *Ukraine*, 56 C3
Lubumbashi, *Democratic Republic of Congo*, 70 E6
Lucena, *Philippines*, 45 H5
Lucerne, *Switzerland*, 62 D2
Lucira, *Angola*, 72 B2
Lucknow, *India*, 48 E5
Luderitz, *Namibia*, 72 C5
Ludhiana, *India*, 48 D4
Ludza, *Latvia*, 59 H4
Luena, *Angola*, 72 C2
Luganville, *Vanuatu*, 39 N3
Lugo, *Spain*, 61 C6
Luhansk, *Ukraine*, 56 D4
Luiana, *Angola*, 72 D3
Lukulu, *Zambia*, 72 D2
Lumbala Kaquengue, *Angola*, 72 D2
Lumbala Nguimbo, *Angola*, 72 D2
Lundazi, *Zambia*, 73 F2
Lupilichi, *Mozambique*, 73 G2
Lusaka, *Zambia, national capital*, 72 E3
Lutsk, *Ukraine*, 59 H6
Luxembourg, *Europe, country*, 60 F4
Luxembourg, *Luxembourg, national capital*, 60 F4
Luxor, *Egypt*, 67 H3
Luzhou, *China*, 46 G5
Luzon, *Philippines*, 45 H4
Luzon Strait, *Philippines*, 45 H4
Lviv, *Ukraine*, 59 H6
Lyon, *France*, 61 F5
Lysychansk, *Ukraine*, 56 D4

### m

Maan, *Jordan*, 51 C5
Maastricht, *Netherlands*, 60 F4
Macae, *Brazil*, 32 K4
Macapa, *Brazil*, 31 H3
Macau, *China*, 47 H6

Macedonia, *Europe, country*, 63 G3
Maceio, *Brazil*, 31 L5
Machakos, *Kenya*, 71 G4
Machala, *Ecuador*, 30 C4
Machu Picchu, *Peru*, 30 D6
Mackay, *Australia*, 39 J4
Mackenzie, *Canada*, 22 G2
Mackenzie Bay, *Canada*, 22 F2
Mackenzie Mountains, *Canada*, 22 F2
Macon, *U.S.A.*, 25 K4
Madagascar, *Africa, country*, 73 J4
Madang, *Papua New Guinea*, 43 L5
Madeira, *Atlantic Ocean*, 68 B2
Madeira, *Brazil*, 30 F5
Madingou, *Congo*, 70 B4
Madison, *U.S.A., internal capital*, 25 J2
Madras, *India*, 49 E8
Madrid, *Spain, national capital*, 61 D6
Madurai, *India*, 49 D9
Maevatanana, *Madagascar*, 73 J3
Mafeteng, *Lesotho*, 72 E5
Mafia Island, *Tanzania*, 71 H5
Magadan, *Russia*, 53 H3
Magangue, *Colombia*, 30 D2
Magdalena, *Bolivia*, 32 F2
Magdeburg, *Germany*, 60 G3
Magellan, Strait of, *South America*, 33 E10
Magnitogorsk, *Russia*, 57 H3
Mahajanga, *Madagascar*, 73 J3
Mahalapye, *Botswana*, 72 E4
Mahilyow, *Belarus*, 59 J5
Mahon, *Spain*, 61 F7
Maiduguri, *Nigeria*, 66 D6
Mai-Ndombe, Lake, *Democratic Republic of Congo*, 70 C4
Maine, *U.S.A., internal admin. area*, 25 N1
Maine, Gulf of, *U.S.A.*, 25 N2
Maio, *Cape Verde*, 69 M11
Majorca, *Spain*, 61 E7
Majuro, *Marshall Islands, national capital*, 36 F4
Makarikari, *Botswana*, 72 D4
Makassar Strait, *Indonesia*, 43 E4
Makeni, *Sierra Leone*, 69 C7
Makgadikgadi Pans, *Botswana*, 72 D4
Makhachkala, *Russia*, 50 E3
Makkovik, *Canada*, 23 P3
Makokou, *Gabon*, 70 B3
Makumbako, *Tanzania*, 71 F5
Makurdi, *Nigeria*, 70 A2
Mala, *Peru*, 30 C6
Malabo, *Equatorial Guinea, national capital*, 70 A3
Maladzyechna, *Belarus*, 59 H5
Malaga, *Spain*, 61 C7
Malaimbandy, *Madagascar*, 73 J4
Malakal, *Sudan*, 71 F2
Malakula, *Vanuatu*, 39 N3
Malang, *Indonesia*, 42 D5
Malanje, *Angola*, 72 C1
Malar, Lake, *Sweden*, 58 F4
Malatya, *Turkey*, 50 C4
Malawi, *Africa, country*, 73 J4
Malawi, Lake, *Africa*, 71 F6
Malaysia, *Asia, country*, 42 B2
Maldives, *Asia, country*, 49 C9
Male, *Maldives, national capital*, 49 C10
Malegaon, *India*, 49 C6
Mali, *Africa, country*, 68 E5
Malindi, *Kenya*, 71 H4
Malmo, *Sweden*, 59 E5
Malpelo Island, *Colombia*, 30 B3
Malta, *Europe, country*, 62 E4
Mamoudzou, *Mayotte*, 73 J2
Mamuno, *Botswana*, 72 D4
Man, *Ivory Coast*, 69 D7
Manado, *Indonesia*, 43 F3
Managua, *Nicaragua, national capital*, 27 G5
Manakara, *Madagascar*, 73 J4
Manama, *Bahrain, national capital*, 51 F6
Manaus, *Brazil*, 31 G4
Manchester, *United Kingdom*, 60 D3
Manchuria, *China*, 47 K2
Mandalay, *Burma*, 44 C3

Mandera, *Kenya*, 71 H3
Mandritsara, *Madagascar*, 73 J3
Mandurah, *Australia*, 38 C6
Mangalore, *India*, 49 C8
Mania, *Madagascar*, 73 J3
Manicouagan Reservoir, *Canada*, 23 N3
Manila, *Philippines, national capital*, 45 H5
Manisa, *Turkey*, 63 H4
Man, Isle of, *Europe*, 60 C3
Manitoba, *Canada, internal admin. area*, 23 K3
Manitoba, Lake, *Canada*, 23 K3
Manizales, *Colombia*, 30 C2
Manja, *Madagascar*, 73 H4
Mannar, *Sri Lanka*, 49 E9
Mannar, Gulf of, *Asia*, 49 D9
Mannheim, *Germany*, 60 G4
Mansa, *Zambia*, 72 E2
Manta, *Ecuador*, 30 B4
Manzhouli, *China*, 53 F3
Mao, *Chad*, 66 E6
Maoke Range, *Indonesia*, 43 J4
Maputo, *Mozambique, national capital*, 73 F5
Maraba, *Brazil*, 31 J5
Maracaibo, *Venezuela*, 30 D1
Maracaibo, Lake, *Venezuela*, 30 D2
Maracay, *Venezuela*, 30 E1
Maradi, *Niger*, 66 C6
Maranon, *Peru*, 30 C4
Marathon, *Canada*, 23 L4
Mar del Plata, *Argentina*, 33 G7
Margarita Island, *Venezuela*, 30 F1
Margherita Peak, *Africa*, 70 E3
Marib, *Yemen*, 51 E8
Maribor, *Slovenia*, 62 E2
Marie Byrd Land, *Antarctica*, 77 Q3
Mariental, *Namibia*, 72 C4
Marijampole, *Lithuania*, 59 G5
Marilia, *Brazil*, 32 J4
Marimba, *Angola*, 72 C1
Mariupol, *Ukraine*, 56 D4
Marka, *Somalia*, 71 H3
Marmara, Sea of, *Turkey*, 63 J3
Maroantsetra, *Madagascar*, 73 J3
Maroua, *Cameroon*, 70 B1
Marquesas Islands, *French Polynesia*, 37 K5
Marrakech, *Morocco*, 68 D2
Marra, Mount, *Sudan*, 66 F6
Marsa Matruh, *Egypt*, 67 G2
Marseille, *France*, 61 F6
Marshall Islands, *Oceania, country*, 36 D3
Martapura, *Indonesia*, 42 D4
Martinique, *North America*, 26 M5
Mary, *Turkmenistan*, 50 H4
Maryland, *U.S.A., internal admin. area*, 25 L3
Masaka, *Uganda*, 71 F4
Masasi, *Tanzania*, 71 G6
Masbate, *Philippines*, 45 H5
Maseru, *Lesotho, national capital*, 72 E5
Mashhad, *Iran*, 50 G4
Masirah Island, *Oman*, 51 G7
Massachusetts, *U.S.A., internal admin. area*, 25 M2
Massangena, *Mozambique*, 73 F4
Massawa, *Eritrea*, 67 J5
Massif Central, *France*, 61 E5
Massinga, *Mozambique*, 73 G4
Masvingo, *Zimbabwe*, 72 F4
Matagalpa, *Nicaragua*, 27 G5
Matala, *Angola*, 72 B2
Matamoros, *Mexico*, 26 E2
Matanzas, *Cuba*, 27 H3
Mataram, *Indonesia*, 42 E5
Mataro, *Spain*, 61 E6
Matehuala, *Mexico*, 26 D3
Mato Grosso, Plateau of, *Brazil*, 31 G6
Matsuyama, *Japan*, 47 M4
Maturin, *Venezuela*, 30 F2
Maui, *U.S.A.*, 25 P7
Maun, *Botswana*, 72 D3
Mauritania, *Africa, country*, 68 C5
Mauritius, *Indian Ocean, country*, 73 L3

Mavinga, *Angola*, 72 D3
Mayotte, *Africa*, 73 J2
Mazar-e Sharif, *Afghanistan*, 48 B3
Mazatlan, *Mexico*, 26 C3
Mazyr, *Belarus*, 59 J5
Mbabane, *Swaziland, national capital*, 72 F5
Mbala, *Zambia*, 72 F1
Mbale, *Uganda*, 71 F3
Mbandaka, *Democratic Republic of Congo*, 70 C3
Mbarara, *Uganda*, 71 F4
Mbeya, *Tanzania*, 71 F5
Mbuji-Mayi, *Democratic Republic of Congo*, 70 D5
McClintock Channel, *Canada*, 22 J1
McClure Strait, *Canada*, 22 G1
McKinley, Mount, *U.S.A.*, 22 D2
Mead, Lake, *U.S.A.*, 24 D3
Mecca, *Saudi Arabia*, 51 C7
Mecula, *Mozambique*, 73 G2
Medan, *Indonesia*, 42 A3
Medellin, *Colombia*, 30 C2
Medford, *U.S.A.*, 24 B2
Medina, *Saudi Arabia*, 51 C7
Mediterranean Sea, *Africa/Europe*, 19
Medvezhyegorsk, *Russia*, 58 K3
Meerut, *India*, 48 D5
Meiktila, *Burma*, 44 C3
Meizhou, *China*, 47 J6
Mekele, *Ethiopia*, 71 G1
Meknes, *Morocco*, 68 D2
Mekong, *Asia*, 44 E5
Melaka, *Malaysia*, 42 B3
Melamo, Cape, *Mozambique*, 73 H2
Melanesia, *Oceania*, 36 D5
Melbourne, *Australia, internal capital*, 38 H7
Melilla, *Africa*, 61 D7
Melitopol, *Ukraine*, 56 D4
Melo, *Uruguay*, 32 H6
Melville Island, *Australia*, 38 F2
Melville Island, *Canada*, 22 H1
Melville Peninsula, *Canada*, 23 L2
Memphis, *U.S.A.*, 25 J3
Mendoza, *Argentina*, 32 E6
Menongue, *Angola*, 72 C2
Mentawai Islands, *Indonesia*, 42 A4
Menzel Bourguiba, *Tunisia*, 66 C1
Mergui, *Burma*, 44 C5
Mergui Archipelago, *Burma*, 44 C5
Merida, *Mexico*, 26 G3
Meridian, *U.S.A.*, 25 J4
Merlo, *Argentina*, 32 E6
Mersin, *Turkey*, 50 B4
Meru, *Kenya*, 71 G3
Messina, *Italy*, 62 E4
Messina, *South Africa*, 72 F4
Metz, *France*, 60 F4
Mexicali, *Mexico*, 26 A1
Mexico, *North America, country*, 26 D3
Mexico City, *Mexico, national capital*, 26 E4
Mexico, Gulf of, *North America*, 26 F3
Mexico, Plateau of, *Mexico*, 26 D2
Miami, *U.S.A.*, 25 K5
Michigan, *U.S.A., internal admin. area*, 25 J2
Michigan, Lake, *U.S.A.*, 25 J2
Michurinsk, *Russia*, 56 E3
Micronesia, *Oceania*, 36 C4
Micronesia, Federated States of, *Oceania, country*, 36 C4
Middlesbrough, *United Kingdom*, 60 D3
Midway Islands, *Pacific Ocean*, 36 F2
Mikkeli, *Finland*, 58 H3
Milan, *Italy*, 62 D2
Milange, *Mozambique*, 73 G3
Mildura, *Australia*, 38 H6
Milwaukee, *U.S.A.*, 25 J2
Minas, *Uruguay*, 32 G6
Mindanao, *Philippines*, 45 H6
Mindelo, *Cape Verde*, 69 M11
Mindoro, *Philippines*, 45 H5
Mingacevir, *Azerbaijan*, 50 E3
Minna, *Nigeria*, 69 G7

Nuremberg, *Germany*, 60 G4
Nyala, *Sudan*, 66 F6
Nyasa, Lake, *Africa*, 71 F6
Nyeri, *Kenya*, 71 G4
Nykobing, *Denmark*, 59 D5
Nzerekore, *Guinea*, 69 D7
Nzwani, *Comoros*, 73 H2

## O

Oahu, *U.S.A.*, 25 P7
Oaxaca, *Mexico*, 26 E4
Ob, *Russia*, 52 D2
Obi, *Indonesia*, 43 G4
Obninsk, *Russia*, 56 D2
Obo, *Central African Republic*, 70 E2
Odda, *Norway*, 58 C3
Odemis, *Turkey*, 63 J4
Odense, *Denmark*, 59 D5
Oder, *Europe*, 59 E5
Odesa, *Ukraine*, 56 C4
Odienne, *Ivory Coast*, 69 D7
Ogbomoso, *Nigeria*, 69 F7
Ogden, *U.S.A.*, 24 D2
Ohio, *U.S.A.*, 25 J3
Ohio, *U.S.A., internal admin. area*, 25 K2
Ojinaga, *Mexico*, 26 D2
Ojos del Salado, Mount, *South America*, 32 E5
Oka, *Russia*, 56 E2
Okahandja, *Namibia*, 72 C4
Okaukuejo, *Namibia*, 72 C3
Okavango, *Africa*, 72 D3
Okavango Swamp, *Botswana*, 72 D3
Okayama, *Japan*, 47 M4
Okeechobee, Lake, *U.S.A.*, 25 K5
Okhotsk, Sea of, *Asia*, 53 H3
Okinawa, *Japan*, 47 L5
Oklahoma, *U.S.A., internal admin. area*, 24 G4
Oklahoma City, *U.S.A., internal capital*, 24 G3
Oktyabrskiy, *Russia*, 57 G3
Oland, *Sweden*, 59 F4
Olavarria, *Argentina*, 33 F7
Oleksandriya, *Ukraine*, 56 C4
Ollague, *Chile*, 32 E4
Olomouc, *Czech Republic*, 62 F1
Olongapo, *Philippines*, 45 H5
Olsztyn, *Poland*, 59 G5
Olympia, *U.S.A., internal capital*, 24 B1
Olympus, Mount, *Greece*, 63 G3
Omaha, *U.S.A.*, 25 G2
Oman, *Asia, country*, 51 G7
Oman, Gulf of, *Asia*, 51 G7
Omdurman, *Sudan*, 67 H5
Omsk, *Russia*, 52 D3
Ondangwa, *Namibia*, 72 C3
Onega, Lake, *Russia*, 58 K3
Onitsha, *Nigeria*, 69 G7
Ontario, *Canada, internal admin. area*, 23 L3
Ontario, Lake, *U.S.A.*, 25 L2
Opochka, *Russia*, 59 J4
Opole, *Poland*, 59 F6
Oporto, *Portugal*, 61 B6
Oppdal, *Norway*, 58 D3
Opuwo, *Namibia*, 72 B3
Oradea, *Romania*, 63 G2
Oral, *Kazakhstan*, 57 G3
Oran, *Algeria*, 68 E1
Orange, *Africa*, 72 C5
Orange, Cape, *Brazil*, 31 H3
Orapa, *Botswana*, 72 E4
Orebro, *Sweden*, 58 E4
Oregon, *U.S.A., internal admin. area*, 24 B2
Orel, *Russia*, 56 D3
Orenburg, *Russia*, 57 H3
Orense, *Spain*, 61 C6
Orinoco, *Venezuela*, 30 F2
Orinoco Delta, *Venezuela*, 30 F2
Oristano, *Italy*, 62 D4
Orizaba, *Mexico*, 26 E4
Orkney, *South Africa*, 72 E5

Orkney Islands, *United Kingdom*, 60 D2
Orlando, *U.S.A.*, 25 K5
Orleans, *France*, 60 E5
Orsha, *Belarus*, 59 J5
Orsk, *Russia*, 57 H3
Oruro, *Bolivia*, 32 E3
Osaka, *Japan*, 47 N4
Osh, *Kyrgyzstan*, 48 C2
Osijek, *Croatia*, 63 F2
Oskarshamn, *Sweden*, 59 F4
Oslo, *Norway, national capital*, 58 D4
Osnabruck, *Germany*, 60 G3
Osorno, *Chile*, 33 D8
Ostersund, *Sweden*, 58 E3
Ostrava, *Czech Republic*, 63 F1
Otavi, *Namibia*, 72 C3
Otjiwarongo, *Namibia*, 72 C4
Ottawa, *Canada, national capital*, 23 M4
Ouadda, *Central African Republic*, 70 D2
Ouagadougou, *Burkina Faso, national capital*, 69 E6
Ouahigouya, *Burkina Faso*, 69 E6
Ouargla, *Algeria*, 68 G2
Ouarzazate, *Morocco*, 68 D2
Oudtshoorn, *South Africa*, 72 D6
Ouesso, *Congo*, 70 C3
Oujda, *Morocco*, 68 E2
Oulu, *Finland*, 58 H2
Oulu Lake, *Finland*, 58 H2
Ovalle, *Chile*, 32 D6
Oviedo, *Spain*, 61 C6
Owando, *Congo*, 70 C4
Owen Sound, *Canada*, 23 L4
Owo, *Nigeria*, 69 G7
Oxford, *United Kingdom*, 60 D4
Oyem, *Gabon*, 70 B3
Ozark Plateau, *U.S.A.*, 25 H3

## P

Paarl, *South Africa*, 72 C6
Pacasmayo, *Peru*, 30 C5
Pacific Ocean, 18
Padang, *Indonesia*, 42 B4
Pafuri, *Mozambique*, 72 F4
Pagadian, *Philippines*, 45 H6
Paijanne Lake, *Finland*, 58 H3
Pakistan, *Asia, country*, 48 B5
Pakxe, *Laos*, 44 E4
Palangkaraya, *Indonesia*, 42 D4
Palau, *Oceania, country*, 36 A4
Palawan, *Philippines*, 45 G6
Palembang, *Indonesia*, 42 B4
Palencia, *Spain*, 61 C6
Palermo, *Italy*, 62 E4
Palikir, *Federated States of Micronesia, national capital*, 36 C4
Palk Strait, *Asia*, 49 D9
Palma, *Mozambique*, 73 H2
Palma, *Spain*, 61 E7
Palmas, Cape, *Africa*, 69 D8
Palmyra Atoll, *Oceania*, 36 G4
Palopo, *Indonesia*, 43 F4
Palu, *Indonesia*, 43 E4
Pampas, *Argentina*, 33 F7
Pamplona, *Colombia*, 30 D2
Pamplona, *Spain*, 61 D6
Panama, *North America, country*, 27 H6
Panama Canal, *Panama*, 27 J6
Panama City, *Panama, internal capital*, 27 J6
Panama, Gulf of, *North America*, 27 J6
Panay, *Philippines*, 45 H5
Panevezys, *Lithuania*, 59 H5
Pangkalpinang, *Indonesia*, 42 C4
Panjgur, *Pakistan*, 48 A5
Pantelleria, *Italy*, 62 E4
Panzhihua, *China*, 46 F5
Papeete, *French Polynesia*, 37 J6
Paphos, *Cyprus*, 63 K5
Papua, Gulf of, *Papua New Guinea*, 43 K5
Papua New Guinea, *Oceania, country*, 43 L5
Paracel Islands, *Asia*, 45 F4
Paraguaipoa, *Venezuela*, 30 D1
Paraguay, *South America*, 32 G4

Paraguay, *South America, country*, 32 F4
Parakou, *Benin*, 69 F7
Paramaribo, *Surinam, national capital*, 31 G2
Parana, *South America*, 32 G6
Paranagua, *Brazil*, 32 J5
Parepare, *Indonesia*, 43 E4
Paris, *France, national capital*, 60 E4
Parma, *Italy*, 62 D2
Parnaiba, *Brazil*, 31 K4
Parnu, *Estonia*, 58 H4
Parry Islands, *Canada*, 22 J1
Pasadena, *U.S.A.*, 24 C4
Pasto, *Colombia*, 30 C3
Passo Fundo, *Brazil*, 32 H5
Pasto, *Colombia*, 30 C3
Patagonia, *Argentina*, 33 E9
Pathein, *Burma*, 44 B4
Patna, *India*, 48 F5
Patos de Minas, *Brazil*, 32 J3
Patos Lagoon, *Brazil*, 32 H6
Patra, *Greece*, 63 G4
Pattaya, *Thailand*, 44 D5
Pau, *France*, 61 D6
Pavlodar, *Kazakhstan*, 52 D3
Paysandu, *Uruguay*, 32 G6
Peace River, *Canada*, 22 H3
Pecos, *U.S.A.*, 24 F4
Pecs, *Hungary*, 59 F7
Pedro Juan Caballero, *Paraguay*, 32 G4
Pegu, *Burma*, 44 C4
Peipus, Lake, *Europe*, 58 H4
Peiraias, *Greece*, 63 G4
Pekanbaru, *Indonesia*, 42 B3
Pelagian Islands, *Italy*, 62 E5
Peleng, *Indonesia*, 43 F4
Pelotas, *Brazil*, 32 H6
Pematangsiantar, *Indonesia*, 42 A3
Pemba, *Mozambique*, 73 H2
Pemba Island, *Tanzania*, 71 G5
Penang, *Malaysia*, 42 B2
Penas, Gulf of, *Chile*, 33 C9
Pennsylvania, *U.S.A., internal admin. area*, 25 L2
Pensacola, *U.S.A.*, 25 J4
Penza, *Russia*, 56 F3
Penzance, *United Kingdom*, 60 C4
Peoria, *U.S.A.*, 25 J2
Pereira, *Colombia*, 30 C3
Perm, *Russia*, 57 H2
Perpignan, *France*, 61 E6
Persepolis, *Iran*, 51 F6
Persian Gulf, *Asia*, 51 F6
Perth, *Australia, internal capital*, 38 C6
Peru, *South America, country*, 30 C5
Perugia, *Italy*, 62 E3
Pescara, *Italy*, 62 E3
Peshawar, *Pakistan*, 48 C4
Petauke, *Zambia*, 72 F2
Petra, *Jordan*, 51 C5
Petrolina, *Brazil*, 31 K5
Petropavlovsk-Kamchatskiy, *Russia*, 53 H3
Petrozavodsk, *Russia*, 58 K3
Philadelphia, *U.S.A.*, 25 L3
Philippines, *Asia, country*, 45 J5
Philippine Sea, *Asia*, 45 H5
Phitsanulok, *Thailand*, 44 D4
Phnom Penh, *Cambodia, national capital*, 44 D5
Phoenix, *U.S.A., internal capital*, 24 D4
Phongsali, *Laos*, 44 D3
Piatra Neamt, *Romania*, 63 H2
Pica, *Chile*, 32 E4
Pico, *Azores*, 68 K10
Pierre, *U.S.A., internal capital*, 24 F2
Pietermaritzburg, *South Africa*, 72 F5
Pietersburg, *South Africa*, 72 E4
Pihlaja Lake, *Finland*, 58 J3
Pik Pobedy, *Asia*, 48 E2
Pilcomayo, *South America*, 32 F4
Pilsen, *Czech Republic*, 62 E1
Pinar del Rio, *Cuba*, 27 H3
Pindus Mountains, *Greece*, 63 G4
Pingdingshan, *China*, 47 H4
Pinsk, *Belarus*, 59 H5
Pisa, *Italy*, 62 D3

Pitcairn Islands, *Oceania*, 37 L7
Pitesti, *Romania*, 63 H2
Pittsburgh, *U.S.A.*, 25 L2
Piura, *Peru*, 30 B5
Platte, *U.S.A.*, 24 F2
Pleven, *Bulgaria*, 63 H3
Plock, *Poland*, 59 F5
Ploiesti, *Romania*, 63 H2
Plovdiv, *Bulgaria*, 63 H3
Plumtree, *Zimbabwe*, 72 E4
Plymouth, *United Kingdom*, 60 C4
Po, *Italy*, 62 D2
Pocos de Caldas, *Brazil*, 32 J4
Podgorica, *Serbia and Montenegro*, 56 C4
Podolsk, *Russia*, 56 D2
Pointe-Noire, *Congo*, 70 B4
Poitiers, *France*, 61 E5
Pokhara, *Nepal*, 48 E5
Poland, *Europe, country*, 59 F6
Polatsk, *Belarus*, 59 J5
Poltava, *Ukraine*, 56 C4
Polynesia, *Oceania*, 36 G5
Pompeii, *Italy*, 62 E3
Ponta Delgada, *Azores*, 68 K10
Ponta Pora, *Brazil*, 32 G4
Pontianak, *Indonesia*, 42 C3
Poole, *United Kingdom*, 60 D4
Poopo, Lake, *Bolivia*, 32 E3
Popayan, *Colombia*, 30 C3
Porbandar, *India*, 49 B6
Pori, *Finland*, 58 G3
Porlamar, *Venezuela*, 26 M5
Port-au-Prince, *Haiti, national capital*, 27 K4
Port Blair, *India*, 49 G8
Port Elizabeth, *South Africa*, 72 E6
Port-Gentil, *Gabon*, 70 A4
Port Harcourt, *Nigeria*, 69 G8
Port Hardy, *Canada*, 22 G3
Port Hedland, *Australia*, 38 C4
Portland, *Australia*, 38 H7
Portland, *Maine, U.S.A.*, 25 M2
Portland, *Oregon, U.S.A.*, 24 B1
Port Louis, *Mauritius, national capital*, 73 L4
Port Macquarie, *Australia*, 39 K6
Port McNeill, *Canada*, 22 G3
Port Moresby, *Papua New Guinea, national capital*, 43 L5
Porto Alegre, *Brazil*, 32 H5
Port-of-Spain, *Trinidad and Tobago, national capital*, 26 M5
Porto-Novo, *Benin, national capital*, 69 F7
Porto-Vecchio, *France*, 61 G6
Porto Velho, *Brazil*, 30 F5
Port Said, *Egypt*, 67 H2
Portsmouth, *United Kingdom*, 60 D4
Port Sudan, *Sudan*, 67 J5
Portugal, *Europe, country*, 61 B7
Port-Vila, *Vanuatu, national capital*, 39 N3
Porvenir, *Chile*, 33 D10
Posadas, *Argentina*, 32 G5
Poti, *Georgia*, 50 D3
Potiskum, *Nigeria*, 66 D6
Potosi, *Bolivia*, 32 E3
Potsdam, *Germany*, 60 H3
Poyang Lake, *China*, 47 J5
Poznan, *Poland*, 59 F5
Prachuap Khiri Khan, *Thailand*, 44 C5
Prague, *Czech Republic, national capital*, 62 E1
Praia, *Cape Verde, national capital*, 69 M12
Presidente Prudente, *Brazil*, 32 H4
Presov, *Slovakia*, 59 G6
Pretoria, *South Africa, national capital*, 72 E5
Preveza, *Greece*, 63 G4
Prieska, *South Africa*, 72 D5
Prilep, *Macedonia*, 63 G3
Prince Albert, *Canada*, 22 J3
Prince Edward Island, *Canada, internal admin. area*, 23 N4
Prince George, *Canada*, 22 G3

# GENERAL INDEX

## Acknowledgements

Every effort has been made to trace the copyright holders of the material in this book. If any rights have been omitted, the publishers offer to rectify this in any subsequent edition, following notification. The publishers are grateful to the following organizations and individuals for their contributions and permission to reproduce material (t=top, m=middle, b=bottom, l=left, r=right):

© **AFP Photos** 95bm (Henry Ray Abrams). © **Agripicture** 55br (Peter Dean). © **Craig Asquith** 11 projections, 12b, 13, 80. © **Corbis** 8tr (Dan Guravich), 9tr (W. Perry Conway), 10 (Christopher Cormack), 12tr (Bill Ross), 20bl (Richard Cummins), 21br (W. Perry Conway), 28b (Galen Rowell), 29tr (Eye Ubiquitous), 35br (Bates Littlehales), 40–41b (Michael S. Yamashita), 41br (Keren Su), 64–65b (Tom Brakefield), 65br (Gallo Images), 74bl (Galen Rowell), 76b (Wolfgang Kaehler). © **Digital Vision** cover globe, 1, 2–3, 4–5 background, 7tr Earth, 14 background, 54–55 background, 74br, 82–95 background, 96–97b, 97tr. © **European Map Graphics Ltd** 7bm & br, 9bl, 14–19, 20–21 map, 22–27, 28–29 map, 30–33, 34–35 map, 36–39, 40–41 map, 42–53, 54–55 map, 56–63, 64–65 map, 66–73, 75, 77. © **Flag Enterprises Ltd** 82–95 all flags except Afghanistan, Bahrain, Comoros, East Timor, Rwanda, Turkmenistan. © **Stephen Moncrieff** 6mr, 8bl globes, 11 globes. © **NASA** cover background, endpapers (data by Marc Imhoff, NASA GSFC, & Christopher Elvidge, NOAA NGDC; image by Craig Mayhew & Robert Simmon, NASA GSFC), 7tr satellite (JPL). © **Science Photo Library** 4tr (Geospace), 6bl (CNES, 1988 Distribution SPOT image), 74tr (Worldsat International), 76mr (NASA). © **Shipmate Flags, Vlaardingen, The Netherlands** 82 Afghanistan & Bahrain flags, 84 Comoros flag, 85 East Timor flag, 92 Rwanda flag, 94 Turkmenistan flag. © **Still Pictures** 34–35t (Pascal Kobeh).

Managing editor: Gillian Doherty    Managing designer: Mary Cartwright    Cover design by Zöe Wray

Usborne Publishing is not responsible and does not accept liability for the availability or content of any website other than its own, or for any exposure to harmful, offensive, or inaccurate material which may appear on the Web. Usborne Publishing will have no liability for any damage or loss caused by viruses that may be downloaded as a result of browsing the sites it recommends.

First published in 2004 by Usborne Publishing Ltd, 83–85 Saffron Hill, London EC1N 8RT, England. www.usborne.com  Copyright © 2004, 2002, 2001 Usborne Publishing Ltd. The name Usborne and the devices ♀ ⊕ are Trade Marks of Usborne Publishing Ltd. All rights reserved. No part of this publication may be reproduced, stored in a retrieval system, or transmitted in any form or by any means, electronic, mechanical, photocopying, recording or otherwise, without the prior permission of the publisher. UE. First published in America in 2004. Printed in Dubai.